A PLUME BOOK

THE LOST NIGHT

RACHEL HOWARD currently covers dance and writes book reviews for the *San Francisco Chronicle*. She has also written for *The Village Voice* and the *San Francisco Examiner*, among other publications. She lives in San Francisco with her husband.

"As a memoirist, [Howard] succeeds brilliantly. *The Lost Night* is enthralling, a skillfully narrated story that begins as a tale of detection but becomes something more." —*The New York Times*

"Powerful . . . this heartfelt memoir is about one young woman reconciling with the past, and in that process discovering the difference between loving the living and missing the dead." —*San Francisco Chronicle*

"Rachel Howard's *The Lost Night* unfolds with the urgency of a thriller, for both obvious reasons—the central fact of Howard's life is her father's murder when she was ten—but also because of the author's clear-sighted, propulsive prose. . . . What begins as a quest for justice winds up a complex, compulsively readable meditation on the nature of reconciliation, whether it is with your family, your past, or yourself." —*Elle.com*

"Not all crimes are solved in the quick sixty minutes, minus commercials, that television dramas or true-crime shows may lead us to believe. But if Howard has not discovered her father's murderer by the end of the book, she has perhaps rediscovered her father." —MSNBC.com (included in year-end roundup of highly recommended books)

"There is a quiet, personal heroism to *The Lost Night*, as an account of a young woman confronting the killing of her father and recognizing the deep loss of that love in her life, but there is also something more. The book is a searing, clear-eyed report on what it's like to be a child fighting for emotional survival in an ever-shifting landscape of broken families, drug addiction, lack of emotional support, and the shame that quickly shrouds an act of violence." —*The Orange County Register*

"Not an attempt at vengeance, but rather a profoundly personal account of a California Central Valley childhood defined by chaotic family life . . . poignant." —*Publishers Weekly*

"An abundantly candid and dramatically riveting account of one young woman's courageous determination to understand the unfathomable." —*Booklist*

Visit www.rachelhoward.com

A DAUGHTER'S SEARCH FOR
THE TRUTH OF
HER FATHER'S MURDER

the lost night

Rachel Howard

A PLUME BOOK

PLUME
Published by Penguin Group
Penguin Group (USA) Inc., 375 Hudson Street, New York, New York 10014, USA
Penguin Group (Canada), 90 Eglinton Avenue East, Suite 700, Toronto, Ontario,
Canada M4P 2Y3 (a division of Pearson Penguin Canada Inc.)
Penguin Books Ltd., 80 Strand, London WC2R 0RL, England
Penguin Ireland, 25 St. Stephen's Green, Dublin 2,
Ireland (a division of Penguin Books Ltd.)
Penguin Group (Australia), 250 Camberwell Road, Camberwell, Victoria 3124,
Australia (a division of Pearson Australia Group Pty. Ltd.)
Penguin Books India Pvt. Ltd., 11 Community Centre, Panchsheel Park,
New Delhi – 110 017, India
Penguin Group (NZ), cnr Airborne and Rosedale Roads, Albany,
Auckland 1310, New Zealand (a division of Pearson New Zealand Ltd.)
Penguin Books (South Africa) (Pty.) Ltd., 24 Sturdee Avenue,
Rosebank, Johannesburg 2196, South Africa

Penguin Books Ltd., Registered Offices: 80 Strand, London WC2R 0RL, England

Published by Plume, a member of Penguin Group (USA) Inc. Previously published in a Dutton
edition.

First Plume Printing, July 2006
10 9 8 7 6 5 4 3 2 1

The Library of Congress has catalogued the Dutton edition as follows:

Howard, Rachel.
   The lost night : a daughter's search for the truth of her father's murder / by Rachel Howard.
      p. cm.
   Includes bibliographical references and index.
   ISBN 0-525-94862-7 (hc.)
   ISBN 0-452-28742-1 (pbk.)
   1. Murder—California—Case studies. 2. Murder victims' families—California—Case
studies.   I. Title.
   HV6533.C2H69 2005
   364.152'3'0979458—dc22   200506982

Printed in the United States of America
Original hardcover design by Eve L. Kirch

To the memory of my father.
And to my mother,
who selflessly helps me remember even things we'd rather not.
With love.

ACKNOWLEDGMENTS

The process of writing this book was also the process of moving on with my life, and so to those who helped me I am doubly grateful. Elsa Hurley, Jessie Sholl, and Adrianne Bee encouraged me when I had only twenty pages of disjointed recollections. Anne N. Marino brought her frank insights to the first draft. Susan Coss and Lindsey Crittenden read every line of the final draft with keen attention and offered incisive suggestions. Stephanie Rapp sounded out many chapters for me under tight deadlines, and Alexandra Tomalonis trained her own sharp eyes on the book's first half. Frank Morris ran to superior court for me on more than one occasion. Ann and Tony Fischer let me use their home as a personal writer's retreat. A shout-out to Steve Schwartz for his generous research advice.

Noah Lukeman not only represented me with enthusiasm, but placed this book with precisely the right editor, Laurie Chittenden, who understood what I was seeking even before I did and helped me tell my story with integrity. Erika Kahn told me what I needed to hear. Carole Baron's notes sparked epiphanies and urged this book toward full maturity. Everyone at Dutton supported and challenged me in ways I never imagined.

To the members of my family who helped me live this story—Grandma Mae, Grandpa Ben, Uncle Brad, Uncle Ric, Nanette, and especially my mother—thank you for your love and trust. Thanks too to Howdy Cullen for understanding my need to retell unpleasant stories.

Most of all, thanks to my husband, Bill, for his comic relief, for his honesty, and for believing in me as much as I believe in him.

This is a true story, though memories differ. The names of several characters have been changed to protect their identities.

Grateful acknowledgment is made to reprint the following song lyrics:

the lost night

PROLOGUE

I SAW MY FATHER CLUTCHING HIS THROAT, trying to speak.

That image taunted me as I walked into the Merced County Sheriff's Department one sweltering August day. I'd come to meet with the detectives assigned to my father's murder, though discussing his death with anyone, let alone the authorities, still made my throat constrict and my right eye twitch. Whenever anyone asked about my father, I replied, in a flat, neutral voice, "My father was murdered." I hoped to stop the conversation cold, and usually I succeeded. But sometimes the questions persisted. *How old were you?* I was ten. *God, I'm sorry, can I ask what happened?*

If I felt strong, if I felt I was dealing with a straight shooter who wouldn't coo with pity, I might push myself to continue. I'd tell of waking up that summer night, and seeing pools of blood on the hallway carpet. I'd describe my father standing inside the darkened bedroom doorway, one hand clenching his throat. I might say he'd been trying to say something to me, his mouth moving soundlessly as he bled, even though I could not swear upon it.

This was the trouble with talking about the murder, the reason I usually blunted the topic. The moment I saw my father clutching his throat was just one among so many details I couldn't verify. Some details remained in doubt because I'd never worked up the nerve to check them out; others, things I'd seen with my own eyes, lay obscured because for sixteen years I'd let them fade like an intense and illogical dream you try to shake upon waking.

The only facts I held with certainty were these: At about three thirty a.m. on June 22, 1986, someone entered, through an unlocked sliding-glass door, my father's house on the outskirts of the central California farming town where he had grown up. The intruder took a knife from the kitchen and stabbed my father as he lay sleeping next to his third wife. He was pronounced dead at the hospital an hour later. He was thirty-two years old, a handsome, laid-back guy who had loved weight lifting and the Three Stooges and Rod Stewart songs, and who seemed to have no enemies. No one was ever charged with the crime.

Beyond this, fact dissolved to suspicion. My father was married to his third wife, Sherrie, for just over a year. I never met her brother Steve, but I heard my grandparents refer to him in mysterious, bitter outbursts. I'd been left to wonder whether Sherrie had conspired in my father's death, and I'd done so—fleetingly—in the privacy of my own mind, never daring to talk to my family about what had happened.

Finally, in my mid-twenties, I'd begun writing about my father, reclaiming moments from our summers together, trying to bring the years before his death into focus. But when I thought of describing the night of his murder or the way I'd felt afterward, my mind stopped short like a horse at a tall fence, unwilling to cross into territory I wasn't sure I could return from.

The story of my father's death was half complete, because I'd been too afraid of what I might remember, and because I hadn't lived the end of it. Now I was ready, and I had a guess as to why. Three days before my appointment with the detectives, I'd joined my boyfriend, Bill, on a visit to his family. We sat around the dining table with his siblings and parents, playing Scrabble and trading jokes as the night grew darker. Finally Bill glanced at me, tapped my foot under the table, and said, "Rachel and I are engaged." You would have thought we'd announced we were joining the circus, the way the air hung with incredulity before the excited gasps. And though he'd proposed months earlier, Bill and I could hardly believe the news ourselves.

I wrote in an ecstatic scrawl in my journal the next day, "I've entered a new era. One in which the murder is past—or almost." Was I ready to face my father's murder because I was getting married, or was I ready to get married because I'd begun to examine the murder? I only knew the two were connected, and that the need to learn all that I could about my father's death now felt urgent.

And so I found myself giving my name at the Sheriff Department's bulletproof reception window and waiting for a detective to open the locked steel door leading to his office. I wasn't on a mission to solve my father's murder or convict his killer. What I wanted was even more elusive, and unlike an investigation, full of leads to pursue, there were no clear steps to tracking it down.

Perhaps I'd thought the detectives guarded all the answers I needed, that their case file held some magic decoder that would make sense of the little I knew about my father's death. They confirmed a few elements of the crime that had always felt too bizarre to be real and gave me new pieces of information that left me even more bewildered. But they didn't present a definitive story of my father's death that I could live with, that I could hold in my mind as truth.

I didn't recognize my story in the detectives' bare-bones accounting, and I wanted to fill in the scenes their facts left out. I wanted to tell them about the summer afternoons of happiness my father and I had shared dancing to "Maggie May" in our cramped living room, the wiggle of his mustache as he winked at me in his janitorial van's rearview mirror, the triumphant smirk on his face when he crossed the finish line in our neighborhood 10K. I wanted to say that all of that had ended with his third marriage. My father had changed in the months before the murder; he'd turned sluggish and controlling, and his love had come to feel more suffocating than protective. My story was still disconnected and inconclusive, but it was more revealing, I felt certain, than anything the detectives could share with me from their tightly clutched case file.

The detectives weren't interested in hearing my story, or in helping me assemble it. They nodded as I tried to condense the most telling scenes, took care to look me straight in the eyes and jot down a few notes. They shook my hand and asked, "Did you get what you came for?"

I answered yes. I said I had just wanted to hear the little that was known about the case for myself. But in truth my need ran deeper. I wanted to understand the facts of my father's murder in order to write about it—and I had to write about his death in order to understand it. Those drives were circular and inextricable as I tried to construct a past that would let me move into the future.

But only I could live the second half of this story. And my father's murder wasn't behind me just yet.

part
one

MURDER NIGHT: JUNE 1986

BOBBY IS AT MY BEDROOM DOOR, in his tighty-whities. "Wake up. Rachel, wake up!" he whispers. "I think Daddy cut himself shaving."

Bobby is nine and I am ten and what he is saying makes no sense. First off, Bobby has no right to call my father "Daddy," even if Bobby lives here year-round and I've only come for the summer. But as I rub the sleep from my eyes and look at the clock, the usual irritation fades into confusion. It's three thirty a.m.—no time for a shave.

Bobby is gone. I sit up and shuffle alongside my dresser, feeling my way to the bedroom door. I can scan our entire house from my room: the living room straight across, the kitchen to the right, the bathroom and Bobby's room down a short hallway to the left, and Dad and Sherrie's room across from it.

It takes a few seconds for my eyes to adjust to the moonlight pouring through the living room window. I make out our powder-blue curtains first, slate gray against the darkness, and as the rest of the view falls into place, I see the house is empty and still. Then I look down the hallway, and what I find there sears itself upon my brain: huge, dark pools in the carpet, like giant grape Kool-Aid spills. Bigger around than basketballs, sticky wet and black in the colorless night. As I stare at them and remember Bobby's nonsensical words about shaving, I know at once that they are pools of blood.

The blood is a flash, a Polaroid snapshot of a shadowy moment, and the next ten minutes come in flashes too, murky images captured and set aside to develop in slow motion. In a flash, I'm at the open door of

Dad's bedroom. Dad is standing bare-chested, deathly white, holding his throat, looking into my eyes and mouthing something I can't understand. In a flash, the door slams in my face, and I hear Sherrie shout "I'm calling 911."

It feels like I stare at that closed door a long time. I don't know if I try the handle, but if I do, it's locked. I don't know how I step around the blood, how I decide to go back into my bedroom, how it is that I eventually walk into the living room and quietly take a seat on the couch next to Bobby. I don't know who turned the lamp on, but the light is throwing just enough illumination around the room to make the shadows look that much deeper. And I don't know how it is that Bobby and I are both now fully dressed. The biggest mystery of all, though, is how Bobby knows someone has tried to kill my father.

He picks up one of Dad's sweat-stained weight-lifting gloves from the glass-top coffee table and slips it over his pudgy fingers.

"Maybe we should take these with us," he says in a serious but steady voice, pulling the Velcro strap open and closed. "Like a keepsake."

I pick up the other glove and let the meaning of Bobby's strange words trickle through my mind. I slide the glove over my hand. The cutoff finger holes are too big for me; the glove is a hard, sweaty shell that doesn't fit, that makes me feel tiny and protected.

But Bobby has a second thought. "Wait," he says. "What if that person touched them!"

He tosses his glove so it slides off the edge of the coffee table and flaps his hands as if shaking off cooties. I set my glove down gingerly, not believing that whoever came through our house could have tarnished it but wanting to play along with Bobby's game because playing along will let us believe that we can still play games after what we've just seen.

The house hums with noiselessness in the dead night of our country neighborhood. I try to think of other mementos we might want to take, to ignore the blood splattered along the wall and soaking on the carpet behind us. The couch is placed so that its back faces the open hallway. I want to curl up in a ball for fear that someone will pop up behind me, but Bobby's presence keeps me from cowering.

Instead I search for cootie-free souvenirs, looking at the airbrushed duck decoy Bobby and I bought Dad at the flea market a few weeks ago. At Dad's old record collection, his beloved Rod Stewart albums, leaning against the TV. At yesterday's cold coffee cup forming a creamy brown ring on the coffee table glass.

When the paramedics charge through our living room, it's like a scene from an action movie crashing down our hallway. A moment later Sherrie is sitting between us on the couch, wrapping her hands around our eyes and telling us, "Don't look, kids, don't look." I look anyway, can just peek over her skinny pinkie and above her shoulder, and I see Dad's legs and his feet streaking by on the gurney. I tell myself to remember that last look well. In my gut I know it will be the last I ever see of Dad.

When we arrive at the emergency room, everyone is there. My grandfather, my aunts and uncles—it's like Christmas without the other children. Grandpa Ben gets up from the plastic waiting-room chair and steps aside with Sherrie into the hallway. Grandma Mae calls me and Bobby over to sit in her wide lap, to each slide upon her bench-sized thighs, clenching us to her enormous bosom. "Don't you worry, kids, your daddy's tough and he's gonna make it!" she says, rocking. I look around the blue-gray fluorescent room at my aunts and uncles, who don't seem to share Grandma Mae's conviction.

It is forever and yet no time at all before a man in blue scrubs walks into the room. He stands in front of Grandma Mae, looking down on us huddled together. He acts as though he's talking just to her. "He lost too much blood," he says. He says something about trying to operate, about a piece of knife stuck in the vein. "I'm sorry but he just lost too much blood, and he's passed on."

I think I feel Grandma Mae's heart stop beating beneath her cushiony chest. She looks up at the man, silent. "Would you like a moment alone with the body?" he asks. He's still talking to Grandma Mae, but it will always feel as though he were asking me too, as though if I'd had the courage to pipe up, I could have visited my father one last time.

I'm not quite thinking this though. I'm thinking of cooties. I'm thinking of dead bodies. I'm thinking that it's gross to see a dead body, even if it is my father's. I'm thinking I have seen enough.

The only entertainment Bobby and I can find on TV at five thirty in the morning is a fishing show. One of the adults has handed us the remote control and headed to my grandparents' kitchen, where the coffeepot is gurgling and Grandma Mae is busying herself filling cup after cup. Sherrie sits at the kitchen table as aunts and uncles seem to sleepwalk around her. She is chattering hysterically. "I just can't believe it, I don't know who could have done this." My uncles stare at her with puffy, annoyed eyes.

The sliding-glass door slams. Grandpa Ben stands outside, wailing and kicking the redwood deck with his short, strong legs. Every pound against the wood makes me cringe. I'm staring at the television, but I'm telepathically begging Grandpa Ben to wipe his foxlike eyes, smooth his dirty-blond hair, and stroll back inside. His whimpers fall silent, but the door does not open.

Bobby and I stay focused on the fishing. Two men sit on a dull, flat lake whispering, waiting for the big one to bite. For the sake of distraction, for the sake of fear, it is the most engrossing program Bobby and I have ever seen. We made it back to the house first, in Grandma's car. Bobby headed directly to the message board next to the kitchen telephone and scrawled "CREMATED 6/22/86" in chalk. I watched, puzzled, not knowing what *cremated* meant and not believing Bobby could use the word so confidently. I'd never felt a kinship with Bobby. His father, Dad had told me, was a bad man. I was brash, outspoken, full of myself; Bobby tended to mumble and communicate in nervous giggles, with wary eyes. Yet, except for that weird remark about the shaving accident, Bobby had shown admirable control during those last two hours at the house and the hospital.

When the knock comes at the front door, I know it's my mom, because only she, the perpetually paranoid ex-wife, would knock. She crouches in the foyer and hugs me, braces my shoulders, makeup-free face twisting with worry. I feel as if I've just been released from a torture camp in which I'd been next in line for the firing squad, but my joy in finally seeing her, in finally heading to our home far, far down the freeway in Fresno, is muted. I look her in the eye.

"Someone killed my dad," I tell her. "But I'm OK."

This is what I say to her, verbatim. I know it now for fact because she never forgets it.

THE FALLOUT

FOUR DAYS AFTER MY FATHER'S MURDER, Grandma Mae, Sherrie, Bobby, and I sat on the Merced County Sheriff's Department steps, waiting for the detectives to send us on our way. Bobby and I had just been fingerprinted. A current of excitement had rippled through me as the lieutenant firmly rolled each of my fingers on the ink pad, followed by a wave of guilt as I remembered that my father was dead, that it was only because of his murder that I was feeling like a guest star on *The Rockford Files*. I would get used to this seesaw sensation over the next few months—a moment of normality, of laughing at my favorite cartoon or delighting in the teddy bear my aunt in Oregon had sent as a condolence gift. And then that jolt of memory, of registering anew a fact that had not yet become a given of my existence—Dad would never watch *Inspector Gadget* with me again; my aunt had sent the bear because my father was dead.

Grandma Mae's salt-and-pepper bob had turned noticeably grayer overnight. The outside corner of her right eye twitched above her deepening jowls. I repositioned myself, tugging at my culottes to cover as much skin as possible—the afternoon was so hot that the concrete baked my backside, even though a breeze blew down the sidewalk. The wind picked up a pile of dead leaves and tossed them into a tiny whirlwind that swept toward us. Sherrie took a deep drag on her cigarette, peering at the miniature tornado with that thoughtful smoker expression. "Stan always said that when he died, he'd like to come back as the wind," she said with a wistful smile.

My own right eye began to twitch. It struck me that what Sherrie said wasn't true. Just a few weeks ago Sherrie, Bobby, and I had all lain together in Dad's bed one late morning, cuddling as he sipped his coffee, musing on the concept of reincarnation. I said I wanted to return as a rabbit, and Dad said he wanted to come back as an eagle, soaring above the mountains.

I let Sherrie's seeming lie wash over me, like so many things that Sherrie had said in the year and a half since she'd entered my life. I'd given up trying to read her motivations long ago. Just before her marriage to my dad, a year earlier, she'd taken me alone to the mall for "girl shopping." She'd hovered over a bin in the Mervyn's lingerie department, dangling discounted thong panties from her skinny fingers and purring, "Your father's going to *love* this!" Was I supposed to enjoy being in on her grown-up seduction? Was she trying to make clear the sexual powers she held over my dad? My face tingled with shame, but my head shook up and down as though she'd offered me a piece of candy, because it was the only way I knew to get through.

All of us were just getting through during those days after the murder, which is why I was sitting at the Sheriff's Department with Sherrie in the first place. I'd spent the first day after the murder in Fresno with my mother, but Grandma Mae requested that I stay with her and Grandpa Ben after the funeral. Sherrie and Bobby had moved into my grandparents' extra bedroom. Unbeknownst to my mother, Sherrie's sworn enemy, I was left not in my grandparents' constant care, but in Sherrie's charge. And so, the day after the Sheriff's Department visit, Sherrie dropped Bobby and me off at a city-run child-care program in Applegate Park and came back for us late that afternoon.

We drove past downtown's vacuum-repair shops and boarded-up cafés, past the vintage movie theater with its peeling orange trim, past the fairgrounds, past the cemetery where Dad's ashes had just been laid to rest. Beyond the freeway overpass, Bobby and I knew the route by heart. No other destination was possible. We were going back to the house, our house, where Dad was killed.

"I've gotta run inside and get some things," Sherrie said as she pulled into the driveway, as though stopping off at Long's for toothpaste and deodorant. She turned the key, set the parking brake. "Come on, guys," she said.

She took quick strides up the walkway while Bobby and I dragged our feet behind. We stopped in the hallway, where the harsh summer light glared upon a trail of blood.

"I guess we'll have to get new carpet before we put the place on the market," Sherrie said with mystifying levelheadedness. She tiptoed around the blood spots, pussyfooting along the wall to the back bedroom. Bobby looked ready to pick his nose, his nervous tic. I grabbed his arm, pulled him into my bedroom, and shut the door.

My bedcovers lay unmade, just as I had left them, and the dresser drawers sat open, clothes tossed around like tissue paper. Just to make believe this was a normal trip home, I picked out some shorts and T-shirts and began folding them. Bobby sat in the corner next to my trunk of stuffed animals bobbing Ralph the Muppet up and down in conversation with Arthur the Cabbage Patch Kid. "Mommy's going to sell the house," he said in a ventriloquist's squeaky voice, nodding Arthur's plastic head. "Yes, and then we'll never come back here again," he huffed, snapping Ralph's mouth open and shut.

There was a soft knock at the door. "You guys ready?" Sherrie said. She had a backpack over one shoulder, and an overnight case in her hand. Bobby and I followed her out of the bedroom and around the blood, not bothering to take anything with us, not knowing if we'd ever come back.

On June 23, 1986, the headline MERCED MAN STABBED TO DEATH appeared on the third page of the *Merced Sun-Star*, beneath a puff piece about locals auditioning for the new *Fresno* miniseries. *Merced County sheriff's officers are investigating the stabbing death of Stanley Howard, 32, who died early Sunday. Sheriff's Detective Sgt. Hector Garibay said Sunday no suspects had been arrested in the case.*

While Sherrie and Bobby and I were revisiting the crime scene, articles about Dad's murder that I was not shown, that I would not see for nearly two decades, were running in the Merced and Fresno papers. News spots about the case I would never view were playing on the local television stations. The story had the makings of a gripping chronicle:

The murder was bizarre even for an agricultural town of sixty thousand despite Merced County's high crime rate—a dozen people were murdered there the year Dad died. And yet the story would quickly disappear, because within a week it would be obvious that the case was going nowhere.

I overheard certain details in those days right after his death, a word dropped by Sherrie, a whisper from someone I didn't even recognize at the funeral reception. Some of these details stuck in my memory. Others I didn't learn until more than fifteen years later, so that it would become difficult for me to sort what I knew then from what I gathered as an adult.

The detectives decided that whoever killed my father had been expert in his operation: He'd stabbed Dad's carotid artery and twisted the knife, breaking the blade off inside his neck. They had a psychologist interview Bobby, who talked of half-waking to see a shadowy figure in his bedroom doorway. They analyzed a hair that had been found in the house and failed to connect it to anybody. They dusted the house for prints but found only the family's finger smudges and a stray print from one of the detectives.

They canvassed the neighborhood and questioned Dad's friends and acquaintances in hopes of identifying someone, anyone, with a reason to want Dad dead. Names were swiftly checked off the list of possible suspects: The owner of a van that had been sighted parked near our house had a strong alibi; a man spotted walking down a road near our home with blood on his hand had buddies vouch that he'd been in a fight, and that he'd been returning from a late night out. One final suspect—Sherrie's own brother—was cleared just as quickly and mysteriously.

But my family was silently beginning to form its own suspicions. The process began the moment Grandma Mae called my mother at four thirty a.m. to tell her my father was dead, with my mother's gut response: "Did Sherrie do this?"

The Howards had accepted Sherrie out of family solidarity. But she was never one of us. She was a good-looking woman, thin, with alluring blue eyes and long legs. She wore typical eighties fashions, acid-washed jeans and big dangling earrings, but she did not dress especially provocatively. Her hair was a flat brown, feathered in a *Charlie's Angels* style, and her face bore big bee-stung lips, black-lined eyes, and carefully arched and penciled brows. If my mental image of her now tends toward caricature, a snapshot of a woman in skintight shorts and heavy makeup, it's because of her carriage, not her grooming. She was incorrigibly flirtatious and suggestive, a habitual eyelash batter, a fan of heavy metal music, a partyer. A tease.

She was the antithesis of my previous stepmother, my father's second wife, Nanette. I had lived with Nanette during visiting weekends and vacations for five years and adored her, and perhaps that helps to explain why I never took to Sherrie, why I distrusted her so staunchly. A week or so before my father died, I dreamt Sherrie was trying to kill me by poisoning my cereal.

But my dislike of Sherrie remained mostly secret before Dad's murder. During Dad's marriage to her, my grandparents had stood by her, defending her against my mother's demands for skipped child support, which Dad had never failed to pay while married to Nanette. And so during those first days after the murder, the facade of that allegiance remained. I had always looked upon Sherrie with wary eyes. Now I sensed, but did not know, that my family was watching Sherrie with that same distrust. From my mother's groggy gut reaction forward, Sherrie would assume a mysterious, mythological status in our memories.

My mother's memory of Dad's funeral is much stronger than mine. She sat with her second husband, Howdy, in the parlor's main hall as the organ music—"I Come to the Garden Alone"—meandered and a minister my father hadn't seen in years attested to Dad's zeal for life. I sat in a curtained side box with Sherrie, Bobby, my grandparents, and a host of aunts, uncles, and cousins. When my mom heard a child wailing, she rushed over to comfort me, parting the box curtains as her former in-laws shot sharp looks. But I hadn't so much as sniffled—it was Bobby who sobbed uncontrollably. My father had been in the process of adopting him, becoming his hero almost overnight. I had lost my father but Bobby had lost his new life.

I didn't cry that day. In fact, I never cried about my father's death in front of anyone. I detested pity and shrank from it in horror, afraid that the murder had made it obvious to everyone that I was broken and hurt. At the funeral, I focused on minute details to blur the reality of a bigger picture. My oldest cousin, Kelly, was wearing electric blue eyeliner and mascara; I stared at her in wonder, longing for the day I'd begin to wear makeup, as we trudged across the prickly lawn to the gravesite.

For many years I remembered Sherrie as also remaining unstained by tears during Dad's funeral. Somehow this impression, which must have taken hold a few years after Dad's death, morphed into a vision of her, blithe and stony-eyed, black mascara utterly unsmudged. Many years later, when she might as well have been some monster under the bed I'd imagined as a child, I fit the piece into my personal Sherrie lore.

But Sherrie did cry at the funeral. Other witnesses remember that now. Her tears flowed more liberally than my grandparents'. For almost two decades, my memory chose not to acknowledge that.

A box of ashes went into the ground that day, marked by a headstone that read BELOVED HUSBAND.

My father was not a wealthy man. He left $30,000 in insurance money. Initially the insurance company told Sherrie and my grandparents that he left that money in his second wife's name, but the policy was restored to Sherrie without whispering a word to the woman who had come before. Accounts differ, but as far as I can ascertain, my father had died owing my grandfather about $16,000. The day the insurance check came, Grandpa Ben accompanied Sherrie to the bank to supervise her deposit, collected his debt, and told her to get lost.

My mother assumed that my father left more insurance money, remembering the way he'd bragged about his policies. She'd wanted to fight for the payout and claim a piece for me. She'd put herself through college, on welfare, to become a registered nurse, and she knew she wanted me to be able to attend college one day without going on the dole. After months of Dad's missed child support payments, she figured a chunk of insurance cash was only just.

My grandparents didn't want any fuss. They wanted to move on, or more specifically, they wanted to get Sherrie out of their house and lives, though they didn't tell Mom that. "Let this pass," Grandma Mae said. "We'll help Rachel with college when the time comes." This ambiguous agreement resulted years later in the near-gift of their used station wagon (Mom bought me a car herself, making it unnecessary) and a check for $500. My mother saw this as stingy; Mae and Ben, born of the Great Depression, with thirteen grandkids and an objective, everything-split-exactly-evenly philosophy of money, saw it as more than fair. Certainly, it wasn't personal: I had been as close to them as any of their other grandchildren, visiting on weekends with Dad, delighting in each family Christmas, even living with them for part of second grade. But all that easy familiarity was about to disintegrate.

Except for Social Security, I never got any money from Dad's death. Mom regretted not fighting for a settlement, however meager, but as I grew up, I never wished for the nonexistent inheritance. It was not the lack of a few thousand dollars that would eventually bring me to emotional collapse, that would build an invisible wall between an only child and the extended family she had once taken for granted.

Instead it was the absence of answers—the desire for an accounting of Dad's death that felt real and made sense—that would shape my life. It would take many years of forgetting to realize that I wanted to remember.

BEFORE:
SUMMER 1981

MY FATHER WAS A LOOKER: a little on the short side at five foot nine, but trim, with thick raven hair and gold-flecked hazel eyes that I feel fortunate to have inherited. I loved him for his toothy, hunched-nose smile, and for the way he'd grab my nose and then slip his thumb between his knuckles as though he'd pulled it off. I missed that gesture after the murder. During our happy "before" era, when I was five years old, I felt his presence could protect me from anything, even the threats I did not share with him.

"I want to talk to you about that man your mother's been running around with," my father said one August evening as we sat on the old tree stump, my hair still wet from running through the sprinklers. His eyes darted as he collected himself. "I don't mean your mother any bad feelings, you know?"

You know? was Dad's tic, the question he asked dozens of times a day, but this time I nodded back with an emphatic bounce of my blond bangs. "I haven't heard good things about him. If he ever yells at you, or does anything to you that you don't like, you come tell me and I'll set him straight." He didn't say *you know?* again, but he didn't have to, because my head was already nodding like a Weeble on linoleum. "That man" was Howdy Cullen, my mother's grumbling future husband.

Dad rose with an exaggerated groan, grabbed me under the armpits to swing me once around, and set me on the ground with a gentle slap on the rear. He was smiling again, and his gold herringbone necklace glinted in the remaining light. "You see these muscles?" he said, flexing his pale biceps so that they pushed up the short sleeves of his polo shirt, and he bent his knees deep so that I could reach up and squeeze his arm. "You just tell him your daddy's got the biggest muscles in all Merced, you got that?" He sent me off to the house to change into dry clothes as he swaggered back toward the garden.

Dad's favorite prank was to say you had food on your shirt and then flip your nose with his finger as you glanced down. He wasn't big on heart-to-hearts. But glancing through the bars of our iron back gate, I had a queasy feeling why he'd taken me aside: Mom's tan Datsun 210 sat empty across the tree-lined road, in front of the picket-fenced house belonging to the Cullen family. In an uncomfortable twist of fate common to small towns, Mom had ended up dating a man whose family lived across the street from her ex-husband. A couple of times, at family barbecues, I'd met the old woman who lived there alone. They called her Grammy Cullen, and during the summer I'd look out my bedroom window and see her pruning her roses over her white lattices, a long, skinny cigarette dripping from her bony hand. All the people in that family had funny names. Howdy's brother was called Tig, and one of his sisters was named Corky. They sounded like characters on kiddie TV shows, but they didn't act like them. They spoke in huffs and grunts, and even Howdy's nickname for me, Ringtail Ignat, had a strangely sinister edge.

Except for those barbecues I hadn't been inside the house. But Mom had been by, many times lately. I'd see her car across the road, and then she'd stop over alone for a minute to visit me, just before she and Howdy were ready to leave. But on this particular night she wouldn't just stop by. She'd pick up my little vinyl suitcase and my Raggedy Ann doll and set them in the trunk, and I'd climb into the backseat. My summer vacation at Dad's house over, we'd embark on the hour-long drive from Merced to Fresno, Mom in the passenger seat and Howdy behind the wheel.

Life with Howdy was already volatile when Dad issued that warning. And yet, the overriding feeling from that summer with Dad is not unease, but contentedness. Living with Nanette at the house on Twenty-fifth Street, Dad and I were happy together. When I think back now, when people hear that my father was murdered and then ask what kind of trouble he got into, what kind of enemies he had, I look to that era as a time when Stanley Howard seemed incapable of coming to any harm.

On a typical day that summer I'd first hear his voice—usually laughing—coming from his bedroom. I'd grab the *Merced Sun-Star* off the front porch and then push the bedroom door open slowly, creakily, until Dad shouted, "Good morning," my cue to dive onto the water bed and set off a tsunami as I nestled between him and Nanette. I'd give them each a kiss and lie with my head pressed to Dad's chest, right next to the little rose tattoo just above his heart. I'd try to match my breathing to his, slow and deep. "Jesus Christ," Dad would say, picking up the front page. "One hundred and two today." That'd be Nanette's cue to throw on her big brown and orange robe and put the kettle on for Sanka.

If Dad were a morning kind of guy, he would have rounded us up in the early daylight to avoid the worst heat. But he worked late hours—way past my bedtime—squeegeeing windows, emptying trash cans, and wiping down counters. He ran a business, Howard's Janitorial Service, with him and his younger brother Brad as the sole employees. So on this as on every Saturday, just as the glaring sun climbed overhead, we donned flip-flops (mine pink with plastic daisies) and sunglasses (purple plastic-rimmed, heart-shaped) and headed out into the back-yard to work the garden as a family. "We're a family": This had been drilled into my head, like prereading flash cards, every time we sat down to dinner or climbed into Nanette's rusty VW Bug for a trip to the new town mall. And we were truly a happy family, never happier than on the weekends, when Dad threw his favorite Rod Stewart album of the moment on the turntable.

Young hearts, be free tonight.
Time is on your side.

All through the summer that scratchy voice wafted across the yard as though carried on the heat waves in the air, aerobic backbeat and exhilarating synthesizer scales keeping us energized through hours of hoeing and weeding. The lot was three times as big as our neat little rectangle of a brown, two-bedroom house. Running across the yard winded me, but I did anyway, chasing our white German shepherd, Chancey, careening like an airplane, rushing after hummingbirds, rubber-bottomed feet oblivious to the prickly dried grass.

You might think Stan Howard came from farming stock, like nearly everyone else in Merced, but if there are farmers in the Howard genealogy, they stretch back a few generations to Kansas, where Dad's parents grew up. From the time I was born my Grandpa Ben had been retired from the air force—which had transferred him to England and finally to Castle Air Force Base, just outside Merced—and employed by the fire department. All that public duty had given him a solid pension and the promise of more retirement benefits, and that stretched a long way in a nowhere village like Merced. Planting and pulling up vegetables wasn't work for Howards, just a peculiarly pleasurable hobby.

Dad's garden was five rows across: zucchini, carrots, squash, tomatoes, cucumbers, celery—more vegetables than we ever knew what to do with, though Nanette transformed the cucumbers into dozens of jars of bread-and-butter pickles every fall. At five, I was an ineffectual gardener—I had to be reminded not to overwater and wasn't allowed to handle the fertilizer—so I spent my time traipsing about, ambushing Nanette's cat or plucking figs from the corner tree. This was fine with Dad, because I was sticking it out with him, after all, in the heat.

This yard was the first plot of land he'd ever had to call his own. The house was a first too, although none of this was really Dad's. It belonged to Nanette's generous family, and just about every piece of furniture in it—the wine barrel converted into a toilet stand, a burgundy and ocher paisley couch, and my favorite, the stuffed bobcat that sat beneath a glass-and-walnut coffee table, giving off a musty death smell—belonged to Nanette. Dad married Nanette in 1979, in a wedding replete with puff-sleeved dress and dinner reception at the Elks Lodge—her first. The photos show me, three years old, tiny toes bundled inside pint-size suntan panty hose. I look bewildered, and happy. I liked Nanette from as early as I can remember. Nanette was good with vegetables, good with kittens, good with stuffed animals and sea monkey kits. She was a pro with instant oatmeal, which she made for me every morning by letting the tap water run until it wouldn't get any hotter, creating a satisfyingly crunchy texture. She never asked me to think of her as a mother, or love her as I did my own mother, and I loved her all the more for that, the way a kindergartner might grow attached to a favorite teacher.

She worked as a checkout clerk at the largest hardware store in town, where she got the employee discount, and so our house was full of the kind of do-it-yourself improvements that made other Merced homeowners jealous. First came the aluminum miniblinds and eggshell-colored chiffon swags to top them, then new carpet—the plush kind marbled with knobby rivulets—and vinyl runners tacked down the hallway to protect it. And the paneling in my bedroom—whitewashed, self-adhesive particleboard with a thin veneer of grass-green grain, with green curtains to match.

Earlier that summer Dad had built a redwood deck over the old concrete back patio, assisted by Grandpa, Uncle Brad, and *Sunset* magazine, and then a new fence. The day they finished, we'd pulled the plastic lawn chairs out of the basement and sat around drinking Tab straight out of the bottle until the june bugs had come out and the three shag-haired members of Dad's band had straggled in. Grandpa ducked out for home and Dad took his place in the garage behind his drum set, testing the snare and revving up for the usual opener, "Maggie May." The band was too undisciplined about meeting regularly for the neighbors to bother complaining. Nanette and I plugged our ears at the mike feedback and pulled the lawn chairs around front to settle in for the show.

Dad was a Rod Stewart fanatic. He had the full collection of Rod's albums and eight-tracks. Sure, we listened to A Flock of Seagulls and Duran Duran and Hall and Oates and turned up the volume for The Cars. After all, our time was measured in MTV heavy rotations: "I'll be back in three videos," Dad would say if he needed to slip out to the garage for a second and Nanette wasn't around.

But the real sound track to summer at Dad's was pure Rod. At night when I'd sometimes join him and Nanette sweeping out doctors' offices, curling up on a scratchy waiting-room couch when my eyelids got too heavy, he'd bring along his brand-new boom box and turn it up so that we could hear "Maggie May" over the whirring of the waxing machine. Of course the song he listened to most was "Maggie May," resetting the needle to the right spot on the turntable at home, bouncing me up and down the plastic runners in the cramped hallway with my feet on top of his. It was his band's best cover.

But that last summer day in the garden I'd swear we listened to *Tonight I'm Yours*. It came out in 1981, though perhaps too late for the hot weather, and yet I'll always associate summer in the garden with that album. It's got all the classic Rod elements: one of those fast, roadhouse bad-boy songs ("Tora Tora Tora"); one of those strangely scheming sensitive-man songs ("Tonight's the Night" is the standard-bearer in this genre, but on this album the tune is "Sonny," in which he tells an ex-girlfriend all about how his new flame doesn't measure up); and one of those fiddle-filled small-town-boy-makes-good—or sometimes bad—ballads (in this case "Only a Boy," another song Dad played over and over). And then, second-to-last, "Young Turks," a track that screams "eighties" so loud you see striped leg warmers dancing through your head. It's a small-town-boy ballad, but instead of sweet, nostalgic fiddle playing, we get a pulsing electronic soundscape and a heroic leitmotif on the keyboard.

Nineteen eighty-one was a prime-of-life summer for Dad, who never let a visiting weekend go by unused. He didn't really take care of me, didn't feed me or clothe me or attend to the mundane details of child rearing—Nanette did those things, as best she could. But every day he told me that I had to come and live with him, for good, and he meant it. "When you're thirteen," he'd shout over the music as he reached around the driver's seat to squeeze my ankle, "you can tell the judge where you want to live—with your daddy." I loved it when he reached around, just to let me know he was thinking of me. But then his hand would clench a bit too tight. And I just couldn't squirm away or whine to him to let go, not with that toothy mustache smile shining at me in the rearview mirror.

I always loved "Young Turks," Rod's sentimental synthesizer tale about two kids in love, even though at five I couldn't quite follow the story. Later, when I could make out all the words, I was struck by the song's last verse. After reckless Billy and Patty leave their hometown with only youth and determination to boost them, we hear Billy's letter back to his folks. His final line: "Patty gave birth to a ten-pound baby boy." "Yeah!" Rod shouts, and you can just about see him raising his fist in the air.

I think Dad could relate to that weirdly celebratory "Yeah!"—that feeling that procreating was like raising a triumphant middle finger to the nay-saying world. He never had the guts to run away from home the way the kids in the song did, so his antiauthoritarian statement was less dramatic, more imagined. But here I was for the summer, with him where I belonged, dragged around town from one cleaning gig to the next in a beat-up van that bore his last name to show everyone in Merced that he was someone, damn it.

Usually he was chatty with my mom when she came over—after all, they'd been good friends through high school before eloping on a whim. But he barely spoke to her when she picked me up that night. Nanette handed my things over and we started down the porch steps toward the Datsun, where Howdy Cullen sat sucking on a cigarette in the driver's seat.

Dad called out to me as Mom popped the vinyl seat forward for me to crawl in. "Remember!" he shouted, flexing.

I watched Dad through the back window as Howdy snuffed out his cigarette and pulled down the street toward the freeway to Fresno.

THE GREAT CENTRAL VALLEY

A TYPICAL AFTERNOON IN THE CAR, circa 1981: I'm playing the role of human jukebox on the drive from Merced to Fresno. It's not an easy job to fulfill at age five, with my limited repertoire of lyrics, but I'm determined to keep Mom entertained. The Datsun lacks a radio and—more crucially in the ninety-degree September heat—air-conditioning. My sweaty legs slip against the vinyl upholstery, picking up bits of dirt from the crevices, as I kneel on the backseat and belt out patchy renditions of "Jesus Loves Me," "You are My Sunshine," and "On the Road Again." The Willie Nelson track is one of Mom's favorites, and I chose it because, from what I can glimpse of her in the rearview mirror, she needs a catchy tune to take her mind off the perspiration matting her short brown hair, and the new baby just beginning to swell her belly. The air from the passenger window blows in one steady, hot gust, sweetly pungent with rotting chicken feed, blasting us with fine grains of soil from the shriveled cotton fields outside. I have to shout against the roaring wind.

> On the road again!
> La la la la making music with my friends!

Mom fills in the words I never could make out as she sings along and smiles—my toneless squeaking seems to have brightened her mood. The gray-brown fields pass, and the rows of almond trees begin to whip by, ticking off fractions of the sixty-five-mile journey in excruciatingly small increments. Los Banos. Chowchilla. Madera. "Almost there," Mom shouts.

This is California, but not the California of the Beach Boys and convertibles and Endless Summer romances, of palm trees and surfing and gentle ocean breezes. Here the climate is far from balmy: scorching and dry in the summer, cloaked by blinding fog in the winter. But the conditions are perfect, when well irrigated, for growing everything from grapes to sugar beets to sorghum—twenty-five percent of all table food produced in the United States. The 99 freeway, which runs down the center of the state like a long, straight zipper, connects dozens of agricultural towns—Bakersfield, Turlock, Modesto, Livingston. Some are little more than a roadside fruit stand, others—like Fresno—are sprawling vortexes of malls and tract homes, but all are dry and hot and flat. The freeway feels as though it stretches into eternity; the Central Valley is 430 miles long and up to 100 miles wide. You can see the Sierra Nevadas, but they seem impossibly distant, far-off ridges walling in reality from the unknown.

This drive is one among hundreds Mom and I will make from Merced to Fresno, drives that blur into each other like an endless road trip. My command performance of Willie Nelson finished, Mom still appears sluggish, lethargic. Only in retrospect will I consider whether it was the wilting heat or our departure from Merced that sapped her energy.

I'm too young to appreciate that Merced has its charms—neatly trimmed park lawns, streets canopied by ash trees, carefully swept sidewalks. Bear Creek wends through the town center, banked by blackberry bushes, barely a trickle in the summer but high enough for fishing and swimming in the early spring. Ranch houses with split-log fences and half-circle driveways face the creek, fronting neighborhoods of prewar three bedrooms with peaked roofs and stucco stoops. JCPenney, Sears, and Mervyn's—fine purveyors of everything a family needs—cluster together a few blocks away on the east end of the city. Toward the freeway, a brick-paved official downtown district with sandwich shops and a vintage fifties movie theater sits largely deserted. Far on the west side of the freeway, Mexican farmworkers live in decaying, overpopulated homes, chasing chickens around yards littered with car parts.

Merced holds memories for Mom, and crucial blood ties. And now she is leaving Merced specifically to be with Howdy, whose child she is carrying, because Howdy is a heroin addict and there are no methadone clinics for him to visit daily in Merced.

Mom has a defeated look on her face as we approach the first Fresno exits, as though she can see all the trouble with Howdy coming but can do nothing to stop it.

And then I spot a big rig approaching in the rearview window and her eyes perk up. "Get ready to wave!" Mom rallies. I scramble to the window, clench my little fingers into a fist, and pump my arm up and down as though to pull an invisible horn. The truck is roaring alongside us now, the cab looming powerfully above our sedan. The driver winks and lifts his cap, and the truck lets out two satisfying honks.

Our exit is fast approaching; in twenty minutes we'll be on the southeast side of town, at home in our cheap apartment with Howdy, who will be rolling another joint.

HOWDY

THE FIRST AND ONLY TIME I heard Howdy cry, I was four, and the sound of his weeping frightened me more than his screaming. Just a few weeks earlier I'd watched him use a screwdriver to gouge the eyes of a rat he'd caught in one of our mousetraps, laughing in amusement as Mom looked on in uneasy silence. They'd split up again the next day. Mom and I lived in a house shaped like a castle near the Merced train depot; my bedroom window was next to the front door. That night I lay in the dark, clenching my *Sesame Street* sheets, as Howdy sobbed like a forlorn dog on our stoop. *Don't do it, don't do it, don't do it,* my heart pounded out, as I telepathically begged my mother to keep the dead bolt locked. But even as a preschooler I knew my mother would open that door, knew that something about Howdy turned her from the strong, dependable woman I saw in his absence into someone weak and powerless. This gave my love for her a frustrated, angry edge. When she briefly took up smoking, I would scream at her, "If you smoke, you'll die, and if you die, what will *I* do?" The real question, the furious silent one, was "How can you *do* this to me?" It was a question I felt in my tense, indignant muscles every time I looked at Howdy.

At first glance, my mother must have thought Howdy had his selling points. He was strong and intimidating and wore big manly silver belt buckles and cowboy boots. His Irish good looks were a little rough around the edges: thick brown hair, steely eyes, pale freckles. Unlike most Merced guys, he'd gone to college, on a baseball scholarship until a shoulder injury to his pitching arm made him drop out. He'd lived in

Costa Rica and spoke fluent Spanish. He had artistic leanings: Shards of stained glass and coils of metal littered the living rooms of our Fresno apartments, and watercolor paintings of dragons, unicorns, and busty mermaids leaned against the walls. I liked the stained-glass landscapes, but not the paintings. They were full of the kind of images that delighted me in picture books, but Howdy's art made my cheeks turn red. The mermaids' breasts bulged in disconcerting ways—you could see their nipples—and the unicorn's eyes twinkled suspiciously.

From the start my father did not teach me to see Howdy's good side. Dad had remained friends with my mother following their swift divorce, even after he remarried. Dad's sister Dana had introduced my mom to Howdy, and therefore my father knew the scoop, knew about Howdy's temper and his history with drugs. That summer evening in the garden with Dad was just one among many lectures that must have started when I was three, from the time my mother and Howdy first began dating. Dad was right to worry about how Howdy would treat me, and yet his motivations were more than protective. He wanted to be the only father figure in my life. And I would respond to his early lectures with fierce loyalty, no matter how formidable a foe Howdy proved.

After that Sunday anti-Howdy pep talk in the garden, I came back from my weekend at Dad's full of pride. "My dad is stronger than you-oo," I sang to Howdy after Mom had left for the grocery store, flexing my puny biceps in front of his face.

Howdy lay on the sagging couch, taking in the baseball game, and slid his eyes to look at me dismissively. "I could kick your dad's ass," he said. My giggling stopped dead.

I'd already gotten the message that Howdy did not fear my father. The first time Howdy took me to the methadone clinic, when I was five, he told me we were going to see the doctor. "Are you sick?" I asked, but he just laughed and twiddled the end of his mustache: "Yeah, kid, I've got a real bad cold."

The woman took a mint-green pitcher and poured what looked like water into a Dixie cup; Howdy tossed it back and we left. I saw the lift in his mood on the way home, as he ran the tuner of his new Ford Taurus up and down the dial looking for Jimi Hendrix, Eric Clapton, Led

Zeppelin. Howdy had tried to set me straight on this a few weeks ago, when I'd come home from Dad's singing.

"Rod Stewart," he'd said, with a finger pointing at me like Uncle Sam's, "is for pussies."

Sometime that first year in Fresno, Mom was pouring cupfuls of water over my head while I screamed about soap getting up my nose, and then she grabbed my arm and pulled it toward her so hard it felt like it would come out of the socket.

"What—what is this?" she shouted. On my upper arm was a red circle the size of a cigarette tip. We had scorched holes the same dimensions on our sofa where Howdy had snuffed out his Marlboros.

"Oh my God," Mom said under her breath. When she confronted Howdy, he blamed a babysitting accident. The babysitter was not a smoker. Mom chose to accept Howdy's story.

She was pregnant with Howdy's child. Just weeks earlier she had put on her only dress, a brown calico wrap-skirt, and Howdy had donned khakis, and we had driven to a Unitarian church shaded by maple trees. The pews were empty, but still I buzzed with the solemnity of the occasion and the excitement of seeing my mother as a bride. My giddiness over the glamorous idea of marriage overcame my distrust of Howdy for that moment, as they stood before a priest and exchanged rings. Only in the pit of my stomach did I realize that Mom's ability to leave him had just been reduced from slim to almost nonexistent.

Since I didn't remember the burns, I can only speculate as to why I didn't tell my father. Loyalty was a double-edged sword. Telling my father about the burns would have meant betraying my mother. I would wage my war against Howdy, with my dad as silent backup. But I would keep the details about the battles to myself.

Howdy nicknamed his son, my brother Emmet, Buckley Weasel. He gave me my nickname around the time Emmet was born, as we stood at the Fresno Zoo staring at the island of ringtail lemurs: "Ringtail Ignat." That's not the name I heard most often, though. *Brat. Bitch. Little shit.* These are names I got used to hearing, delivered at window-rattling decibels with clenched fists, accompanied by spectacular displays of physicality—a freshly delivered pizza skating across the kitchen linoleum, a potted plant smashed against the wall.

We had moments when I worried that I might come to like him, days when I saw his charm in full bloom. During our early years together, he'd sit me on his bicycle handlebars for the ride to work at the Sunnyside Tennis Club, balancing me securely between his beefy arms. Throughout the spring I'd trail him around the club, dazzled by his effortless rapport with the club members, as he checked the pool's chlorine levels and hosed down courts.

The Sunnyside Tennis Club was a clean, carefully mown landscape populated by lawyers, doctors, financial planners: incessantly smiling men with carefully creased shorts and hair like a Ken doll's. Howdy called them by their last names, no *Mr.*: "Hey, McGillis, how's that backhand today?" And then, lifting me onto his shoulders: "Yeah, this here is the Ringtail Ignat. She's a handy one. Listen, if you're looking for a doubles partner, I could manage to put down this hose awhile." He and McGillis might have me keep score as they hit a few volleys under a system that defied my limited counting abilities. "Forty–love, you got that?" Howdy would shout, and I'd repeat it dutifully, smiling back at his well-groomed opponent, legs swinging beneath the plastic bench. Howdy might take a graceful loss, shrugging his head in a mock disbelief that charmed the Ken doll, winning us an invitation to a back-yard barbecue next weekend. "I'll bring the little woman and the Ring-tail Ignat," Howdy would say with a wink.

These mornings at the club had their perks, but three in the afternoon was my golden hour, the time when Mom woke to let me shadow her around the apartment as she lugged laundry or watered Howdy's jungle of spider plants. It wasn't until six each night that the dread set in. Because five nights a week or more, depending on how many double-time shifts Mom was trying to pull, we sat down to a dinner of London broil or Shake 'n Bake, and then Mom began gathering her nursing scrubs and stethoscope and preparing to leave for work. She left at six thirty, sensing my anxiety and setting my favorite Mickey Mouse Discomania record on the player, which Howdy would take off the moment the door closed.

Sometimes Howdy and I drove her to the community hospital

across town. The journey meant I could hear her voice for twenty-five minutes more and gain extra time to memorize her brown eyes in the rearview mirror. But after she kissed me good-bye, I would have to face one red light after another with Howdy, never knowing when thick traffic might send him cussing and slamming the steering wheel.

Back at the apartment, Howdy took out his packs of rolling papers and his Ziploc bag of pot. He smoked it all night, every night, sometimes at home, and sometimes at buddies' houses, weird redwood structures shaped like domes or shadowed by thick pines and carpeted with Navajo rugs, in the foothills outside Fresno. I would occupy myself with coloring books as Howdy and his friends took their drags, relieved when Howdy would dig for his car keys, my excitement at heading home only dampened by a vague worry over whether Howdy should drive.

He smoked it in front of Mom too, usually while we watched our fuzzy black-and-white television on her nights off. I'd try to join them in the living room, holding a dusty macramé throw pillow against my face to filter the sickly sweet pot smoke from my breathing. The eighties drug war had not yet turned me into a poster child for the DARE campaign, but already I hated the pot, disgusted and terrified by the way it made Howdy's eyes glaze over. "Relax," Mom would say, and try to pull the pillow from my face, but I'd press it harder to my nose, flashing Howdy a pissy look.

"Go to your room," he'd shout, and I'd trudge off, happy to fulfill his brusque orders.

My mother atoned for staying with Howdy by loading me with material goods. When Guess? jeans were the lower-middle-class status symbol du jour, I was one of only three or four kids at Easterby Elementary to sport them. We didn't live on the rich side of Fresno, the northeast end lined with Tudor-style mansionettes. Through fourteen years and four moves, we lived a half-hour drive down the city's six-lane streets, past strip malls and parking lots and through endless red lights, in the opposite corner, the southeast's Sunnyside area.

We lived in cardboard-walled apartments and then in a cozy 1950s three-bedroom, one block down the street from Section 8 housing, and were rich only in comparison to the kids at my school, the children of grocery store tellers and auto mechanics. Mom's nursing night shifts brought in upward of $80,000 a year in a city where a 1,600-square-foot home with a swimming pool ran $72,000. And so Mom bought me $80 Guess? overalls when others wore OshKosh. She bought me $45 Reebok high-tops when Payless Shoe Source was the norm, and $150 limited-edition teddy bears and one of the first Texas Instruments home computers and gold Anne Klein watches that I lost (three times) in my PE locker. She wrote checks for ballet classes and horse-riding lessons. Howdy's money didn't pay for any of these things. Through his various Fresno careers as a sports club groundskeeper, an assistant undertaker, and finally a life insurance salesman, most of his modest salary supported his dope habit, his golf practice, and his enduring love of tanklike American luxury cars.

Mom did not have as much time to share with me as she did money, but the time we did share felt luxurious. I was never happier than when she let me play hooky from first grade on one of her rare days off. We drove through the rain all morning in our musty little Datsun, dashing from mall to mall to stock up on household goods, Mom cheerfully examining sheet sets and charging toward sale signs as though on a treasure hunt. Our hair wet from running through the parking lot, we pulled into A&W and ordered yeasty-smelling burgers delivered to the window of our car and ate happily, my intense enjoyment undermined only by the dread of returning home to Howdy.

In exchange for mom's dependability, I made halfhearted attempts to placate Howdy. This mostly involved completing chores at night as Howdy smoked a joint on the couch and toddler-aged Emmet tottered around trying to play with me, after Mom had gone to work. By first grade, my dishwashing technique had improved, and I could now wrangle our Hoover up and down the apartment stairs, thudding one step at a time. The housecleaning campaign to gain Howdy's favor seemed to be working: Earlier that year Howdy had given me a new bike, sans training wheels, for Christmas, with a special note from Santa's elf that I recognized as his handwriting. It was the most affectionate gesture I had ever seen from him.

Then one night as I set to vacuuming per Howdy's instructions, Emmet invented a new game. He'd stick his pudgy little hand out just as the vacuum roared toward him, pulling it away and squealing and jumping up and down as the Hoover neared. His blond bangs were so cute, and his laughter was so sweet, that I started getting into it, lunging toward him to his dimple-producing delight, shouting "ha ha" as I pulled back just in time and his eyes glittered.

Emmet crawled under the kitchen table. I heard his laugh, and I lunged without looking. I felt the vacuum climb up over something, and then I heard Emmet's giggles turn to shrieks. At that time we owned a guinea pig that would make heinous, ear-piercing shrieks when he wanted more lettuce. Emmet sounded like the guinea pig, but louder and more frenzied.

I dropped the vacuum handle and fell to my knees to see what had happened. Emmet lay crying with his hand up inside the vacuum as the motor kept roaring. And I just knelt there looking at what I'd done, mouth gaping at the vacuum as though it were a creature from a Stephen King movie. The motor whirred to a stop and I felt Howdy standing behind me with the electrical cord in his fist. He didn't hit me with it. He didn't touch me.

"You fucking bitch!" he shouted. Spit flew from his mouth as his chest heaved. I cowered as he screamed, hunching into the corner, steeling my eyes against inevitable tears. Shaking, carrying Emmet in his arms, Howdy loaded us into the car and drove to the emergency room. Almost two decades later, at Emmet's graduation from army boot camp, Howdy recounted the scene with a chuckle. "The look on your face at the hospital!" he said. "You were going to take those doctors aside and tell them I'd done it to him." The irony that in fact he had been an abuser, even if he had not vacuumed Emmet's hand, seemed not to touch him.

Right after the vacuum incident, Mom's friends around the apartment complex took to calling Emmet "Michael Jackson," because he had to wear a white sock over the hand that had been sucked right through the rotating brush, crunching bones. They'd shout across the Village Green Apartments parking lot as Mom and Emmet and I got out of the Datsun, "Hey there, Michael Jackson!" Mom would laugh and wave; Emmet's injuries were a joke, the kind of rough-and-tumble accident that happened between careless little kids. She didn't seem to notice that I wouldn't laugh or smile, but instead drop my head toward the gravel.

The vacuum incident marked a definitive point in my relationship with Howdy. That night, as I stared into his screaming face, full of guilt and worry over how I'd hurt Emmet, full of hatred toward Emmet's father, all pretenses between us shattered. We would not, even occasionally, pretend to like each other anymore.

And I would never call on my father for backup. Soon enough my father could not save me any longer, not even in my imagination. He was already sliding toward his sudden death.

part
two

THE BEGINNING OF
DAD'S END: FALL 1983

LOOKING BACK, I'D SAY Dad's decline started with his divorce from Nanette. I'd just come to live with Dad for the second grade, his trial run at caring for me. Mom hoped it might offer respite from the ongoing war between Howdy and me, that I might come back matured and more accepting of him.

But the timing was off. The summer before second grade, Nanette's father hung himself from a backyard tree. Mom broke the news to me in the credit-union parking lot. She told me Grandpa Frago (I called him Grandpa even though we weren't close) had been taking medication that had made his heart stop. She didn't tell me that the medication in question was an antidepressant, and that the only way it had caused his heart to stop was by failing to prevent his suicide.

I didn't need to know about the suicide to see that something was terribly wrong when, one fall evening, Nanette and Dad and I sat watching MTV. *Who's gonna drive you home?* The Cars implored while Nanette sipped her tea and I posed my Strawberry Shortcake dolls on their plastic picnic bench. "What's the deal with the exercise bike?" Dad asked, eyes still fixed on the screen.

Nanette had loaned the stationary cycle to Grandma Rose in hopes that riding it would rile her endorphins and perk her up. In her sixties, Rose Frago was more vibrant than the thick layer of dust covering the statues of praying hands in her house would suggest, able to pull me down the street in a rusty red wagon the whole length of a block. I could easily imagine her donning a polyester jog suit and tearing it up on a dinky metal bike.

Dad was dubious. "Is she even using it?" he demanded, as Nanette faced the television rather than hold the hard gaze he'd turned on her. I scanned their expressions, perplexed. With or without the bike, Dad was in great shape. " 'Cause you know if she's not using it, I sure could," he said. He turned the channel for our weekly dose of *Solid Gold*, the show's glittery dancers bounding past as Dad glared.

That argument was not about the exercise bike, but about Dad's annoyance at Nanette's persistent grief. The summer before I arrived, Grandma Mae and Grandpa Ben had accompanied Nanette to three churches, trying to help her find a religious service that could soothe her pain. None eased her sadness or transformed her back into the playful wife Dad had known. Not that I could get a clear read on their marital problems. Howdy had accustomed me to shouting, but at Dad's house the unrest was mostly silent. My father's impatience was subtle, playing out through withheld kisses and tense dinner conversations.

Depressed but resolute, Nanette continued to take good care of me. She took me swimming at the public pool, hung my tempera paint artworks proudly on the refrigerator, and bought me a pair of low-maintenance hermit crabs. When Mom arranged for me to continue ballet classes in Merced, the task of outfitting me fell to Nanette. She took me to Mervyn's and had me try on black house slippers, pinching the tips. "Plenty of growing room," she said, glowing with accomplishment at her resourcefulness. Soft and spongy, the slippers turned my feet to marshmallows on skinny-leg sticks. They were all wrong, and standing at the barre alongside girls in pliant leather shoes, I knew it. But I didn't complain to Nanette, because I was too embarrassed for her, and because in her heavy brown eyes I could see how hard she was trying.

I attended three schools that year. The first was John Muir Elementary, which Dad rechristened John Manure Smellamentary. In fact John Muir was overly scrubbed if anything, its clean, modern buildings rising like nuclear bunkers atop the play yard. My teacher was even starker. Miss Adams had a jet-black bob and coal eyes. And she hated me, because of my mother.

Mom had called to let Miss Adams know that her child had passed the Gifted and Talented Education test, and if her dad hadn't made her move, she'd be going to a GATE school in Fresno. Mom demanded challenges: homework. Ms. Adams obliged with pages of math drills that she never checked over.

"Let me see those," Dad said one day after faithfully meeting me by the hopscotch grids. He wadded the drill sheets, looked for a trash can, then shoved them in the pocket of his leather bomber jacket. His eyes twinkled behind the tobacco lenses of his aviator sunglasses. As for the row of S's for "Satisfactory" on my report card, where once I had gotten straight O's for "Outstanding": "Lots of S's for stinky, smelly, John Manure," Dad said. "Don't sweat it."

I didn't. My most significant education that year would be in nonacademic subjects, like the Russians. A boy on the jungle gym had informed me they were evil. Another kid let me know the tooth fairy was a sham. The final blow came that winter. "There's no such thing as Santa Claus, stupid!" one of my classmates said, laughing after I'd told him about my letter to the North Pole.

"He's wrong!" I told Dad as we waited for Nanette in front of Grandma Rose's house, the janitorial truck's engine humming. "I read all about him, the real St. Klaus, from Germany."

Dad laughed. "Good thing you do all that reading," he said. A few weeks later, on Christmas morning, a four-foot-tall teddy bear wearing a gold tuxedo and top hat awaited me under my grandparents' tree, marked "From Santa." I knew who had put it there, but I loved Dad all the more for his deception.

I moved to Franklin Elementary that winter. Dad and Nanette had bought a new house, a 1,600-square-foot distraction from the problems with their marriage. It was in a newer tract neighborhood out by the mall, and it was almost twice as large as the place on Twenty-fifth Street. The amenities were all there: automatic dishwasher, garbage disposal, garage-door opener. It had a double-car garage, and yet Dad's old drum set sat boxed in the corner. A built-in swimming pool, not a garden, consumed the backyard. We'd moved up in the world, but none of us was happy.

Dad and Nanette's silence echoed through the extra space. I tried to combat it with volume, crying at bedtime. When Dad and Nanette invited friends over for a housewarming, I wailed with newfound lung power. "I want my brother!" I cried from my bed, working myself into a hyperventilating froth. "Emmet! Emmet! I *want* my brother!"

"I don't know what's gotten into her," Dad and Nanette said, dismissing themselves to calm me. "You can see your little brother this weekend, honey," Nanette said as I kept the tears rolling. But the problem was not that I missed two-year-old Emmet. As I took in a deep breath to power a new scream, a guilty voice inside said I was just using him to make Dad and Nanette snap out of it.

Then one day I came home to find Dad's bedroom door open, and Nanette nowhere to be found. I peeked in; Dad lay in the middle of the water bed on his back like a corpse floating on a placid lake. His face was a mass of bandages wrapped across his nose, under his chin, and over his forehead like a cartoon character that had just had a tooth pulled. His eyes, ringed in black like a boxer's, squinted.

"Hey, pumpkin." His voice was soft. "Come over here and say hi to your old dad for a minute."

I sat on the water bed's leather rail with perfect ballet posture, not leaning in to hug or kiss him. It seemed he might break or lurch at me like a mummy.

He must have seen that I was spooked. "Did you forget about your old dad's operation today?"

I leaned away. "What happened to you, Dad?"

"It's all right, babe. They fixed the inside of my nose, so I won't snore. Come here, don't treat your old dad like a leper."

Earlier that year, Dad had posed for a drawing at the Merced County Fair, one of those caricatures you pay a few bucks for. In it Dad's hammering away on a teeny-weeny set of drums with his Smurf-sized body, enormous head flashing his usual huge, mustached grin. But the focal point of the drawing was his nose. It hunched toward his forehead when he smiled. It wasn't really cartoonish in life. It gave him a healthy jolt of masculinity.

The bandages from Dad's operation came off within a few weeks. The swelling went down and the dark eye circles faded. If you didn't see him every day, you might not have noticed the nose was smaller, just a little chip off the top. He'd had to fix a deviated septum and decided to get a subtle nose job while he was at it.

He slapped on extra aftershave the day the bandages came off, gave his thick black hair a few extra strokes with the comb. "Your good old dad is back!" he said, helping me into the janitorial van for a ride to school, a special treat. "Same as ever."

Dad and Nanette split in February, and Dad took a bachelor pad with another divorcé. He was getting his life back together, and there was little room for me in that process. Mom advocated the obvious solution: that I return to live with her in Fresno. Dad and my grandparents had other notions. I would live out Dad's "transition" with them. This might have made sense if it had allowed me to stay in the same school for more than three months, but I switched schools again. The true reasons for the arrangement were unspoken but transparent to everyone involved except me: Mae and Ben could not let Dad default on his year of custody, could not allow him to be deemed a failure. Mom's lingering fear of her in-laws' censure was strong back then, and she had her hands full in Fresno with Howdy and Emmet. She gave up the fight.

Mae and Ben's house was not the worst fate a kid could ask for. Ben was, as befitted his son's business, obsessively clean, and Mae and Ben's taste in furniture was not stuck in the 1960s, but formed by whatever happened to be on show at Slater's. The backyard had a pond full of tadpoles good for catching in styrofoam cups and an enormous weeping willow tree whose curtainlike branches formed the perfect pretend house. My bedroom, the same one Dad had slept in as a teenager, was plain. But I made it my own by meticulously arranging an ever-growing collection of My Little Pony toys on the folding card table Grandpa Ben had dragged in, lining up each rubber horse with the color-coordinated brush provided to comb its candy-hued mane. Grandpa Ben's office was next to my room, handy for help with school reports on the flying squirrel and the state of Alaska. My new teacher at Ada Givens Elementary liberated her GATE students to pursue "creative free time" most of the day, which meant I got to curl up happily in a beanbag with books of my choosing.

But living with Grandma and Grandpa had drawbacks. Few children populated this neighborhood of retirees. Grandma took it upon herself to furnish my wardrobe, selecting cheap turquoise pants with white piping off the sales racks at Newberry's. Dad rarely came by and Mom could only make the drive from Fresno when she had a day off. Worst of all was the heavy sense of limbo, the knowledge that this life was temporary, one of those visits to Grandma's house that stretches a few days too long as you sit with your ear to the front door, waiting for someone to drive up and take you home. Wherever that might now be.

Living in limbo colored my mean streak, which jovial Grandma Mae was not prepared for. She picked me up at 3:20 on the dot every afternoon, and in gratitude I called her stupid when she tried to help me with homework. Mae signed me up for the Brownies to mask the fact that, after switching schools three times, I had no friends. Once a week I crossed the yellow field behind the school to one of the members' houses, where someone else's mother helped us glue Popsicle sticks together or make insects out of bottle wire. I flashed my gap-toothed smile at the other Brownie members in hopes of instant connection, since I could never know when I'd be moving on once more.

The tension between Mae and me grew thick in a matter of weeks as I began picking at the ham-and-Miracle Whip sandwiches I used to savor. Grandpa Ben and I still had our bright moments belting out "Puff the Magic Dragon" in his office after school while he balanced the books for Howard's Janitorial Service. But the three of us were struggling together through their guardianship, not relishing it.

We did as well as could be hoped. Grandma Mae bought me the real ballet slippers and sparkly costume required for the annual dance concert. She took a Polaroid of me on the redwood deck before the performance, dolled up in sequins for my part as a jazz rainbow, fluffy fuchsia feather stuck in the top of my blond bun. My mother drove from Fresno to see that concert, and Nanette came too. Dad did not attend.

*   *   *

Just before the split, Dad bought a sports car, a crucial accessory to his imminent man-on-the-prowl status. One day after I'd settled in at Grandma's, he came by for me, zipping down Marthella Avenue in his silver Nissan 280ZX, the radio blasting. Rod Stewart had a new album and a new hit single that obviously fit Dad's frame of mind as he tapped his fingers on the steering wheel in time.

Some guys have all the luck
Some guys have all the pain
Some guys get all the breaks
Some guys do nothing but complain.

I crooned along to the roller-coaster lyricless part of the chorus. Poor Dad. Single again, with nothing but bad luck, so he thought, to blame.

We stopped at a liquor store, where he bought a cigar and lit it as we sat in the parking lot. The leather Nissan interior filled with a rich, manly smelling smoke. "To celebrate," he said, and though I could not figure out what merited celebration, I thought he looked glamorous puffing away. Ten minutes later, the cigar just a stub, Dad snuffed it in the empty ashtray. The ivory-colored plastic mouthpiece remained. I pulled it off the stub and shoved it in my pocket as Dad started the car.

At the apartment, Dad's roommate sat in a La-Z-Boy recliner watching the evening news. My heart sank as we walked into the kitchen and I saw that the school drawings I'd given Dad hadn't made it onto the refrigerator. He threw a take-and-bake pizza in the oven and had us carry our dinner upstairs to his bedroom. We sat on his bed—a mattress stacked on the floor—and chomped contentedly. This was Dad's new good life. But I took tiny bites to make my slice last. I hadn't seen Dad in a week, and I might not see him again for weeks more.

An hour later, Grandma Mae and Grandpa Ben asleep, I placed the cigar holder on the folding card table next to the My Little Pony toys. I picked it back up and pinched it between my fingers like a cigarette. I sniffed it—it smelled good, rich and spicy like the cigar smoke. I put it between my lips for a delicious inhale.

I spit it out across the room. It didn't taste the way that delicious cigar smelled. It tasted bitter and dirty, worse than black coffee. It was the most disgusting thing I'd ever tasted.

I felt my way down the dark hall to the bathroom, the floorboards creaking beneath the shag carpet. I reached straight for my toothbrush and squeezed on extra paste, piling it high like the picture on the Aquafresh box. I was no fanatic for dental hygiene; already I had six fillings. But I brushed until my gums bled, my tonsils stung, and the taste of the cigar holder, and with it Dad's new life, was just a gross memory.

MEETING "MOM": SPRING 1985

"YOU'RE GONNA LOVE HER," Dad said, pushing eighty-five on the freeway from Fresno to Merced. "She's pretty and she's fun. You can do girl things together, you know? Like shopping. She loves to shop. And, you know, makeup. She's got lots of *that* for you to play with." It was as though he had brought home a new Barbie doll from the toy store and couldn't wait to watch my face light up as I unwrapped her.

Dad had passed on months of weekend visits since I'd moved out of Grandma Mae's and back to Mom's in Fresno, and everything had changed. He had a new girlfriend. I'd never met her. They had an apartment together already, where they lived with her son, who was "just a year younger than *you*," as Dad waxed enthusiastic.

Dad's right hand clenched my knee. His left knocked the ash from his cigarette out the window in one efficient flick and returned to the steering wheel. I'd never seen him so ecstatic, mustache fanning like a dust broom above his slightly yellowing smile as the files of almond trees whooshed by. I flashed my new full set of front teeth, happy for him and hopeful.

The bristles of his mustache gathered together again on top of a straight, dead-serious lip. "I'm in love her," he said. "Just wait. Pretty soon you'll come live with us where you belong and we'll be a real family."

He had picked her up at the Sweetwater Saloon, a bar on the Merced Mall: the sexy insta-mom who would turn his life into a rerun of *The Waltons* by day, and a private showing of *Debbie Does Dallas* by night. I met her in the living room of the bare-walled and nearly empty apartment. A flocked cathedral ceiling loomed above us, and crates stood upended next to the sofa to create a coffee table. She was slim, with curvy hips beneath acid-washed jeans, and perky breasts. I squinted at her as she stood before me, trying to decide whether she was pretty. She looked more like a catalog model or a soap opera star than either my mother or Nanette: puffy lips, sharply arched eyebrows, feathered hair, flat waistline. When I brought her into focus, though, the deep bags under her eyes and the rough surface of her skin sent me into confusion. The intensity of her stare made me want to deny her good looks, the way I might tell myself that the most popular girl at my school wasn't really that pretty.

"Go on," Dad said, nudging me with his knees. "Give her a hug." I stepped inside Sherrie's lank arms. Her hair scratched my shoulder like wool, and her smell—perfume and cigarettes—made the inside of my nose itch.

"Your daddy's a special man," she whispered. "I hope you can share him with me."

Sherrie's presence turned all the rules in Dad's house upside down. And she was not the only stranger I had to share Dad with now. I first met Bobby in his bedroom, as he sat on the carpet sending Hot Wheels whizzing around a plastic track. He glanced up the second I stepped into his doorway, as though he'd been waiting for me. "Here," he said in a whisper, pointing excitedly to a row of toy cars. "Pick one. We'll race."

"This one," I said. I looked him over suspiciously. The first thing that struck me about Bobby was that he was Mexican, with rich golden brown skin and spiky, dark hair. That was all right by me—I had plenty of Mexicans in my third-grade class in Fresno and had nursed a serious a crush on Michael Escoto. It was Bobby's fragility, the way he cast his gaze as though in shame upon the carpet even as he spoke to me, that made me keep my distance. His hands were unsteady as he hooked the pieces of the racetrack together. It seemed that if you said the wrong thing, you could break him, and coupled with the idea that he'd be stealing half of Dad's affection, that vulnerability irritated me.

"Dad gave me that one," he said. He picked up the yellow car and displayed it on his palm.

"You mean your dad or *my* dad?"

"He's my dad too," Bobby said. "He's going to adopt me." He grinned as though he'd just found out we were all going to Disneyland.

We set the cars in their starting place and Bobby pulled the plastic rip cord. The cars hung on for the straight length of the course but flew off the rails at the first hairpin turn, launching spectacularly into the bedroom wall.

The next morning I heard laughter and got up to put on Dad's coffee. But the coffee machine was already hissing, the kettle half-empty, surrounded by brown puddles. "Honey?" Dad called. "Come here."

The bedroom door stood open. They all lay in bed, a real mattress on a four-poster frame, not the old water bed. Sherrie wore a silk slip trimmed in lace, her nipples erecting perky domes in the shiny fabric. She held her cigarette and coffee cup in the same hand and cradled Bobby in her other arm. Bobby lay in the middle of the bed, his head resting on Dad's chest.

"Climb in, babe," Dad said. I slipped in next to him under the covers, which were warm and smelled like his sweat and deodorant. He set down the mug and wiggled an arm around me, and I lay my head on his shoulder and touched my finger to his rose tattoo, taking covert glances at Sherrie. She caught me looking and winked. The wink felt too sly. I cast my eyes away.

"A real family," Dad said quietly, to himself. "Listen, baby, let's have a quick talk. Bobby is your brother now, you know? It's all just paperwork. This, us here together, this is what matters." He paused, kissed me on the forehead.

"You're a lucky girl," Sherrie said. "Your daddy won't stop talking about how much he loves you."

I picked my head off Dad's chest to grin at Sherrie. "I know," I said. I had a bad habit of saying "I know" instead of "thank you" anytime an adult gave me a compliment. Sherrie smirked.

"Sherrie's going to be your new mom," Dad said. "So we'd really like it if you could call her that—Mom."

"Okay," I said, and tried the word anew on my lips. "Mom," I whispered, staring at the rose tattoo. The word made me homesick, made me want to run for the freeway and take my chances hitchhiking back to Fresno, maybe catch a ride on a smelly chicken truck. But it was so warm under the covers, and I could feel Dad's chest rising and falling against mine. I pressed against him as he picked up the paper, and after a few minutes I drifted back to sleep.

Saturdays and Sundays zipped by. Real life was back in Fresno, where Mom, dead tired from too much overtime, rarely asked about Dad's new girlfriend. I missed Dad during the week, when I hid out from Howdy in my pink, heart-plastered bedroom. Seeing Dad on weekends was a contact high that crashed quickly by Sunday, when I longed for Mom and found myself all too eager to wave good-bye to Sherrie and Bobby.

I knew little about Sherrie. She had a job driving a forklift, which she told my grandma made good money. Dad said her ex-husband, Bobby's father, was a bad man, like Howdy. Every once in a while, not often, Bobby would have to visit him, and I'd crane my neck out the car window when we stopped by to collect him, trying to read the evilness on his dad's face. The ex-husband was short and dark, dressed in a flannel shirt and holey jeans as he watched us drive off with a dead set in his jaw. I saw echoes of Howdy in that expression, and I understood some of what Bobby had been through.

Dad picked me up or had me ride Amtrak down every visiting weekend. There was big fun to be had if I could get past Sherrie's presence: pizza, a swim in the apartment complex's pool, or a visit to the Merced zoo—which held a pen full of goats and a handful of chimps. Dad took us to see *Goonies*, even though he never saw kids' movies. And then, in the early evenings, the fun ended. Dad directed me and Bobby to play with our new toys in Bobby's room, at the opposite end of the apartment, while he and Sherrie shut themselves in their bedroom, something he and Nanette had never done. "Good night, kids," Dad would say after dinner, as Bobby and I began pulling out toys for the hours of self-entertainment ahead. "Good night, Dad!" we'd chime, trying to one-up the other's obedience.

I was loath to share my father with a new kid, but I saw that the best way to keep Dad was to pretend Bobby was my own flesh and blood. And so Bobby and I chatted, about cartoons, Dad, and sex. At eight, Bobby knew his basic birds and bees, but he was hungry for details the sex-ed books wouldn't tell him. We'd wait in the back of the janitorial truck, our legs dangling from the benches and kicking at the cleaning gear, as Dad and Sherrie ran into the grocery store for smokes and beer. "Did you know if a girl hasn't got her period yet, and a boy sticks it in her, she can't get pregnant?" Bobby would say.

I was mystified by sex too. I'd spent nights awake during first grade fantasizing about having a baby with the class's most popular boy, imagining him squirming on top of me on my closet floor, vague on the mechanics of the act. But I'd never let Bobby know. Whether because we were supposed to be brother and sister, or because his own mom telegraphed SEX like neon lights on a porn shop, the subject felt too icky between us. "Of *course* I know *that*," I'd say, with an air meant to project all the mysteries my extra year of life had revealed to me.

"Yeah, but did you know if a guy pulls his thing out . . ." We'd hear Dad's keys jingling in the car door, sending Bobby giggling and me blushing.

"Earthquake!" Dad would shout, rocking the camper shell so that the mops and brooms crashed.

"Stop it, Stan!" Sherrie would say, laughing, and from the little camper shell window I'd watch her toss her hair back. Then she and Dad would climb into the cab and we'd be off for our next errand.

Late spring of third grade, about six months after I'd met her, Sherrie and Dad bought a house together. Unlike our old house with Nanette, in the middle of town, this place was in the sticks. About three miles beyond the freeway, just a few blocks past one of Merced's notorious drug strips, lay acres and acres of pasture, and a row of five houses. Ours was a fixer-upper with yellow rectangles on the lawn where the old owners had parked broken-down stock cars. Thick puddles of oil stood on the driveway. We spent our weekends painting, planting, and pulling up weeds, Dad blasting Rod Stewart just like the old days on Twenty-fifth Street. I tried not to think about Nanette and the old place. All that was history now. Dad had bigger ambitions for his latest homestead. He'd start by repainting inside and out and installing a porch made of railroad ties. But no more garden for him. We'd have a scalloped landscape with fancy drip irrigation and, because we still couldn't afford a pool, a fishpond replete with waterfall.

The weekend we took on the pond, Dad threw on shorts and a muscle-T and handed shovels to Bobby and me. He might as well have equipped us with spoons, at the pace we dug, but Dad didn't care. The May afternoon sun shone blindingly, the backyard smelled of cow patties from the neighboring pastures, mulch, and mown grass, and Sherrie stood in the kitchen, stirring a jug of iced tea.

"That's the way to put a little muscle into it," Dad said, and I thought I caught him rolling his eyes. He took the shovel from my hands and tossed off a few heaps, doubling the size of our hole in three strokes. "You get that nice and deep and we'll get you guys some fish." The fish were the incentive, so Bobby began shoveling again, with bigger loads. I knew he'd been lazy with those teaspoon-sized shovels and bit back the urge to tell him so in front of Dad. My pitiful scoops were bigger than his, and I was a girl for crying out loud.

Bobby and I held down the plastic lining as Dad pinned it in place with heavy slate rocks. Dad beamed as the electric waterfall pump gurgled into action, and Sherrie applauded, knocking the ash from her cigarette into the air like confetti. "Warm nights, we'll pull around those chairs from the deck," he envisioned, holding his hands in L-shapes like a camera, "and have ourselves a little oasis."

He'd pieced his dream life back together. All he had to do was glue it secure. So late May 1985, Grandma Mae, Grandpa Ben, Uncle Brad, and Ric and their families came over to our house wearing suits and dresses on a Saturday afternoon. Bobby got to serve as the ring bearer, dressed in high-water gray slacks, white shirt, and a clip-on tie. Sherrie had taken me to JCPenney's to find my flower-girl outfit. The white wrap dress with pink piping was simple enough, but we accessorized with lace, fingerless gloves and a floppy lace bow tied on the side of my head, à la Madonna circa *Desperately Seeking Susan*. I had never felt so glamorous and uneasy at once. The family sat on the sofa and on chairs dragged in from the dining room as Dad and Sherrie processed down the hallway and exchanged rings in front of the television. Afterward Bobby and I sugar-overdosed on Hawaiian Punch while the grown-ups slugged their beers on the back porch. No matter how many Budweisers emptied, the mood stayed tense. Several of the relatives knew what I didn't: Dad's divorce from Nanette had been finalized days earlier.

It was time for a family portrait. Dad had another caricature drawn that year at the Merced County Fair, but not just of him. In the drawing we're standing in a row next to a mailbox that reads THE HOWARDS, Dad with his bushy mustache, Sherrie with her twiggy arms and pert breasts, Bobby with his sideways baseball cap, and me with my potbelly. Dad had made the clan official just in time for my summerlong visit.

THE INCIDENT

ONE DAY IN PARTICULAR stands out from Dad's year and a half with Sherrie. I remember it, my uncles remember it, my grandparents remember it, and my mother remembers it. Yet none of us can say with certainty when it happened: before the wedding to Sherrie or after, weeks before his death or months.

There's a related question, and no one can definitively answer it, either: How much cocaine did Dad use? Did it come out at night, while Bobby and I were sleeping? Sherrie had a strict policy of making us sleep with our bedroom doors closed. "You're safer that way," she said. Lying awake in the dark, I'd hear the deep moans and grunts of soft-core porn playing in the living room.

Dad picked me up at the train station for a visiting weekend that day. The moment he bent down to hug me, I felt it, the woozy haze surrounding him. I pulled back, stung, and then tried to cover up my gut repulsion by muzzling his shoulder as he gave me a noogie. He was drunk.

I tried to paint my visiting-day smile on, but he caught that flash of narrowed eyes and bunched eyebrows. "It's been a rough day," he said, sheepishly hanging his thumbs from his belt loops. I looked at the station clock: ten a.m. Dad cut a straight diagonal across the parking lot blacktop, but with shuffled steps. His palm was sweaty against mine, but not warm.

In the cab, engine sputtering, he set the radio dial to Top 40, just because he knew I liked it. Since the first grade I'd become a count-down fanatic, following the fate of my favorite singles and stewing with indignation when Prince's "Purple Rain" beat out Wham!'s "Wake Me Up Before You Go-Go" for the crown spot. That morning Kasey Kasem read his weekly song dedication letter, then hit us with a deluge of commercials, but Dad didn't turn the dial during ads the way he usually would. Perhaps he just didn't want to deal with me bouncing up and down and begging him to switch it back in time. He always seemed charmed by my seriousness—"But, Dad, Dad, we're going to miss number *seventeen!*"—but a shame of my past whining washed over me. "Dad, don't you want to turn the station?" I asked.

He jumped as though just realizing another person sat in the cab. "Huh?"

"They're only on number *thirty-five*," I said. It sounded like one of those impatient kiddie complaints I felt I ought to have outgrown, like *Why aren't they on nineteen, already?* I was desperate to snap him out of this mood and incapable of saying anything that didn't sound like whining. "Dad, I want you to listen to *your* station." Finally I'd gotten the tone right, and still he just gazed at the road ahead, which pointed north. I didn't know it was north. I just knew that our house was in the opposite direction.

"You hungry?" he said. I'd eaten the Pop-Tarts Mom had packed for the train ride, but that never stopped me those days, as my potbelly continued to balloon atop spindly legs. Dad, on the other hand, was the skinniest I'd ever seen him, so I brightened at the question. Dad drove so slowly that his janitorial equipment didn't crash against the camper shell during turns like usual, just glided back and forth.

At Perko's I ordered extra whipped cream on my mound of pancakes, and Dad picked at his omelet. The booth's vinyl upholstery squeaked as he leaned deep across the fake-wood-grain table.

"Your mom and I, we've got some things to sort out between us today," he said, looking up under heavy eyelids, referring not to my real mother, but to Sherrie. "And when we get home, your mom and I are going to have an adult conversation. So I need you to go to your room, go play with Bobby, while we work things out." I nodded vigorously even though Dad's slurred delivery inspired less than full confidence.

We stopped at the liquor emporium on the way home, and Dad left on the Top 40 countdown as he ran inside. He returned three songs later, empty-handed.

Back at the house I felt like an insider on a sting operation, afraid of what might happen but gloating with my privileged information. I headed straight to play in Bobby's room as Dad had ordered. Bobby reached into the aquarium where his pet iguana lived to peel a layer of dead scales off the lizard's back, counting on it to gross me out.

"They're having a talk," he said. He suspected I knew something.

"Um-hm," I said, with a high lilt on the *hm* to tell him I did know something. Bobby wouldn't press for more. That would mean admitting Dad was maybe a smidge closer to me than to him, and Bobby would never do that.

He placed a ribbonlike peel of lizard scales in the corner of the tank and plunked himself on the carpet, dumping out the bin of LEGOs in an avalanche of plastic. He sifted for axles and I dug for a green foundation. Over the last year our LEGO play had become well defined. Bobby always took his inspiration from the stock cars he loved to watch roar by in their smoke trails of glory at the county racetrack. I always built houses, stockpiling same-colored bricks to avoid leaving bright patches in the walls. Houses were the easiest structures to attempt, true, but I never tried to make cars or airplanes or any other kind of building. I think I loved to build the kind of house I dreamed of living in someday, when my life was my own. It would be small and perfectly square like the house Dad had shared with Nanette on Twenty-fifth Street. At that moment the only hurdle that stood between me and architectural harmony was the hunt for three blue bricks.

And then the first shout struck like an earthquake. "*No*, I won't fucking . . ." Dad's voice trailed off, but the force of the first shake promised more tremors. Bobby and I sat motionless, waiting to see if they'd come. Nothing. Another pause for extra security. All quiet. We leaned over and rustled the LEGO pile again, the soft jangle of plastic pieces filling up the tense silence, soothing us like wind chimes.

"*NO!* Now fucking *listen* to . . ." Dad's voice blasted and it didn't die down. This time the shaking wouldn't stop. Bobby and I looked at each other, and then he bolted out of the bedroom and put his ear against Dad's door, as if we couldn't already hear way too much.

Dad was roaring, shouting not just in that saddening or hurtful way, but in a frightening way. Howdy's way. A way that meant business, that meant hits and slaps might follow. For a second I mentally coached Sherrie, telling her the right things to say—nothing, don't say anything—and the right way to look—that's much more important: look him in the eyes and look pathetic—to simmer things down.

"Stop, Stan, fuck, Stan, stop!" Sherrie's screams were bereft of calculation. He was beating her.

The shock in Bobby's eyes was of a certain type: not surprise, but recognition. That's when I realized he had heard her scream and cry like this before, with another man, not my father. Bobby kept his ear to the door as his eyes began to well up. But my first concern was not for him, not for his mother. We had to make this stop, immediately. For my dad's sake, before he did something he'd regret.

Bobby and I rushed into the living room for a strategy session. We didn't bother with figuring out who to call. I knew Grandma Mae's number by heart but I didn't want her involved, didn't want to get Dad in trouble. Besides, Bobby and I needed somebody right here, right now.

"There's Tom next door," Bobby offered. Tom was the one guy we actually knew in the neighborhood, a bachelor who sometimes came over to barbecue and have a beer. But because he was single and about Dad's age, he didn't seem grown-up enough to handle this. And after all this was over, whatever was going on in that room that was definitely not a good thing, he probably wouldn't want to come over for barbecues anymore. We wouldn't go to Tom.

That left two other houses before the next block of wide-open pastures. But those houses had brown stains from dirt flowerbeds washing up their white-stucco siding, and broken-down stock cars in their driveways. I wasn't quite sure why that immediately ruled them out, but it did.

"There's the old man," I said. He lived on the other side of our house. We'd seen him in the front yard watering his rosebushes, and he'd smiled at us even if we'd never spoken.

Without speaking another word we were sprinting out the door and along the crunching dirt roadside to find the old man.

The old man was even nicer up close than we remembered from our glances in the front yard. It must have been clear from our clenched jaws and fearful eyes that we'd come on a mission, because he didn't ask us whether we were selling chocolate bars for youth group or something. He just said, "What's the matter?" and ushered us inside.

His house was flower-wallpapered and reeked of Ben-Gay. We were safe. He would make the shouting stop with his grandfatherly calm. Bobby let me do the talking, and somehow I sputtered that my dad was shouting at his wife, and we didn't want him to hurt her.

The old man told us to follow him into the kitchen, where he pulled out a phone book. "I think what we need to do," he said, his wrinkled face grave, "is call the police."

So he would force Bobby and me to call the shot. He could have just picked up the phone. Instead he said "we" and "I think," so that it sounded like a group decision, our decision, as if he were just giving outsider advice. This was the point where we could have stopped him, said no. But we just looked at each other.

The old man dialed. "Domestic disturbance" were the words he used.

Bobby hung his head, unable to look at me. We'd failed. We'd come with a common goal and separate allegiances, but we'd both ended up traitors.

Bobby and I sat at the edge of our front lawn and watched the two cops wait at the front door. Bobby threw a rock into the road, aiming at the dotted yellow line, and missed, and soon I picked up a stick and started a contest. It beat talking.

We turned back toward the house when we heard dirt crunching under heavy police boots.

Dad stood, or more accurately drooped, in between the two policemen, and I watched, unable to understand how he had become the bad guy.

Howdy was a bad guy, I'd decided that a few years ago, though I wouldn't dare admit it to anyone, not even Dad, because Dad would just turn it around and use it against Mom. I wished someone would come to the house in Fresno, the house I suddenly crumbled in homesickness for, and cart Howdy away. With sirens and everything, a big noisy send-off before Mom and Emmet and I and all of the neighbor kids crowded into the backyard for celebratory Baskin-Robbins ice-cream cake.

Dad lifted his eyes as the cops dunked his head into the backseat. His gaze rested on me, I just knew it, even though Bobby and I stood right next to each other. "I love you," he said, before the car door slammed.

When Sherrie came out, I couldn't look at her. She wore her black cat-eye sunglasses and she shook as she grabbed Bobby by the hand and led him to the car. Bobby took the front seat and I slid into the back, sneaking glances at Sherrie's red and swollen cheeks.

"Are you okay, Mom?" Bobby asked, but she waved him off with a trembling hand.

"I'm fine, sweetheart, it's all right." It sounded to me like a lie she was used to giving, but unlike her other lies—the ones I couldn't even admit to myself were lies because after all I had to live with her, I was supposed to love her—it made my heart sink.

"I hope you're OK." My condolences came out feebly as she dropped me at my grandparents and zoomed away down their quiet street.

Inside my grandparents' house, Mae set another cup of coffee in front of Dad, no milk, no sugar. The coffeemaker had been hissing and dripping from the moment I entered and found Dad sitting, surprisingly upright, at the kitchen counter. I wrangled myself into one of the high-backed stools while Grandma got down the Tang and mixed a glass for me.

Grandpa Ben came and leaned over Dad, grabbed his shoulders, and shook them a little in a "that's my boy" kind of way, but he looked troubled, as if he wanted to shake him a little more, as he pulled away and patted him on the back. He leaned in again, arm around Dad's back, talking close in the ear farthest from me. I caught some mumbling about "how this happened" and figured I wasn't meant to listen, so turned my attention to watching little pieces of Tang float like sea monkeys in the glass of water.

Uncle Brad sat at the table, dealing himself a game of solitaire, while Uncle Ric flipped through a magazine. The house had become a summit for silent, long-in-the-tooth men, gathered, I sensed, to set my father straight.

A knock came from the front door, a soft knock, but everyone perked up, immediately attentive to it.

Grandma Mae ambled back into the kitchen. "Stan," she said, and crooked her head toward the entryway.

"Who is it?" he asked, sliding off the stool, but Grandma Mae just crooked her head again.

No one took the empty seat next to me. Grandpa Ben headed, with peculiar resolve, into his billiards room, and a moment later I heard him racking up. Uncle Ric followed, Uncle Brad turned to filling out a crossword puzzle, and Mae put on another pot of coffee. Suddenly I sat alone and uncomfortable in this once warm, familiar house. It was the first time I'd ever felt that way around Dad's family, an outsider at a place where I had spent every Christmas Eve since I was born, around people who had known me and loved me since before I could talk.

Mae set the Maxwell House can aside. "A long day, Rachel my belle, do you remember your song, 'Rachel, my belle, set off to sea for a hook and a whale . . .'" She belted the "my belle" song, and the "bonnie lies over the ocean" song, somehow segued into "Puff the Magic Dragon," then launched into a rousing chorus of her favorite:

> There's a mosquiter on my peter
> Knock it off! Knock it off!

This made her laugh heartily for mysterious reasons. But she didn't look at me as she sang it, just rushed from one song to the next.

She'd begun recycling material, nervously belting out reprises, when Dad walked back in. He came over and kissed me on the crown of the head as she rambled on, and then he ducked into the billiards room, from where I heard the click and thunk of a well-executed shot, and my Grandpa's "Hey hey!"

"Grandma," I said, interrupting. "I have to go to the bathroom." And I climbed down from the stool as she moved on to another selection from her silly-song repertoire.

But I stopped in the foyer and peeked out the lattice-window top half of the door. A dark, thin figure sat on the front deck. She looked up and saw me through the beveled glass and walked to the door, and I opened it and stepped outside into her arms. She was warm, her polyester tank top surprisingly soft and her long hair herbal-shampoo-smelling, and I kept my head pressed to her chest as she shut the front door and shuffled me to the side a bit, like a slow-dancing couple, as though afraid someone might see us.

I looked up into Nanette's pale face, the oversize whites of her cartoon-big eyes red-veined, tear tracks meandering down the powder on her cheeks and landing on sticky bits of fuchsia lipstick. Her face glowed in the setting sun.

She spoke softly, but then again that's the only way I'd ever heard her speak, some variant of soft ranging from whisper to not-quite-loud. "Your dad and I have been talking," she talk-whispered. "We're going to work things out."

The sunset had reached the point where even the bright red planks of Grandpa's deck turned to gray, but my chest felt full of light. She hugged me again and headed down the driveway, and I slipped back inside, making sure to hold the door handle until I could slide the latch in soundlessly.

That night I dreamt of my old bed and our old house on Twenty-fifth Street, assured that Dad, and by extension everything, would be all right because Nanette was back. But the next time I saw Nanette, my father would be dead.

ENDLESS SUMMER:
JULY 1985

I DREADED GOING TO LIVE with Dad for the summer of 1985, but I whined only to my best friend in Fresno, KC Mason, and not to any adults. Dad was on the custody warpath again, trying to rub his new wife and house in Mom's face, and I couldn't bring myself to betray him. My half-conscious strategy was to ride out the visiting periods, silently longing for Mom and my grade-school friends. After what had happened in second grade, a deep internal logic told me Mom would never hand me over. I could let Dad tug, and Mom would tug back harder, and I'd make it through without ripping in half. The terrifying age of thirteen, that fabled day when I would have to go before a judge and admit to Dad that I didn't want to live with him, loomed as ominously as puberty itself.

That whole summer was so distressing that for more than a decade I managed, by a trick of chronology, to erase it from my memory. When, in my midtwenties, I felt prepared to examine the facts of Dad's murder, my mind stuck on the date of his death: June 22, 1986. That would have been just a week since I'd finished school and moved in with him and Sherrie for the summer. And yet what I could recall of that summer seemed interminable, like a never-ending stay at a sadistic summer camp; it couldn't possibly have transpired over one week. Finally, after piecing bits of fact from newspaper articles with the dates on the backs of pictures, calling relatives and sketching time lines, the truth clicked in my head. I *had* spent an entire summer with Dad and Sherrie—the year *before* he died. Between then and his death, the whole of fourth grade in Fresno had flashed by full of four-square games and slumber parties, as if a memory from another girl's life.

Could it be that I refused to believe Dad had been married to Sherrie for that long? One year wasn't exactly a golden anniversary, but it was more of a marital long haul than I wanted to give Sherrie credit for. Or had I not wanted to acknowledge that the agony of living with Dad and Sherrie had stretched an entire three months?

The summer of 1985 did not start auspiciously. Sherrie, I suspected, was playing me for a fool, and I couldn't figure out the rules of her game. Around Dad, she'd rub my shoulders and tell me I was pretty. The minute he went to take a shower or ran to the store, she'd transmogrify, like Jekyll turning into Hyde in the Warner Bros. cartoon. "Your father has turned you into a brat," she'd say in front of Bobby while we waited for Dad in the car, gritting her teeth. This was typical nasty-stepparent stuff, behavior I'd become accustomed to with Howdy. I was a professional stepchild, well prepared for this fight.

But the game changed the weekend Sherrie unveiled my redecorated bedroom. I'd told her about how Mom—"my other mom," as I'd have to correct myself around Dad—had fixed up my bedroom in Fresno with heart wallpaper and lace curtains. Soon after, Sherrie had me flip through the JCPenney catalog, examining comforters. The thin page crackled excitingly under her pen as she circled my choice bedroom ensemble—fluffy and ballet pink, as always.

The next weekend she picked me up at the train station while Dad slept in after a late-night cleaning gig, heavy metal guitars blaring from the truck's speakers as we made the rattling drive from the center of town out to the countryside. A jolt of fear rushed through me when I saw her standing alone in the parking lot. And just as I feared, she did not speak to me during the drive, as I fumbled to break the silence. Compliment her nail polish? Remark upon the pretty horses standing in the field? I failed to find the confidence to try any. But back at the house, where Dad groggily sipped his midmorning Sanka, she turned into a different person. "Welcome home, sweetheart!" she announced.

"Mom has a surprise for you," she said as Dad blew on his steaming coffee, and I caught myself from flinching at the M-word. She wrapped her hands around my eyes and maneuvered me to my bedroom door. "You're going to love this," she whispered in my ear, but more like a command than a prediction. She lifted her hands from my eyes.

My white furniture—iron bed, toy chest, and dresser, all from the house on Twenty-fifth Street—had been coated in a convalescent shade of peach with lavender accents, the kind of color scheme I'd seen in the geriatric wards Mom used to work. It all coordinated with the bedspread, which was peach with gaudy purple flowers. "The one from the catalog," Sherrie said firmly and evenly, eyes locked on mine. Finally I realized that the edges of my mouth had turned down and the bridge of my nose had wrinkled up, and that Dad had ambled over in his bathrobe to watch me erupt in sheer delight.

"I love it!" I squealed, throwing in a few halfhearted bounces for full effect. "Thanks so much, Dad." Having blurted it out, I knew I had to say the other half too. "Thanks, Mom."

I hadn't picked out that comforter, but I couldn't tell Dad that. And I couldn't understand why she would tell me I'd chosen something I hadn't, or put my finger on why I felt too intimidated to point that out to her. But if Sherrie could make Dad believe I'd picked out that tacky comforter, what else could she make him believe?

Dad's new house had strange rules. I was not allowed to take anything Dad and Sherrie bought for me back to Mom's in Fresno. And after I moved in for the summer, I was not allowed to call Mom or speak about her.

"Long distance is expensive," Sherrie said when I asked to telephone home.

"I can call her collect." The words slipped out too matter-of-factly; before the summer was over, Sherrie would cold-stare my smart-ass tendencies right out of me.

"What made you think I meant expensive for us?" she said. "I meant expensive period. And you just saw her."

I would have backed off had Dad not walked into the kitchen. I could plead with him, my sympathetic party.

"No, honey," Dad said, stroking my hair. "You're home now."

Rarely was anyone really home with Bobby and me. Technically Dad was there, locked in his bedroom sleeping after a late-night grocery-floor wax. The change had come on suddenly. He slept more than ever. When he was awake, he was either hazy and lethargic or buzzing with energy. While he dozed, Sherrie was usually off running mysterious errands. So Bobby and I sat alone in the living room, wearing our pajamas well past noon and watching *Inspector Gadget* reruns on Nickelodeon, turned down low so as not to wake Dad. The unsupervised kiddie TV was wicked fun, for about three days. Finally, heads ringing like a bad hangover from staring at the screen, we'd turn off the set and make faces at each other. Bobby would swivel the baby-blue wing-backed chair away from me to pick his nose, and I'd catch his reflection in the huge window, which turned our living room into a stuffy greenhouse. "Eeeewww." I'd draw it out to make the extent of my disgust clear. Bobby would dig deeper, no longer worried about impressing me now that we were stuck together.

Soon enough, food started running low. We'd eaten all the cereal, and instant oatmeal, and fruit roll-ups. One afternoon, all we could find were a few boxes of Rice-A-Roni, which I wasn't skilled enough to cook, and a head of wilted iceberg. I remembered hearing from Grandma Mae that Thousand Island dressing was just ketchup and mayonnaise mixed together, so I took out the condiments and stirred them in a bowl, instant dressing. Bobby, who would eat just about anything, who'd eaten dog food off the floor of the garage on a dare, pointed his finger down his throat and made elaborate gagging sounds.

When Bobby and I could no longer stand the house and the television and each other, we'd head to the big empty field. No use playing in the backyard anymore. The pond had dried up after holes had ripped in the plastic lining. The fish had died and been tossed in the trash. Dad's dog, the white German shepherd he'd owned since living with Nanette on Twenty-fifth Street, had run away on the Fourth of July, and it wouldn't be until a few months later that Sherrie bought a new dog, a boxer she named Rocky, to replace it (this dog too disappeared, not long before the murder). A huge satellite dish had been installed in the middle of our now underwatered, dried-out crabgrass. Just as well: I wasn't athletic enough to kick a ball around or play catch, and anyway those kinds of activities would probably wake Dad, whose dark-shuttered bedroom window faced the back of the house.

But beyond our fence, five acres of stabbing yellow hayfield stood like a vista from one of my *Little House on the Prairie* books. Best of all was the horse, a stocky, swaybacked nag that belonged to our neighbor. We took it carrots, until all our fresh vegetables had either been eaten or rotted to goop in the crisper drawer. Petting its dusty backside thrilled us for about all of fifteen minutes.

After daring each other to climb on the horse's back and both wimping out, we'd set out to the far side of the field, kicking dirt clods along the way with our flip-flops, coating our feet in dust. At the very back of the field, running alongside the barbed-wire fence, was what we called the "creek." It was really an irrigation ditch, five feet or so across, flowing with pesticide-polluted water that came up to our thighs mid-stream. Dense evergreen grass magically carpeted the banks. There were no trees along the ditch; the tallest plants were knee-high milk-weeds. But we could catch tadpoles and smash dragonflies and look for ladybugs on the mustard flowers, and to us this unvisited strip felt like a lush glen. It was just ten minutes from our house, but we made it another world in our minds. Bobby dreamed aloud about heading home to find Dad awake and alert, ready to take us out on the town. I fantasized about letting the gurgling water lull me to sleep under the stars, which were so clear and bright out there in the countryside, about never having to walk back home in the first place.

We didn't protest to Sherrie about her absences. We didn't dream of waking up Dad, when he'd worked so hard, when Bobby idolized him so deeply. We thought our loneliness, hunger, and boredom were our own fault.

Bobby had screwed up first. Sherrie had bought us fancy modeling clay at the art supply store next to her hair salon. We'd decided to sculpt clowns out of it, and then Bobby had introduced the bright idea of using fuzz from the dryer's lint trap to give the figures hair and beards. When we tried to smash the clowns down and start over again, the lint turned the clay into a crumbly, worthless blob. "I should have known better than to buy you two anything expensive," Sherrie said, pitching a fistful of clay into the trash like a baseball.

I'd screwed up too, wearing a tube top to our big afternoon at Rollertowne. Sherrie dropped us off, and before I could even finish lacing my brown rental skates and start clinging my way around the rink's edge to the strains of "Karma Chameleon," a manager carted me to the office for violating dress code.

"Here," Sherrie said after I'd called home for a new wardrobe, thrusting a wadded T-shirt against my belly. I wasn't thrilled to walk back into the rink. I couldn't put my finger on why my face had turned so red, why I couldn't meet any of the other kids' eyes. None of them were getting called on dress code for showing too much skin. I should have known there was something shameful about the way I had dressed. Sherrie was trashy. I was trashy now too.

Mom saw a change in me. I came home from that summer withdrawn, mousy, on edge. I recovered as fourth grade wore on, even though Dad called for me every other weekend, demanding that Mom put me on the Saturday-morning train to Merced. A weekend was all right. I could play with Bobby and the new dog and stifle my longing for Mom for a weekend, because I knew I'd be heading back.

But another summer was creeping up, and the stakes were rising. Early that spring, Sherrie and Dad started threatening to sue Mom for more custody. They staged melodramatic phone calls in which Dad would ask Mom if he could keep me for another day. When she said no, he'd start barking, sometimes holding the receiver away from his mouth for theatrical effect. "We've got a lawyer, Aleta. We're *not* fooling around." He was going to save me from "that man"— Howdy. I hated Howdy, but I feared Sherrie equally, and I missed my mother desperately. I loved my father, but he had become my captor.

Dad's child support, all $150 a month of it, stopped showing up in the mailbox in Fresno, and my mother demanded to know why. Sherrie called her from Grandma Mae's house. "You're *harassing* us," she shouted, and my mother heard my grandparents in the background. "We *paid* you. You're *harassing* us and we're going to get a lawyer." Mae couldn't hear Mom on the other end of the line, straining to remain calm, to stick with reasoning, to ask why Sherrie couldn't provide a canceled check if she'd actually sent the payment.

Dad intensified his offensive over Easter, after I'd ridden the train down to stay the week. Mom's father, my grandpa Dirks, was celebrating his sixty-fifth birthday that weekend, and Aunt Norine and all my cousins from Oregon had flown down for a reunion at Grandma Dirks's house, out among the grapevines of Livingston. But when Mom asked to pick me up for just a few hours, Sherrie screamed at her over the phone. "Everyone's coming over today, Aleta. It's Easter. *Our* day. She's not going anywhere." I sat at the kitchen table as Bobby peeked up at me over his cereal, winking, assuming I was on his mom's side.

Later that afternoon, as my aunts and uncles played volleyball on the front lawn, Mom's Datsun pulled into Dad's driveway. I wanted to run toward it but knew everyone would see my betrayal. So I walked over quietly, hoping no one would notice me, as Uncle Ric lobbed another serve and Aunt Lisa sat in her lawn chair, sipping a Budweiser. No one waved or said hi to Mom, who stood with Aunt Norine next to the car. Dad strode up behind me and grabbed my arm, wrapping his whole hand firmly around my bony elbow. "Relax," Mom said. "Can't I bring my sister over to visit?" But it took a few seconds of stare-down for Dad to let go.

Once he backed off, I had nothing to say, because I was under surveillance. Even too eager of a hug would be suspect. "What's the matter?" Mom said, but I just shuffled my feet. After about ten minutes they drove off again, and I longingly watched her car pull down the road, out of the corner of my eye.

The next day Dad and Sherrie drove me out to my other grandparents' house, in Livingston, for my grandpa Dirks's birthday party. "It's just for a few hours," Dad said as they dropped me off. "And if you want to come back early, you just call."

I'd missed all the excitement—yesterday the Doughboy pool had exploded, turning the backyard into a scene from Hurricane Andrew as Mom captured it on her rented video camera like an evening-news correspondent on the scene of a natural disaster.

The big movie a few years earlier was *Ghostbusters*. All the kids had seen it, some two or three times. So as the sun started to set, Mom popped the theme music into the cassette deck and had all eight of us sing it for the camera, popping up from behind the sofa to shout "Who ya gonna call?" On the tape the other kids are grinning like gremlins, hamming it up for the screen, and I'm just bobbing along, watching carefully to take my cues. Dad and Sherrie would be knocking at the door for me any minute.

Two and a half months later Dad and Sherrie picked me up at Mom's in Fresno. On our way out of town we stopped for dinner at the Spaghetti Factory, where the warehouse ceilings rose above us like a cathedral, and the booths, rigged out of old bed frames, made Bobby and me feel as if we were visiting an amusement park. Dad let us slurp our pasta, marinara sauce splattering our faces, and afterward ordered us all a banana split. This was a celebration. Dad was whisking me "home" for another dreaded summer, back to Merced.

At the start of that summer, Rod's latest hit flooded the airwaves. I remember hearing it for the umpteenth time one afternoon as the whole family drove into town to run errands. Sherrie had just let Bobby and me take turns trying to drive our sedan down the empty two-lane country road; I'd performed miserably, focusing right on the yellow line instead of gazing ahead, swerving madly even at twenty miles per hour while Dad and Sherrie snickered. Dad had proudly reassumed the wheel and turned up the volume, as was his driving custom, when Rod's scratchy voice filled the car, going on and on about giving someone his "love touch." It was part of the sound track for the new movie *Legal Eagles*, and the video sprang to my mind, lawyers in pinstripe suits dancing on desktops as Rod lip-synched before a scandalized judge. But Dad killed the station, wagging his head in laughter at the tune.

"Sellout," he scoffed. I could hardly believe my ears. Rod Stewart had always been our hero, our personal sound track to happy times. And now, like so many other people in his life, Dad had forsaken him. He didn't even see Uncle Brad that often anymore. In repudiating Rod, no matter how crappy the hit, Dad was repudiating his old self. I had a sick feeling then that I would never get him back.

* * *

A few nights later I woke at four a.m., my bladder insistent. Bobby and I had thrown too much tissue paper into our bathroom toilet that day, and Dad's most valiant plunging hadn't removed the clog. If I used the hall bathroom, it would overflow, and if I used Dad and Sherrie's bathroom, I would wake them. So I tiptoed to my bedroom door and, looking out upon the shadowy living room, gathered my courage. The moon was nearly full, the path along the couch and around the kitchen table to the back sliding-glass door illuminated. I stepped outside barefoot, the dried lawn prickling my feet, and crept to the side of the house, where I slipped my pajama bottoms down and crouched, sighing with sweet relief. Black night had turned gray; dawn was about to break. I paused to drip-dry, no longer afraid of the lifting darkness. The stillness and silence felt intensely peaceful. I took every step back deliberately, gently, so as not to let the grass poke me any more than necessary, and locked the sliding-glass door behind me.

GOOD NIGHT:
JUNE 1986

THE ZOOM OF THE STOCK CARS almost drowns out Bobby's voice. "Six fries on number twenty-seven," he shouts.

I size up the pile of French fries greasing their red-checkered cardboard boat, then follow the stock cars with my eyes—zip! zip! zip!—pupils darting left to right.

"Seven on number nineteen," I squeak above the roar, cupping hand to mouth in Bobby's direction. We're sitting at the bottom of the stadium, exposing our ears to certain hearing impairment with the pride of teenagers at a rock concert. I'm still high on the monster trucks that opened the show, slamming and crashing their way over a line of cars the length of the football field, my ears pleasantly ringing in between conquests. I got into the sounds, engine growling as the front of the truck reared high like a bucking stallion, metal screeching as it stomped the first casualty; I got on the monster truck's side, and I won eight fries for that.

Here at the fairgrounds, I'm on Bobby's turf. Three of his school friends, all old pros at the stock car scene, sit circled around us, considering their gambles. They're dressed in stained T-shirts and trucker's caps their dads must have given them, ducktails trailing down tanned necks. This is the first time I've realized that Bobby actually has friends, the first time I've really had fun with him. "You might win," he yells as the crew of number nineteen changes tires and sends my pick off again in a smoke trail of inevitable victory. If I do win, I decide, I'll give Bobby my fries.

Moths swarm the stadium lights overhead, renegades among them dive-bombing our faces, but we take no notice. The night is warm, and even though I can't see a single star through the glare of the stadium lights, I can imagine them in the sky, still and quiet above the chaos of the insects and the thrilling hard-metal symphony of half a dozen souped-up engines.

My car crashes the sidewall and spins onto the field, too mangled to hit the road again. Bobby's car falls behind the pack. We hand the fries over to our fellow bettors with mock-resignation, but we feel victorious. Bobby throws his arm around my shoulder like a master proud of his protégé as another monster truck takes the stage.

Dad and Sherrie meet us at the stadium entrance at the appointed time, all smiley and lovey-dovey from their grown-up movie. We drive way across town to the pizza parlor, the dark one with enormous lacquered benches and signs painted on barrels hung overhead. Dad orders half Canadian bacon—his favorite—and half pepperoni and lets Bobby and me shake all the Parmesan cheese we want on it. We drink root beer in giant frosty mugs. Dad fishes a few quarters out of his jeans pocket and puts some tunes on the jukebox, dragging Sherrie out onto the floor. They dance to classics—the Beatles, Hall and Oates—none of that angry heavy-metal stuff Sherrie likes. Dad and Sherrie hug each other and sway during a slow number while Bobby and I toss our crusts onto our plates, and then on the next fast song Sherrie rushes over and grabs my hand and Dad lugs Bobby off his bench and then we're two couples on the floor, holding hands, swinging madly until the jukebox runs out of juice.

It's nearly midnight when we get home. Bobby and I change straight into our pajamas, but we take our time brushing our teeth. This night, we know, is the most fun we'll have all summer, and we want it to last forever. Sherrie turns out the living room lights and shuts our bedroom doors. "Good night!" Bobby shouts, as if he thinks he's John-Boy on *The Waltons*. The race cars buzz in my head like a nice memory as I close my eyes. I'm so tired I feel I could sleep forever. But in just three hours I'll be awake. In just three hours Bobby will be standing before me in his underwear, saying nonsensical things about Daddy cutting himself shaving.

part
three

SLEEPING: SUMMER 1986

I SPENT MY FIRST DAY after Dad's death awaiting nightfall, knowing the fear it would bring. The dread of that fear hung so thick that I barely had room in my consciousness for the first pangs of grief.

The morning of the murder, on the way out of Merced, Mom broke down sobbing while we waited for a train crossing. I stared at her, dumbfounded, not offering my hand or touching her shoulder as the crossing bells clanged. "*Why* are you crying?" I finally said.

"Because," she said as the tears rolled, looking at me in disbelief as though I'd just announced I was the Antichrist, "your father was my *friend*."

The idea that she might miss him too didn't compute. I didn't even miss him, in that moment. I wiggled my fingers, which had gone as numb as my emotions. At last the train's caboose chugged by, the traffic gate lifted, and Mom slammed the car into first gear.

Back at the house, Howdy was watching TV in his underwear. "Hey, sorry about your dad," he grumbled. It was the last I ever heard from him on the subject, and I relished his silence.

I ate a bowl of Lucky Charms at the kitchen table, then headed to my bedroom and locked the door. I lay on my daybed and stared across the room at my closet door. It was just a plain honey-lacquered door, just a point to stare at. After twenty minutes of staring, the first realization hit. *I'll never see Dad again. Ever.* I strangled my lace-crochet pillow to my chest and cried so hard that I felt I would collapse inside myself, like a black hole, and cease to exist. After fifteen minutes of uninterrupted crying, the second realization hit: *I'm stuck with Howdy now.*

Finished crying alone, I shadowed Mom from room to room like a puppy that wanted to be let outside. "What is it, honey?" she said, cracking the bathroom door after she'd flushed the toilet.

I cast my face down in embarrassment. "I'm afraid I won't be able to sleep." Mom got on the phone, and within hours we were at the psychiatrist's.

I sat in a leather chair in an office on the top floor of Mom's hospital and refused to say a word about my father or the murder. I kept my gaze on the carpet; I answered curtly "Yes" and "No." I knew it was beyond the psychiatrist's powers to help me, however serious his demeanor and shiny his tie. No matter what I told him, I would still have to live with Howdy. My father would still be dead. And my brokenness, hard enough to hide during the custody wars, would still be shamefully public because of the murder. If I cried here, in front of this stranger, I would only have to cry harder back home, alone.

"She's in shock," the man in the suit said, scribbling out the prescription for Valium. "She'll let you know when she wants to talk." The elevator ride down felt like a never-ending descent to hell, Mom and I alone for floors at a time as orderlies and nurses rolled their carts and gurneys in and out. The walk across the parking lot, where heat waves wrinkled the dry air like fun-house mirrors, felt like crossing the Sahara. I counted steps between lines on the asphalt to keep from looking at Mom. "I really wish you'd talk, honey," she said, but I kept my eyes on the pavement, taking the widest steps possible—*one, two, three, four, line!*

After the appointment we drove to the grocery store, where I wandered the aisles as Mom filled my prescription. Mrs. Ouijian spotted me in the hair-care section, looking up in delighted surprise from reading a box of scarlet hair dye.

"Hey there, how's my favorite student doing?" she said. I'd gotten top marks in Mrs. Ouijian's fourth-grade class last year, scoring big after our field trip to Monterey Bay Aquarium with a six-page story about a whale, which my friend Rhiannon and I planned to turn into a best-selling series of children's books.

"Doing any good summer reading?" she said, punching my arm lightly. "Where ya been?"

"I was at my dad's in Merced." I looked at my toes peeping through my jelly sandals. "But I'm here now." I made a conscious effort to look up and smile, because I hoped a smile would keep her from sensing a gap between the two pieces of information I'd offered.

"Well, great!" Mrs. Ouijian said. "And how's your mom?"

"She's looking at vegetables," I said, knowing full well she stood in line a few rows over at the pharmacy.

"Well, tell her I said hi," Mrs. Ouijian said. "Guess I'll see you in September." She plunked the red hair dye in her basket and strolled down the aisle.

In the car, Mom kept the radio off. "I ran into Mrs. Ouijian in the grocery store," I said.

She stopped the car, back end already pulled into the stream of parking lot traffic. "Did you tell her about your dad?"

"I just said I was home for the rest of the summer."

Her shoulders relaxed and her hand reached over to touch my knee. "Oh, good," she said, and looked back over her shoulder to continue pulling out.

I puzzled over her reaction. It seemed clear she didn't want me blabbing about the murder to people outside the family, and I couldn't square that with her earlier plea to talk. But I liked this new strategy better. It agreed with my instinct. I would try my hardest not to talk about Dad's murder, to Mom or anyone else.

"Vitamins," Mom explained when I walked into the kitchen and caught her crushing the pill and mixing it with the spoonful of peanut butter. I knew better. The only vitamins she'd ever given me and Emmet—and only sporadically, in one of her fleeting wannabe super-mom moments—were shaped like Flintstones and washed down with sweet, pink leftover milk from our daily bowl of Cap'n Crunch berries.

But I ate the Valium-laced peanut butter, no whining about the bitter aftertaste, no questions asked.

We tried darkness first, with the bedroom door open and a night-light plugged into the corner socket. I could hear the sitcom on the living room TV and I tried to focus on the laugh track, to let it roll over me like soothing, crashing waves of chatter. Mom lay next to me on the rollout trundle as I closed my eyes, faking sleep. It took all my willpower not to cry after her when she rose gently, slowly, so as not to creak the springs, and headed out.

The moment she stepped out the door, I popped my eyes open, resolved to stand my own guard. But I couldn't stop worrying about the windows. They were covered on the outside by bushes and on the inside by fluffy lace curtains, but didn't have blinds. I worried that someone, whoever killed my father, could peer in and find me and break one of the windows and climb in. That was why they were all closed, even though the night was warm and my room was stuffy. That was why my blanket—not just the sheet, it seemed too thin and insubstantial, but my heavy comforter—was pulled up to my ears, to protect my neck from anyone who might break in and want to slash it.

Still I feared that if I ever did fall asleep, I would roll over and uncover my neck, and I'd be unprotected, so even though I would rather have volunteered to wash next week's dinner dishes than tell Mom I was scared, I screamed.

One of those awful, eardrum-piercing, preteen screams. I knew it would cost me with Howdy, that interrupting his TV shows didn't win you any points with him, that if Mom weren't here to shut me up and if he didn't have to feel sorry for me, he'd tell me to shut up or—depending on how many beers he'd cracked open—call me a sissy bitch.

Mom came back to my room with our German shepherd on a leash and tethered him to the door handle. "Luther's a big dog," she said. "No one could get past Luther."

Luther was also an ill-trained dog. He paced and whined when Mom went back to watch her TV show, and then he barked, and then he pulled my bedroom door closed. It was pitch-black in my room, so I ducked my head under the blanket. And I screamed.

Mom came back and turned the light on and took the dog away. Her face was not annoyed, but genuinely worried. She grabbed a pillow and lay on the trundle mattress next to me under the glaring light until, hours later, I fell asleep, my blanket pulled up to my ears.

When I woke up at six a.m., the sun was already rising, but Mom wasn't lying on the trundle bed.

"You left," I said to her over my bowl of Cap'n Crunch.

"I'm sorry, honey," she said. "You were asleep."

"You can't leave tonight," I said, but it wasn't a bossy little girl's demand, just a sheepish plea.

That afternoon, the second day after the murder, we sat at the hottest, dullest, most treeless lake in Fresno County, picking our way through a bucket of Kentucky Fried Chicken. The nails in the picnic bench scorched my thighs like lit cigarettes when I accidentally sat on them. Next to our dusty lakeside perch, shiny jacked-up pickups backed fishing boats down a giant concrete loading dock.

This was Mom's new idea of helping me feel better: dragging Howdy and Emmet along for an afternoon of swatting flies and fidgeting through awkward silences. In just one day her strategy had shifted from coercing me to talk to acting as though nothing had happened, and even though the pressure to splash around in the water like a giggling kid from a Slip 'N Slide commercial was crushing ("C'mon, you're supposed to be having *fun!*" the lake's echoing silence seemed to shout), I was relieved at the new approach.

There was a kind of sweet vengeance in watching Howdy forced into playing the family man after he'd been off the hook so many years. The greasy bucket of Colonel Sanders emptied, he slumped over the table, chain-smoking but not uttering a single complaint; even he felt a duty to walk on eggshells around me.

"Hey, Rachel, how about you and me and Emmet take a walk on the beach?" Mom asked.

I looked at the tiny waves monotonously lapping the hot sand, and at Emmet, poking Mom in the side and making grabbing motions with his hands for a drink of water. He hadn't whined the whole trip, as though even at four years old he too had received orders to treat me as if I were made of glass.

"I'd really rather just go home," I said, studying Mom's face for that wince of disappointment it pained me to cause her.

"A-men," Howdy said, and patted me on the back as though he liked me for a change.

I didn't bother going inside when we got home, but struck out barefoot across the neighbor's lawn to KC Mason's house.

KC was my preternaturally pubescent best friend. She was a year younger, but her parents Shirley and Dorsey were in their fifties, gray-haired, leather-skinned, Ben-Gay scented; they owned a liquor store five blocks away called The Mason Jar. It gave them a special stature in our blue-collar neighborhood, and they often parked their spare car, a perfectly preserved silver Corvette, in the driveway to remind everyone of it. One weekend during the school year I spilled Capri Sun on that car's perfect wax job, and KC freaked out in front of the other neighborhood kids. We didn't talk for a week, but finally we couldn't take being apart, and we'd spent just about every school-day afternoon together since.

I walked through the front door without knocking, as usual, and found Shirley and Dorsey just where I expected them: sitting in their high-backed kitchen-counter barstools, sipping their customary syrupy, amber drink over ice ("Scotch on the rocks," KC had taught me, fascinated by her parents' drinking) at two in the afternoon.

"Well, lookee here, Dorsey," Shirley said, raising her highball.

"Good old Rachel," Dorsey said, and motioned me over for a hug. Even from where he sat, his long arm draped around me from high above on the barstool, he smelled like alcohol and hair tonic, but I didn't mind.

"Kaaaaay-Seeeee!" Shirley shouted, and shooed me over to the spare stool at the other end of the bar. "She's on the phone with a *boy*," she half-whispered. And then loud again, that too-loud voice she would get at that time of day, like someone talking into a bad phone connection: "Sit down, sweetie. We didn't expect you in these parts for a while! Had enough of your Dad's for the summer?"

A big gaping pause, filled with the cool darkness of their house, the brown and orange kitchen carpet, the fake-grain cabinets, the breeze of the ceiling fan brushing my hair. And then I just said it.

"My dad's dead."

"Christ Almighty," Shirley said under her breath. Dorsey set his highball down.

"Did you just say your dad's dead?" KC said, stepping from behind me into the kitchen. She wore her bikini, ready for a dip in their Doughboy.

"Oh, honey," Shirley said, talking to me, not KC.

"What happened?" KC said.

"Shush," Shirley said. "You all right, honey? You don't have to talk about whatever you don't want to."

But suddenly I wanted to.

"Somebody stabbed him," I said, and the three of them gasped together.

"Oh my god," Shirley said. "Too bad you can't have a sip of this, calm your nerves."

But I felt calm, and normal, finally. "No thanks," I said, as KC raised her eyebrows and nodded toward her mom to encourage me—KC would take that sip in a second, always wishing they'd offer her one.

"What happened, sweetie?" Dorsey said. I had his complete attention. And for some reason—the fact that they knew no one in my family, the fact that they had no grief of their own to attend to, the fact that with a few more drinks in their system they might not remember half of what I said—talking to them didn't bother me.

"My stepbrother, Bobby, woke me up," I said. "Really late. Three thirty in the morning. And then I came out of my room, and there was blood all up and down the hallway." I wriggled my legs beneath the barstool, embarrassed, as Shirley and Dorsey drooped with disbelief. There was shock in their eyes, but not grief. I could go on.

"Someone had stabbed my dad, but he was gone. So I sat with Bobby, waiting. And then the ambulance came, and they took my dad away, and we went to the hospital, and Dad died there. Yesterday morning."

"And they don't know who did it, honey, or why?" Dorsey said.

"Uh-uh."

They just sat in silence, and then Shirley called me over to her barstool, slapping the leather seat. "Come here, kiddo." She locked her arm around my neck and stroked my hair, a bit rough, but then she'd had a few, and kissed the top of my head. I let her do that for a while, melting under the touch of her wrinkled hand.

"All right, Mom," KC said, and grabbed my wrist. They made teasing, tongue-sticking-out faces at each other until KC tugged me down the hallway to her bedroom.

KC lay on her water bed as I tinkered with the dress on one of her pricey porcelain dolls, the collector's-edition kind I'd envied since I'd met her. "About your dad," she said. "That's intense."

"Um, thanks."

"But maybe it's a good thing, you know? I mean, now you won't have to worry, about him wanting you to go live with him . . ."

I dropped the doll's ruffled hem as a tinge of anger passed through me. But then it became something else, something I would have preferred to forget. Because I'd had that exact same thought, lying in my room crying yesterday morning. Right after realizing that I would never see Dad again, right after realizing I was stuck with Howdy, it hit me that the custody fights were over, that I wouldn't have to fret about letting Dad down when I turned thirteen, when the judge asked me where I wanted to live. Dad's murder had simplified everything. All I had to do now was keep my head down and shut my door and ignore Howdy until I reached adulthood. I'd been overcome with relief. And then, guilt.

KC sprang up in her bed, the water mattress rippling around her. "Hey, you wanna spend the night?"

I did. I wanted it more than anything. Because I didn't want to go home, now or ever. But then I thought of lying there on the water bed with all the lights out, just KC's night-light casting shadows, and knew I couldn't. And I couldn't tell her why either, couldn't tell her how I'd been transformed into a sissy-freak overnight, how I didn't know if I'd ever turn the lights out again.

I lifted up my tank top to flash my pink Ocean Pacific one-piece. "I wore my suit," I said. "Let's get out of here."

We spent the rest of that summer chasing boys and bees. KC had crushes on the teenage skateboarders who'd built a ramp in a neighbor's backyard, and we'd hang on the alley's chain-link fence for hours, hoping they'd notice us. Back at the Masons', we'd hole up in KC's backyard playhouse, where we had set up a laboratory using a children's science kit: scalpels, petri dishes, beakers, and best of all a microscope. We made bee mortality our research subject. They swarmed around the tree with the red bottlebrush flowers—we had to be careful not to step on them in the moss underneath. But KC was fearless. She'd clap a bee inside her cupped bare hands, and after watching her do this dozens of times without getting stung, I'd catch them plain-fisted too. Somehow we'd maneuver our captives into test tubes, and then the real fun would begin. We had to chop the bees up to get them under the microscope, in the name of science. And so we devised all kinds of ways to kill them—drowning, stabbing, suffocation. We experimented with semitoxic liquids, using a stopwatch to verify how long it took the bee to die, and decided that for drowning, rubbing alcohol was most efficient.

We turned that summer into a bee holocaust, killing dozens each day. Dorsey and Shirley would nod half-drunk approval at our scientific "findings," never warning us to stay away from the bees, that we might get stung. At first I felt uneasy about the torture we inflicted on our insect subjects, but the guilt soon gave way to sadistic pleasure. We were gods. We were powerful. The bees could try to sting us, but we would torture them and have the final word.

I got stung a few times, clapping those bees inside my hands. But whereas the summer before I would have cried with pain and run home for help, the summer after Dad died I just gritted my teeth and had KC extract the stinger with her tweezers. With my tough buddy KC as a mentor, pain couldn't touch me.

By the end of the summer I was spending nearly every night of the week over at KC's place. KC's parents were always around when we wanted them, for example, to help us scrounge up lunch in the fridge. But in their steady drunkenness they were conveniently unconcerned about what kind of trouble we were getting ourselves into. They never asked me about the murder, just treated me like their own daughter. They might get embarrassingly slop-faced and say ridiculous things, but they would never yell at us or threaten us.

The arrangement allowed me to be just one house away from Mom without feeling that my grief was under constant scrutiny. And it provided a respite from Howdy. Mom let me traipse off with a change of clothes every night, seeing that I seemed to be holding together. With KC's night-light plugged in, I could make it through till morning. I didn't breathe a word to her or anyone else about how afraid I still was at night, about the visions I'd have of men cloaked in black climbing through KC's window, about waking at three a.m. from nightmares that someone was stabbing me. I'd just lie on KC's water bed in fear, willing my eyes wide-open, sometimes for hours, until sleep overtook me. And when the next summer day arrived, hot and blinding, I'd pretend Dad's murder had never happened.

BREASTS: 1986-87

TEN IS AN ESPECIALLY INCONVENIENT age to lose your father.

It didn't help that Dad had caught a glimpse of my incipient puberty, days before he died. He walked into my room one morning as I was pulling off my shirt and just about dropped his jaw at the sight of my burgeoning breasts, far from round but undeniably softening like cream cheese left out on the counter. They weren't noticeable when clothed—my chest was still basically flat, with only a slight triangulation around the nipples. But there my imminent puberty was, full frontal in the bright sunlight. "Oops, sorry," Dad said, shutting the door quickly, but that suspended split second of astonishment in his eyes told me my chest had become a snapshot in his mind, more wistfully potent than any *Playboy* pinup.

The next week, at the funeral after-party, Sherrie crouched to reach my ear as my cousins and I sat on the carpet playing Skip-Bo, a card game beloved by retirees everywhere and especially my grandparents. Focusing on my hand was getting me through the gathering, where in my sailor-stripe dress and tightly braided hair I felt like a pathetic orphan on display at a charity fund-raiser. Mom had bought me that dress during a special trip to Macy's, Fresno's premier department store, when I'd bounced up and down begging her to let me get a frothy pink Jessica McClintock number. Those flower-girl frocks, which looked as glamorous to me as any prom night getup, were not "appropriate," Mom pronounced sadly, picking through the racks. The black-and-white sailor dress would look "classy," she said with a lilt her weary eyes undermined. The dress was not meant to please me. It was meant to please the Howards, or rather, one-up them. To this day Mom likes to remind me that I was the only family member dressed "appropriately" for Dad's funeral.

I pulled the stiff-pleated hem of the dress to cover my thighs as Sherrie leaned in. "Do you know what your dad said to me the other day?" she whispered, exhaling nicotine and Scotch. "He said, 'My little girl's growing boobs!' You should have seen him, he was *so* upset!"

My face stung as if slapped. I froze a beat and then giggled to appease Sherrie, who seemed to think this story would amuse me. She picked her drink up from the floor and slunk off through the party, laughing to herself, and I turned back to the card game without a word to my cousins, face as tomato red as the bow tied in my hair. Above us, adults in starchy suits and dresses stirred their drinks with hushed clink, clinks, like far-off wind chimes, and talked slowly, in near-whispers. The smell of flowers throughout the house tickled my nose like cheap perfume. I lost that round of Skip-Bo without a fight, even though my cousins Carrie and Amy were both younger, and snuck off to the telephone in Grandma Mae's bedroom to call Mom and ask her to pick me up.

The summer just after Dad's murder, my chest lay mercifully dormant. But the next summer my boobs sprouted as surely as a wet Chia Pet. What was worse, the rest of me grew too, and not just taller. As July and August stretched on full of nothing but swimming and bee torturing, I treated myself freely to the economy tubs of licorice and beef jerky that Mom bought at Fresno's new Costco and stored in our pantry. My thighs and middle turned fleshy in obvious, humiliating contrast to KC Mason's petite, prepubescent muscularity. Forever chasing boys, she detested her flat-chestedness, but I memorized her taut lines while we showered together, imagining my head on her body. She looked like the lean, angular models in fashion magazines. Teenagers laughed off her precocious flirtatiousness, but they looked her up and down too, and so did grown men stopping to buy cigarettes at her parents' liquor store. I knew that if anyone paused to look at me, they were not admiring my fit, Lolita-like form. They were looking at my belly, or worse, my chest.

The boobs were getting hard to hide. Even Howdy would snicker to himself at them, so hopelessly mal-shaped beneath my tightening summer tank tops. Finally Mom announced that we were heading to Macy's to pick out my first bra. I tried to push back memories of Dad's astonished stare, but this was not a triumph of femininity for me. I didn't want to be a "young woman." I wanted to stay frozen, to remain forever the little girl he had loved, not the sexual creature whose fore-shadowing had horrified him.

Normally I jumped to my feet at the chance to buy clothes at Macy's, but I put Mom off. I told her I was too young to wear a bra (though KC, forever overachieving in all things sexual, already wore one), hoping against hope that the perky pyramids beneath my shoul-ders would spontaneously deflate, like popped balloons. "If you don't cooperate, I'll have to pick a bra out for you myself," Mom said with waning sympathy. "But if you come along, you could pick out a new skirt too." The bribe worked, but I still had my pride—or rather, all-enveloping shame. "No! No, Mom!" I whispered, tugging at her side when she approached a saleswoman for help. Back in front of my bed-room's full-length mirror, I meticulously experimented with safety pins to make sure my bra strap would never slip out from under my tank tops. Maybe no one would notice my new garment.

After the murder I didn't talk to Mae and Ben much. Mom would have me call them occasionally, despite my obvious reluctance as she handed me the receiver. They did not call me, and far from being bothered, I was relieved.

I was too terrified of talking about the murder, and too young to appreciate that Mae and Ben are funny people, the stuff good Benny Hill reruns are made of. They have no decorum. A framed sign in their guest bathroom implores company, "If you sprinkle when you tinkle, be a sweetie and wipe the seatie." Their sense of all things sex-ual is pure farce. Once when I was twelve and staying the night, I bor-rowed Ben's long johns for pajama bottoms. "See, that hole there's for grandpa's wee-wee, but you don't have one, do you, girlie?" Grandma announced with zeal, pointing at my crotch as I walked into the living room.

At ten, blushing my way through fifth-grade sex ed, I was not amused by these jokes. I kept a fear-inspiring mental list of things I could not talk about with Mae and Ben, sex and Dad's death the two most obvious topics, the two most obvious reasons not to see them. Still, Mom would drive me over to see them every six weeks or so, never coming inside but insisting I go in. It was important, she said, that I keep in touch with my dad's family. The importance seemed to me purely theoretical, something good for you to be swallowed like cod liver oil—otherwise why didn't Mom herself keep in touch?

The first Thanksgiving and Christmas after the murder I showed up at the Howards' alone and behaved as though nothing had happened, as though my father were just in the other room and would walk back in any moment, as though my life were as hunky-dory as ever. I didn't want anyone to see my pain, but you can read it in the half-smiling photos I took in front of the tree.

The summer one year after the murder, just before I got my first bra, Grandpa invited me camping in Yosemite along with Uncle Brad and Aunt Lisa. Photos from that trip show me grotesquely thick around the middle atop persistently skinny, long legs. We roasted marshmallows around the campfire, and Brad and Lisa slept in a tent. Grandpa and I slept in the back of Dad's old janitorial truck, which Grandpa had converted into a bed, except that I didn't sleep much at all. I lay listening to the last of the fire crackling outside, and to mysterious creaks among the trees, and thinking about how weird it was to be sleeping in the old truck now that Dad was dead, and wanting to get home.

On another visit, stumped for anything better to do, Mae and Ben decided to take me to tour the old Merced County Courthouse, a nicely preserved white turn-of-the-century building set in a shaded park in the center of town. We wended our way past rooms done up to replicate 1906 life, with antique desks and writing quills and yellowing Victorian dresses displayed on creepy mannequins. At the end of the tour, Grandpa noticed a plaque with brass plates bearing the names of donors, with room for more entries. "Let's give a donation in your father's name," he said with a twitchy smile, "and they'll add him to that plaque."

I looked on with faked appreciation as Grandpa ponied up the money and printed Dad's name on the donor form in neat, upstanding letters, but I felt anything other than pride or gratitude. I felt like two people: one shrunk tiny deep inside her body, terrified of her own pain, and another larger-than-life, floating outside her body, taking herself right out of the situation at hand and fast-forwarding back home, to Fresno. This was how I felt nearly anytime Dad's death came up in family conversation. This deep-inside/floating-outside sensation kept me from crying, a skill I perfected in my early teens, when I trained myself not to drop a tear at sad movies, walking out of a matinee of *Dying Young* with such a dry face that Mom looked at me as though I'd become a psychopath.

I lived my separate existence in Fresno, eating piles of junk food and massacring whole colonies of bees and sleeping over at KC's every night to pretend that Dad's murder wasn't crushing me. I missed him and sometimes daydreamed about what had happened to his soul, entertaining theories that he had been reincarnated as my black Lab, Shadow, or that he was now in heaven and able to see my every move. But I tried not to think of him too often. And I didn't think about the Howards much—or if I did, I would quickly force myself not to.

By the time a second Christmas Eve rolled around, something had hit me. I had always visited their house with Dad, as Stan's little girl. Now I was a dead son's only daughter. It struck me, standing there with my finger hovering above the doorbell, that I would never be the same person to anyone in my family.

The holiday was in full swing when I arrived, Grandpa leaping spryly around the family room, scorching us all with his rack of overhead lighting as he captured the yearly gift-opening ritual on his new video camera. I held up my peach sweater and gold-plated necklace from Grandma, who had stuck to her policy of spending $50 on each grandchild, as my uncles showed off their new tackle boxes and grilling sets. But there were more presents for me under the artificial tree. Uncle Brad handed me a flat package the size of a manila envelope wrapped in turquoise paper; the tiny cursive across it said it was from Nanette's mom, Grandma Rose.

I tore the paper discreetly, trying not to attract notice. Underneath was a shiny, cardboard-framed picture of two doe-eyed children holding an umbrella, the kind of thing you might pick up at the flea market. Grandma Rose had inscribed the back: "To Rachel, Christmas 1987: With love." I tilted it toward my chest, trying to hide it. The idea that Grandma Rose, whom I hadn't seen in years, had thought especially of me that Christmas made me grateful and mortified at once; grateful because none of my Howard aunts and uncles were paying any special attention to me, and mortified because I didn't want to admit I needed special attention. But Uncle Brad peeked over my shoulder. "Hey, let me see that," he said, holding it up for inspection. "Gee, that's nice, you should get that framed." I looked again at the picture; it took a second to register that he was being sarcastic. I tugged it out of his hand before he could ask his wife, Lisa, for her opinion and folded it inside the peach sweater.

Brad got up and rummaged around the other side of the tree. "This is for you too," he said, handing me a teddy bear dressed in a blue jogging suit. "From Sherrie." He spit the name out as if it were a bad taste he couldn't get rid of fast enough. It was the first time I had heard her name in months, and the way Brad said it, the way he thrust the teddy bear at me, suggested Sherrie was not in good standing with the Howards anymore. But here Brad was, handing me this teddy bear—I couldn't trust myself to read his body language correctly, couldn't be sure. Should I act enthusiastic about the bear or toss it across the room?

The bear looked expensive, with jointed limbs and plush fur. Because it was obviously a boy bear, I knew Bobby had picked it out, and I wondered for the first time in months how he was doing. Would he and Sherrie bring me a gift every Christmas? Was I still supposed to think of them as family, even if I would probably never see them again? Was I supposed to remember them fondly? The next day, back in Fresno, I showed the bear to Mom, watching carefully for her reaction. "How nice of them," she said, but her words rang curiously hollow. I put the bear on my bedroom shelf with the rest of my teddy collection, but there was something tainted about it, I knew. I just couldn't put my finger on what.

Mom had chosen the ensemble I would wear for Christmas Eve, 1987, deliberating over it as though I were going on a date. She'd been especially attentive to my clothes since Dad died, taking me to the toniest kids' shop in Fresno, a boutique where an outfit could set you back upward of $100. During the six-block walk to Easterby Elementary that fall, I would tally the cost of my day's wardrobe: $50 for the Guess? overalls, $40 for the button-down shirt, $40 for the shoes. "Wow, my outfit today cost more than a *hundred* dollars," I announced to my friend Rhiannon, who wore hand-me-downs and blue-light specials, one day as we waited for the crosswalk. That bit of spontaneous boasting cost me a week of lunchtime loneliness and an onslaught of vicious schoolyard gossip.

My Christmas Eve outfit was expensive too, and fire-engine red. It consisted of a knee-length skirt and baggy turtleneck sweater, accessorized with a black belt worn loose on the hips and black high-top Reeboks. Problem was, the shirt was cut of fluid jersey knit, which draped across my every curve. My chest became a spectacular landscape of summits and valleys, every stitch of my bra clearly outlined. I didn't see any problem with the getup, because I had trained myself not to see my own chest.

When Christmas Eve dinner came, the Howards seated me at the grown-up table for the first time, Grandpa Ben offering a seat between him and my uncle Brad's wife, Lisa. I was the only kid at the table, and as we passed around the food, I stayed silent while the adults topped off each other's wineglasses and gassed about the latest 49ers game. Then Grandpa Ben paused as he turned to hand me the mashed potatoes. "Would you look at that?" he announced. "Rachel's wearing a bra now!"

The sound of silverware on china rang through the silence. "Of course she is," Aunt Lisa broke in. "She's a young woman." I smiled at her, grateful, and then I kept my watering eyes on my plate.

I called Mom to pick me up early that night, and when the next holiday season rolled around, I dreaded seeing my family. By the time I reached junior high, I'd feel relatively comfortable with my new body, barely flinching when the flag team named me "Best Chest in the West." But I'd still shy from seeing my grandparents. They sent blank birthday cards with fifty-dollar bills but they didn't call or write. In other words, they treated me just like any of their other grandchildren, the ones who still had both parents, the ones whose parents took them over to Grandma and Grandpa's house for regular visits, the ones who didn't need any special checking on. Back in Fresno, shut in my bedroom with the door locked or staying over at KC's, I was all too happy not to talk to them.

MOM TAKES ACTION: 1989

ONE MORNING I WAS GETTING READY to leave for junior high when I heard my brother's seven-year-old voice coming from the room Mom shared with Howdy. Mom had worked the night shift and would not be home for another half hour; it was Howdy's job to get Emmet to school that morning. Like any other family obligation, this was not a duty he performed with pleasure, and my brother usually washed and dressed himself before climbing into the car with his dad at the last minute, after I had left to catch my bus.

I knew approaching Howdy for anything before midday was ill-advised, so I walked to the master bedroom to check on my brother and stood in the frame of the open door. Howdy sat at the edge of the king-size bed in his underwear, his elbows leaning against his knees and his face in his hands. Emmet stood before him, quietly whining, "Daddy, my lunch. You have to make my lunch." I was about to enter and collect Emmet, perhaps even offer to make his lunch for him (I was quite lazy about helping out myself), when Howdy dropped his hands from his puffy face. In one efficient rush of anger, he stood, clenched his fists, and delivered a swift kick to Emmet's stomach. He kicked Emmet again as he lay on the floor, and once again as Emmet begged him to stop.

"What are you doing?" I shouted, running in to protect Emmet, as Howdy stared on like a dog that had finished his attack and was not sure what to do with his prey. I checked my brother over, helped him to his feet, and led him to his room, where I tied his shoes and wiped his face before dashing off to catch my bus, hoping Mom would be home soon.

I had shouted "What are you doing?" with genuine surprise and shock. I'd never seen Howdy lift a hand against his son. He hadn't physically threatened me in something like two years, and his raging outbursts were now so infrequent that I had come to regard Howdy more like a boorish housemate than a fear-inspiring authority.

Since my father's death, Howdy and I had reached a begrudging truce. I stuck to my bedroom or stayed at friends' houses, and he stayed on the couch. I performed whatever chores he commanded— he was especially fond of making me weed the garden—without comment, and thereby earned my right to avoid him. On the rare occasion when he came on a family vacation, Mom and Emmet and I would splinter off and leave him behind to brood, happily riding the monorail into Disneyland as an adventuresome trio while Howdy watched sports at the Disneyland Hotel. Mom, who had once faithfully trailed him to his friends' backyard barbecues only to be referred to as "the old ball and chain," made cursory efforts, at best, to include Howdy in our trips to the park or our nights out at the movies. Whereas once she had been in his thrall, desperate that I try to see why she loved him, their marriage now seemed one of convenience, maintained to keep Emmet's father under the same roof. That scenario I could live with.

Our new tract home seemed the final seal on these improved relations. We moved the summer before I entered seventh grade, after Section 8 housing in our old neighborhood brought with it tire slashings, graffiti, and suspicious, slow drive-bys. The freshly built two-story we fled for was in Fancher Creek, a huge development bordered by orchards and an irrigation canal. Howdy set to making his mark on the property, claiming dominion over the backyard. He paid thousands of dollars to have a putting green planted and never once rolled a golf ball across it. He bought a high-strung German shorthaired pointer to train for his dove-hunting expeditions, shut it in the side dog pen for a few weeks, then took it to the pound.

At all of these projects, Mom rolled her eyes, and even I had come to find Howdy's presence annoying but comical. He had stopped smoking pot and had taken to shutting himself in the upstairs master bedroom, so that I could now have friends over without fearing they'd find his drug paraphernalia. Little did I know that he was now shooting up cocaine behind that closed bedroom door while Mom was at work.

I was too preoccupied with adolescence to wonder what Howdy was up to. Our June move to Fancher Creek reunited me with my third-grade crush, Michael Escoto, who had moved to the housing development and out of my old school district just before my father died. Back at Easterby Elementary, where we were the only kids in our grade sent to a fourth-grade class for our reading lesson, we would recount the previous night's episode of *Moonlighting* as we crossed the blacktop from Mrs. Lehman's to Mrs. Ouijian's and back. Michael imagined himself as Bruce Willis and me as Cybill Shepherd. But we had a year until our peers became obsessed by "going around" with members of the opposite sex.

I first saw Michael again after KC and I had spent an afternoon wading through Fancher Creek, my shorts rolled up to my fleshy hips and our legs covered in mud as we emerged, like swamp creatures, from the orchards and onto the newly paved street. Michael stood with his gang of friends, looking dumbstruck. He said, "It's just like you, Rachel, to be such a mess," and the line struck me as a movie-romance kind of moment. A few days later he brought a teddy bear tin of Mrs. Fields cookies that he had bought with his mom at the mall to my doorstep, and we were boyfriend-girlfriend.

Michael was more sexually advanced than I. He had a poster of Budweiser girls in bikinis on his bedroom wall. He initiated our kiss one afternoon following a trip to Baskin-Robbins. We were sitting on the bumper of Howdy's black Park Avenue, and Michael set down his ice cream cup and pressed his lips to mine. "Wait," he said. "I didn't do that right." He pressed his lips again and I felt his tongue, like an overgrown worm, part my mouth.

He seemed to like me in spite of his own good taste. When I met the other kids in the neighborhood, he said, "They liked you. Chris said, 'She's no Miss America, but she's real nice.' " But I didn't break up with him because of that insult. I stopped returning his calls because he insisted on closing my bedroom door and squirming on top of me as I tried to pretend to like it, and because KC asked me, "Are you guys going to have sex?" Michael kept calling. He had his five-year-old brother shout stupid things into the receiver until Mom had our phone number changed and unlisted.

We broke up in August, with a full interminable month left until the start of the school year. KC lived eight miles away and could only come over when her parents would give her a ride. Howdy left me alone, and Mom worked or slept all day. For the first time in my life I had no distractions and no crises to hunker down and get through, no custody battles to strategize, no screaming matches to avert. I hadn't thought much about my father since he'd died, and I didn't think about him then. I lay on the mauve floral couch in our "formal" living room, the one with the soaring split-level ceiling, and stared at the white walls and felt that I might as well die. I had never felt that way before, and it frightened me.

But seventh grade arrived, navigating the new social order kept me occupied, and the death feeling passed. Michael Escoto marshaled a couple of older kids, high school freshmen who shared our bus, into calling me a slut and throwing stones at me as I walked home. After a few days of this, I broke down and told Mom, who enlisted Howdy. I stepped off the bus that Friday to see Howdy's Park Avenue at the corner and Howdy, dressed in boots and jeans and holding his hands on his hips to emphasize the expanse of his chest, standing before it. "Hey, Rachel," he called to me in his mirthless bass as the kids started to call me names, and then he looked each of them in the eye, one by one. They never bothered me after that day. I smiled at Howdy and said thanks, and I actually meant it.

I didn't guess that Mom was gearing up to leave him, and that she'd been wanting to leave Howdy for good even before we moved to the new house. Perhaps her resolve to get rid of him began with her third pregnancy. I was eleven and Emmet was five. She sat down with me on my daybed to break the news. I had a fit.

"You can't have another baby!" I shouted. "We don't have room for a baby! What about us? What about Emmet? What about me?"

Part of the panic arose from pure jealousy, not wanting to share Mom with another kid. It was so hard to win time with her as it was. But another part of me worried that a new baby would tie her even closer to Howdy, and the scene was ugly. "You can't have a baby! You just can't!"

I pouted all night. "It'll be fun," Mom said. "The baby will sleep in Emmet's room. You'll like the baby. You'll see." A day later I came around, and Mom took me to Mervyn's to help her pick out maternity clothes.

I grew to accept the idea of the baby and even got excited about it. Forget about Emmet's room: The baby would stay in *my* room. I'd be the ultimate protective big sister. I'd make up for the affection this baby would probably not receive from Howdy, and Mom would love me more for it.

And then a few days later Mom knocked on my door for another sit-down on the daybed. "The baby's not coming," she said.

She said she'd miscarried. Her eyes remained mist-free, but I could hear her voice waver beneath her "that's life" delivery. We took the un-worn maternity clothes back to Mervyn's, and I cried alone in my room, careful not to let Mom hear, wishing I could rewind to the moment she had first told me about the baby and hug her with my full support.

It wasn't until five years later, snooping through Mom's drawers, that I found a spiral-bound notebook in her nightstand and flipped through the first few pages. They were filled with her handwriting, smooth forty-five-degree-slanted cursive, and each page had a date at the top. I scanned a few entries, and then I stopped on one, dated 1987. *Home today from the abortion*, it said. *Howdy didn't even pick me up at the hospital.*

I felt too sick to read further. So it had been my fault all this time. The baby might have lived were it not for my tantrum. I'd been a brat, and I'd caused Mom pain when she already bore too much hurt to bear. Never mind Howdy not being there for her—*I* hadn't been there for her, too panicked over whether we'd still have enough money to buy Guess? jeans with another mouth to feed. And then I heard the front door slam downstairs and nursing shoes squeaking on the parquet entryway, and I knew Mom had just come home. I put the notebook back in the drawer just as I'd found it and never said a word to her about it.

A few weeks after Mom had told me the baby had miscarried, she drove me across town to a psychologist's office. Mom and Howdy had just started marriage counseling, and as part of the therapy, the psychologist thought I should come in for a few sessions too.

I had a history of shunning therapy. A year after the murder Mom had enrolled me in a support group for kids with family problems, and I'd dropped out after two sessions. The other kids moaned and cried about their daddies moving away, and not understanding why mama and papa didn't love each other anymore. How was I supposed to chime in and say my father had been murdered, without feeling like a freak? How were those kids supposed to help me feel better about that?

But I felt hopeful about the marriage counselor, open to the idea of talking with her. It was a chance to put in my two cents about Howdy, to enter my plea in a court of law. I took a seat in her dark-shuttered office. She looked a tad severe, but I registered that as a sign of her fairness and impartiality. I told her about Howdy screaming, about how he'd call me names if I didn't do the dishes with the sink plugged, how he'd cussed me out because I'd dropped a heavy pot of spaghetti on the floor. I didn't tell her about the cigarette burns, of course, because I didn't remember them, and I didn't tell her about the drugs. My strategy was to crack her open a bit, test her sympathy, and when I had her full confidence, spill all.

She waited until I finished my opening piece. I was a confident kid, an incurable know-it-all, so I didn't stutter or fidget, just laid out my gambit. She paused and touched the side of her glasses, and then she posed a question. "What could you do to make things smoother with your stepfather?" she said, leaning forward in an intimation of tenderness from which I instantly recoiled. "Could you do your chores more thoroughly, maybe, or help out around the house more?"

So that was it: I had no hope of turning to anyone. I would have to endure the next seven years or so with Howdy in silence, until I could get my own place and my own life at eighteen. I'm sure the therapist saw my eyes flare with shock and anger, and I'm sure she pinned me for a brat in serious need of discipline. I clenched my teeth and glared at her ugly shag carpet. "Maybe I could put the stopper in the sink when I wash the dishes," I answered quietly, trying to project submissiveness. I would lie my way through the rest of this session, and if need be, I would lie my way through the rest of my childhood too.

That meeting sealed a certain distance between me and Mom. I stopped complaining about Howdy to her, which was easy to do since Howdy had withdrawn on his own, and Mom no longer insisted that I try to act chummy with him. I was closer to Mom than to any other adult, but I kept my serious feelings for my journal and the scraps of paper I took notes on and tucked into a heart-covered box. When I got my period the year after "going around" with Michael Escoto, I contemplated breaking the news to Mom by placing a note inside her car. In the end I waited until she had left for work and called her at the hospital, figuring I could keep the conversation brief and avoid her in the morning.

I didn't know that one day after moving into the new house, Mom went to see a different therapist, on her own. The therapist told her not to come back until she'd left her husband; the marriage was over and there was no use returning to counseling until she'd kicked the louse out. Mom cried with gratitude. This was her permission, her green light, though she wouldn't act on it just yet.

And then shortly after we moved into the new place, Mom's checks started bouncing. She went to the branch office and they walked her through the account's recent activity. It was a joint account, and Howdy had been pulling out hundreds of dollars at a time without telling her, sometimes days in a row. She knew he wasn't telling her because he was spending it on crack. Instead of confronting Howdy with the bank statements, she called a paralegal and asked him to tell her how to file for bankruptcy. With all the money Howdy had spent and the car payments and credit card bills they'd racked up, bankruptcy was the only way for Mom to climb out of the marriage.

✳   ✳   ✳

It's hard for me to understand the thick layers of self-doubt that kept Mom married to Howdy, but they must have weighed heavily, because when Emmet came home from school the day that Howdy had kicked him, Mom reacted with incredulity. "Oh, Emmet, Daddy wouldn't have done something like that to you!" she told him.

But I was watching from the doorway, waiting to seize my big moment. I had found a way to live with Howdy, but the memories of his many transgressions were fresh. Revenge beckoned powerfully, and the promise of freedom overrode the small store of sympathy I'd built for him in the last few months. "I can't believe you're going to let him get away with that!" I shouted at Mom, in a frenzy. "I saw everything!"

Mom lifted Emmet's shirt to find bruises forming on his ribs. We were all silent as she traced her fingers across them. "Get me the phone book," she finally said.

She called Child Protective Services that minute to report Howdy and get a restraining order. Howdy gathered some clothes and left our house that evening with little more than a whimper.

This is the true story of Howdy's departure. But in the years after he left, as Mom and Emmet and I coalesced into a fiercely loyal family, as I saw that her only care now was for our well-being, I developed my own version of Howdy's last day with us. I wrote the account as a short story for my college literary journal, and it morphed into my personal truth.

In my version, Mom had already arrived home from work that morning and had run upstairs when she heard Howdy screaming and seen Emmet crying for herself. Her face boiled with long-repressed rage, and she screeched at Howdy like some scorned woman on a Lifetime movie of the week. "Get *out* of here!" Her face shook as she pointed down the staircase to the front door. "Get *out*!"

Howdy didn't say a word. He looked at Mom, and then he looked at me, eyes steeled like a silverback gorilla's, as if to let us know he'd return to hurt us again. But he wouldn't. I felt his heavy footsteps on the stairs rattle my bedroom walls. I stood at my window to watch Howdy climb into his black Park Avenue and cruise, like a hulking metal shark, down the street.

The way I imagined the scene, Mom got to see Howdy's full cruelty for herself, got to take full agency in his banishment, got to scream at him with all the anger I'd kept wrapped up for so long. Mom was at last a savior and a hero, which was true enough to me in fiction as well as in fact.

SHERRIE CALLING: 1992

I THOUGHT IT WAS my boyfriend calling.

Or rather, my so-called boyfriend, the twenty-two-year-old radio deejay who liked to come around for me at night, after Mom had fallen asleep. He had a habit of checking in with me in the early evenings, after I'd returned from flag team practice, to arrange our nightly rendezvous. In a few months I would have my driver's license and my own car. In the meantime I patiently awaited his instructions to stand under the corner light post at the appointed hour, looking for his white '65 Mustang to cruise down our deserted country-suburb roads.

So I picked the receiver up on the first ring.

"Is that Rachel?" The voice was syrupy yet hard-edged, like crusting molasses, and weirdly familiar. "It's me, Sherrie." My heart stopped, recovered from the blow, and resumed beating in double time. "You know, your old mom."

"Oh my God."

I stared over the kitchen counter and out the vertical blinds of the family room, into our vast backyard, edged with browning shrubs and jagged boulders hauled in from the foothills.

"How have you been?" she said. I pulled the phone cord over the kitchen counter and slid into the corner of the sectional sofa, positioning myself to scan the whole house. Mom, I knew from the mini-van parked out front, was home, probably napping in her bedroom just above my head.

"I'm fine," I replied, in a shaken version of the no-nonsense tone I usually reserved for telemarketers.

"Oh, you must be so big now! What are you these days, a freshman. . . . ?" I was a junior, but I didn't correct her. "A young *woman*. I bet *all* the boys are chasing you." I might have blushed, if all the blood hadn't left my face moments earlier.

She paused. "Well, I was just *calling* because I'm coming through Fresno next week, and so I thought of *you*, and I realized, you know, that I have some things of your father's you might want. Old records and stuff?"

"Okay."

"So I'll need your address so I can bring it all by."

"I don't know about that." My answer was pure instinct, and as I said the words, it struck me as a strange instinct to have. I'd never been given any orders not to talk with Sherrie or see her or been told that she was bad news. I hadn't spoken about her in six years. But as I held the phone to my ear, inexplicably terrified, my body gave its own orders—don't tell her where you live.

"You still there? My God, can you believe the way time passes," she rattled on, but I was already rising from the couch.

"I'm going to get my mom," I said, dropping the phone. And I bolted up the stairs two at a time.

I had never tried to sort out how I felt about Sherrie after my father died. I'd kept the teddy bear she and Bobby had given me for Christmas years ago, placing it on a shelf with my other stuffed animals. Sometimes when I was sitting in my room and my eyes came to rest on it, I'd register an uneasy feeling. But I never pursued that reaction, never tried to figure out why the bear's continuing presence in my room made me uncomfortable or why, despite the queasiness it occasionally aroused in me, I kept it.

I suppose I kept that teddy bear because I wanted to deny I had any feelings of note toward Sherrie to contemplate. My time with Sherrie, I told myself, was in the past. Howdy, vanished for three years now, was a regime from another era. Custody battles were the stuff of TV miniseries. Murders happened on *Miami Vice* and *L.A. Law*, shows I studiously avoided. My father was gone, had been for a long time, end of story.

The kids at school had let me skate by on that last line. I'd lost touch with KC Mason after we'd entered separate junior high schools. I told certain new friends, my junior high clique, that my dad had been murdered and left out the particulars. I wouldn't even have known where to begin with a fuller story, since I had never seriously contemplated who might have killed my father, or how Sherrie had treated me. Once, while I waited for a bus after school, a friend let leak to a group of popular boys across the lawn that my father had been stabbed. "No way!" they shouted, far too zealously, as though they'd just killed the bad guy for the high score on their favorite Nintendo game. They wanted to hear all the details, but Becky Jackson, tall, redheaded, brainy, and in tight with all the teachers, intervened on my behalf. "It's not funny," she said. Subject closed. I slunk onto the bus, too mortified to tell Becky thank you.

That was back in seventh grade, back when I had pudgy thighs and frowsy hair and report cards stacked with A's. I had hung with the egghead crowd, winning spelling bees and history fairs, attaching myself to a brilliant fellow nerd named Michelle, whose missionary parents took us to Presbyterian youth groups on Friday nights. I played alto saxophone in marching band and Michelle played flute. We bought a "Best Friends" necklace set at the mall, Michelle becoming BE FRI and me taking on ST ENDS, code names we used in our meticulously folded notes, which we passed between classes.

Then came high school and, more importantly, the flag team: a serious, full-time endeavor in the vast, well-funded Clovis school district, which framed Fresno to the south and west in an L formation. Hundreds of Fresno residents lied about their addresses to get their children in; our housing tract lay just inside the easternmost district line, saving me from the gun searches and overcrowded classrooms endured by my peers just across Clovis Avenue.

After giving up ballet in grammar school I had wanted to take up dancing again and wear a sparkly uniform, preferably one with bloomers. The choices were color guard or pep squad, and I knew only skinny, rich girls with perfect spiral perms made it into cheerleading.

But my routine to Madonna's "Vogue" passed muster at color-guard tryouts and won me entrance to a ready-made social set. Marching in formation and tossing a big pole into the air took up an elective and a PE period, two to three hours daily after school, Friday evenings performing football halftimes, and a Saturday of competition nearly every weekend. The shows were spectacularly silly high-budget productions. One halftime set using the music from *The Ten Commandments* featured a giant fabric Red Sea that split down the middle of the field. The "winterguard" routines, which we performed inside a gym without the band, were particularly over-the-top. Our number to Sade had us draped in Barbarella-style fake hair falls, crawling seductively through plush white carpet, and holding the blades of our sabers between our teeth. The district's otherwise conservative parents turned a blind eye to the overtly sexual antics.

My soft, round tummy turned firm and tan during late-summer band camp, and my hair, no longer permed, retained brassy blond streaks without the help of Sun-In. I had evolved from simply "geek" to "band geek," but boys, even some passably attractive ones, liked me. So I shocked everyone that freshman year of expanded romantic options by taking up with a lanky Goth senior, Scott, who listened to Pink Floyd and The Cure and wore black denim jackets he'd painted skull-and-bones patterns onto.

My grades nose-dived. I got a D in biology and another D in geometry and accepted without protest my school counselor's directive to downgrade from honors courses to bonehead classes. I got D's in those classes too. I spent all my free time with Scott, who marched with the baritone saxophone, heavy-petting with him on the charter bus backseat during drives to competitions, and sneaking away from school in the trunk of his rattling green station wagon during lunch (seniors had "off-campus lunch" privileges). We'd go back to his house and make out beneath the glow-in-the-dark moon stickers plastered on his black bedroom ceiling. He loved the way my sleek new body looked in my shiny hot-pink practice leotard. I loved his impassioned knowledge of melancholy pop music and cult films like *Brazil* and *Clockwork Orange*, movies few of the Future Farmers of America types at Clovis High School had ever heard of.

Scott marked the first case of my pattern with men, a pattern that played itself out with the radio deejay, with my college love, and even with my future husband. From my first few weeks with Scott I was taken with a fear that his affection toward me, like my father's, was too good to last. My logic was simple: Even before he died, my father had turned undependable; my mother had failed to protect me from Howdy; my grandparents hadn't called me after the murder. You couldn't trust others to stay with you, no matter how close you felt to them. Scott would grow tired of me, he would realize he had never liked me that much after all, he would leave me sooner rather than later unless I lived every day in crisis mode, securing promises and proofs of his loyalty. If Scott passed me a note between third and fourth periods one day but skipped on letter writing the next, this was a red alert that we were on the swift slippery slope toward breakup, and we would have to talk about it immediately. If he went to the mall with his good friend Stephanie, toward whom (in the underutilized rational part of my brain) I knew he felt no sexual attraction, this was a betrayal waiting to happen, and I would have to grill him on it that night. Everything he did and said was under scrutiny, possible evidence that, like my father, he would suddenly disappear.

No surprise then that Scott dumped me. At least three times. The startling thing to my mother and friends was how badly I took it, crying not with the self-conscious high drama of most teenagers, but with an all-consuming bodily reaction, as though someone had died. My grief over the first breakup was so intense that the color-guard members assumed Scott must have said something unspeakably awful to me and glared at him across the field during practice. After the second breakup it must have become obvious that I was a culpable agent in this soap opera, and yet the color-guard girls always took me back.

They were a prefabricated social set you could pull out of and plug right back into again, quick to pardon with a discreetly passed note or an invitation to Sunday's pool party when you'd transgressed by choosing the wrong boy. Within the overall flag team circle I moved in, there were two cliques, the girls of my class and the girls one class ahead. The girls in my class—Jenny, Kristal, Heather, Britten, Cori—were good girls, determined virgins who never drank or snuck out at night. The girls one class ahead—Jennifer, Lisa, another Heather, Candice, Lynette, Jessica—were edgier. They dyed their hair. One of them was definitely not a virgin. Two others gently talked me (or did I talk them?) into letting half the varsity basketball team party at my house one weekend when Mom and Emmet were away, an escapade that might have passed undetected had one of the drunken revelers not stolen a camera and Emmet's Game Boy. I idolized the older girls, especially flamboyant Jennifer Cooper, but they were cattier and could turn on you more quickly. The girls my age were safer, more dependable. Distrusting relationships as a rule, I was not as good a friend to them as they were to me.

But many of the color-guard girls, older and younger, had no idea my father had been murdered. The ones I'd told never pressed me on the topic. We were much more likely to discuss the virtues of matching your socks to your ponytail holders, extol the hair-hardening miracles of Aqua Net, or belt out the latest Michael Bolton hit while cruising home from Taco Bell.

As for my demolished grades, they weren't bad enough to get me kicked off the flag team, which was all that mattered. I was moving up the ranks, becoming by sophomore year a member of the saber line, which got to twirl marine ceremonial swords in the front of the band. In the winter, we performed pseudosophisticated routines to songs like "Try a Little Tenderness" and "Smooth Operator" without the band, inside gymnasiums across the state and as far away as Dayton, Ohio, a locale we found positively exotic during our national championship travels. In the summers I joined the Blue Devils, an independent drum and bugle corps for diehards aged thirteen to twenty-one, and we toured the country on charter buses, practicing daily from nine a.m. till nine p.m. or later in the blistering heat and sleeping on gym floors.

Color guard was my life. When my English teacher assigned a paper researching our future careers, I chose to write about becoming a color-guard instructor, interviewing my squad's twenty-three-year-old leader, who roomed with my family for a season in the spare bedroom. I thought of color guard as my destined vocation, and even today when I watch videotapes of old shows, I miss it intensely.

Mom thought color guard a godsend of extracurricular activity, impressed by the initiative I'd take tossing the saber around in the front yard on nonpractice days, picking the sword right back up again when a miscalculated throw cut my eyelid. The flag team kept me so busy and healthy that she only fleetingly complained about the hours spent driving me to practices and competitions. She noted with displeasure the disparity between my dismal grades and my top-percentile standardized-test scores, but she didn't have the rigid strength of a disciplinarian. She might threaten grounding me or disconnecting the private phone line in my bedroom, but rarely had the heart to carry punishments out.

And so I brought home speeding tickets with two a.m. time stamps. I drove fifteen miles on a flat tire at the break of dawn, knowing Mom needed to drive my car to work that day, and let her discover the damage for herself in the morning. I took off to Santa Cruz with a guy I barely knew at midnight and only got caught the next morning because of the sand in the backseat. I sped one hundred miles an hour down the 680 freeway to a weekend of drum corps practice, blew out another tire, and flipped the car twice on the center divider, miraculously sparing the lives of my three teenaged passengers. No matter how astonishing the stunt, Mom huffed for a few hours, felt guilty for shouting, and let me off scot-free.

So began my double life. Color guard filled my days, but I dreaded lonely nights. In between and after the months with Scott, I snapped up one boyfriend after another, most of them not from high school. I would meet them at the mall or by calling late-night radio deejays and flirting. Whether I liked them much was immaterial. They would pick me up at eleven thirty or midnight, or after Mom bought me the Plymouth Colt, I would drive across the city to meet them, brazenly walking right out the front door. We'd drive around town and make out in the empty parking lot behind Pic-N-Save, or even in the shadowy plum orchard just behind my neighborhood. Scott had initiated me early to the techniques of oral sex, and I felt confident in my seductive abilities, unconcerned whether I still liked my target the day after. Even with my prissy sense of style, I got in with a group of high-school-dropout grunge rockers and moved from one loser to another within the social set. They'd sneak me into dingy nightclubs and hand me beers I didn't drink. They smoked pot, which I still detested from my Howdy years, and passed around pipes packed with something foul-smelling they called crank. I never took a drag on any of that stuff. I didn't want their alcohol or drugs.

I just wanted late-night company, to come home so dead exhausted at three thirty in the morning that I dropped straight to sleep. Otherwise I might start to remember the murder, might be tempted to flip through the photo album of Dad that Grandma Mae had given me. The occasional nightmares were bad enough. Once, after reports of a severed foot found in the grape-fermenting fields a few blocks from our street, I dreamt that someone had climbed into my second-story bedroom window and was standing above my daybed, machete gleaming in hand. And I regularly dreamt that my father had lived and simply hadn't wanted to see me all these years, shaking off vivid memories of that scenario as I curled my bangs and applied my mascara in the early mornings.

But running around with guys wasn't just a way to avoid thinking about the murder. It wasn't only the distraction that I needed—the sex felt urgent too. It was a fix against loneliness, against the unbearable temporary absence of a man's attentions. They stared into my eyes, entranced by the sway of my hips, the arch of my back, the smile on my face. I was the aggressor, urging them to go further, as though a blow job might secure their affections, knowing at the same time that pushing too far would brand me a one-night stand and guarantee their departure. Night after night, I lived out a cycle of trying to hold on to my father's love and knowing I would lose him.

Through all the kissing and necking and fondling and oral sex, I had resolved to remain a virgin. I was simply too scared of pregnancy, though I'd had Mom help me get birth control pills under the pretense of regulating my periods, when things started getting heavy with Scott. But during my appointment with the doctor, I couldn't coax the pediatrician to confirm that the pills she'd given me would keep me from becoming pregnant, and I wouldn't ask outright. So I kept Scott from going all the way, and after a month of battling hormonal nausea, I stopped taking the tiny mint-green tablets altogether.

Two years later, the twenty-two-year-old deejay said he couldn't believe I was holding out. Obviously I was just too young for him. By that point I saw that he was not long-term boyfriend material; he was insecure and snappish and possibly destined to spend most of his adult life living with his mother. But I saw that as I approached eighteen, older men would expect me to go all the way, and I would have to give it up to him or someone else soon. We did it on the downstairs couch while Mom slept in her room above, and I stared at the ceiling and wondered if she would hear us. He was miffed that I didn't come and that it didn't hurt. But I shrugged off his disappointment, too stupid to see how desperately I was trying to compensate for my father's lost affection, how intensely I was playing out his love for me and his sudden disappearance, night after night.

And then there was Sherrie's voice on the line.

Mom was standing at her bedroom door, about to shout downstairs and ask who'd called, when she saw me running toward her. "It's Sherrie," I said.

She narrowed her eyes for a moment, scanning her mental address book for a Sherrie entry. Coming up with nothing, she saw the urgency in my face and it hit her. "You're kidding."

She crossed the bedroom and picked the phone up from the nightstand as I took a seat at the foot of her bed. "This is Aleta," she said, as though dealing with a bill collector. ". . . No, you don't need to bring them here. Well, just . . ." I could barely hear Sherrie's voice chattering on as Mom wrapped the phone cord around white knuckles. "No, you can take them . . ." The chattering grew louder, faster, like a song on high-speed playback.

"Listen," Mom said, cutting the chatter midstream. "If you want her to have those things, you can take them to her grandparents. You know where they live." Mom hung up the phone and then laid it off the hook, dial tone droning and then beeping.

A few minutes later, she dialed my grandparents. I didn't speak to them, but sat next to Mom in silence, not wanting Mae and Ben to sense my presence, trying to guess at the conversation from Mom's terse statements. They spoke for ten minutes or so, Mom making restrained replies. "I see," she said. "I wish you had consulted me."

"Goddamn it!" she said under her breath when she hung up. She pressed her hands against her knees, stretching her jeans down her thighs, then braced my shoulder, which felt so comforting. "It's about your father's grave," she said.

The story took some explanation. My grandparents had decided to change my father's grave marker from BELOVED HUSBAND to BELOVED SON. But Sherrie, who along with me was designated Stan Howard's next of kin, wouldn't sign off on the revision. For some reason that eluded me, my grandparents had then given her my phone number.

My mother made it a policy never to say anything negative about my grandparents, just as she barred me from disparaging Howdy in front of Emmet. But the tension in her shoulders and the tight set of her jaw told me she was outraged. Her anger only confirmed the previously unidentified instinct that had so shocked me when I picked up the phone: Sherrie was trouble. Sherrie was someone to stay the hell away from, someone to fear.

I snuck out that night to fool around with the twenty-two-year-old deejay. And then, after I dropped quickly to sleep at three in the morning, the most disturbing dream I have ever experienced came to me. In the dream, someone had again climbed into my bedroom window. But this time the masked person didn't just hold the knife above me. Instead, I crawled out of my bed and across my floor, trying to escape from him. I cowered in the corner between my closed door and my pink heart wallpaper, arms wrapped over my head. In the dream, the intruder plunged the knife straight into my chest. I could feel the pain of it tearing through my sternum. He stabbed me with the knife again and again, half a dozen times, each stab more painful, more bloody. In the dream, I died. And then I woke up.

I never did quite shake off that dream. I still ran around at night to stave off loneliness, but I started to think about the murder during the daytime, while zoning out in class, say, or between dinnertime and nightfall. My favorite magazine was *Sassy*, to which I had subscribed three years running. In one of the regular features toward the front of the magazine, readers about my age told their true-life stories. The slot was called "It Happened to Me," and though often girls wrote about things like their first screening of *The Rocky Horror Picture Show*, every once in a while some brave teenager recounted getting raped or being abused by a stepparent. I saw the submission address at the bottom of the page and decided to write about Dad's murder.

I wrote about waking up at the house in Merced that night and facing the pools of blood, seeing Dad clutching his throat, watching him being carried out on the gurney. But I gave the second half of my story, the "after" half, a false spin. A tale that grim needed some redemption, I could see that. So I decided to make the piece into a fable for the wonders of psychotherapy, claiming that one-on-one counseling and support groups had helped me deal with the past, with what I'd seen.

Of course, I had been to a therapist precisely three times: the day after the murder, the night Mom tried to enroll me in a support group for "broken families," and the day Mom's marriage counselor suggested I could help Howdy with the chores more. All three encounters had seemed to make my situation worse, not better. My great appreciation for the wonders of therapy was a bald-faced lie.

I wrote the article in Mom's room with the door locked, working on the new word processor she'd bought at Costco. You typed on a blue screen and saved your work on the hard drive or on a disk, and the processor hammered your writing out on a typewriter built into the top of the machine. I saved the document under false names that hid the content, but wasn't inventive enough and titled one version "XXXXX." Nosy Emmet, then ten years old, saw the suspect file name and opened it.

One afternoon in front of Mom, he told me I'd been found out. He didn't do it in a bratty, mean-spirited way, but exposed it tentatively, apologetically. "Have you been writing about your dad's murder?" he asked quietly. He scuffed the linoleum with his tennis shoe. "I read it on the machine."

Mom looked at me as though holding her breath. "That's great, honey," she said gently, flashing a let-it-go-or-I'll-kill-you-later glance at Emmet.

But it didn't feel great to me. I picked up the remote and started flipping through channels as though the topic bore no further comment, but half an hour later I snuck upstairs to Mom's room, printed out a few copies of my dark secret article, and erased all the fake files

I'd saved it under. I hid the copies deep in my bottom dresser drawer but put one in a manila envelope and addressed it to *Sassy*. I never heard back from the magazine, and my father's belongings, the items Sherrie had wanted to deliver, never did show up at my grandparents' house.

THE GRAVE:
SUMMER 1994

TWO YEARS LATER, for the first time since the murder, I found myself sitting across the street from the house I'd shared with Dad and Sherrie, too scared to open the car door.

The neighborhood where my father was killed, a far cry from the tidy streets near Applegate Park where Dad lived with Nanette, is the kind of desolate locale criminals seek for starting crystal meth labs. It's outside the Merced city line, on the wrong side of the freeway, past the flea market grounds and marooned among dry grazing fields. You cruise along the cemetery and then down Cone Avenue, a notoriously drug-riddled strip of rotting houses where broken windows are fixed with cardboard, and litters of unwanted pit-bull puppies frolic in unfenced yards. There are no sidewalks. Two blocks over you hit the corner of Gerard Avenue and Tyler Road. An irrigation ditch borders the horse pasture on one side of the street, and on the other sits a row of five houses. The home Dad, Sherrie, Bobby, and I once shared is a squat, cheaply built one-story with two square windows staring out upon a yellowed lawn. It looks as though a tornado had lifted a fixer-upper tract home and plopped it along with a few other random victims onto this patch of nowhere.

It was August when I first returned to that house, and therefore unbearably hot, sunlight glinting off the flecks of pollution in the valley air. I had just come from the cemetery. There I had felt safe; here, my back tingled with danger, and the apprehension had less to do with unsavory Cone Avenue's proximity than with the visceral reawakening of

the past. Just surveying the house from across two lanes of baking asphalt made me double- and triple-check over my shoulder that I wasn't
being watched. I imagined a tall, shadowy figure sneaking up behind
me, noiseless footsteps kicking up a trail of dust. Of course the only
person I really had to be afraid of was myself, my own memories.

That spring I'd decided to invite Nanette to my high school graduation. My mother insisted that I send the gold-leaf announcements to
my Howard uncles. Since Dad's death, I'd spoken maybe three sentences to them each on the Thanksgivings and Christmases that I'd
made it to Merced, and I could not imagine that they would care about
my graduation. In the midst of my painful resistance to Mom's forcing
of the issue, it occurred to me that the one person in Merced I truly
wanted to send an invitation to was Nanette. She and her eight-year-
old daughter had driven eighty miles to hear my name read over the
football stadium's loudspeakers as a stream of nearly a thousand classmates rushed on. Afterward, at the graduation party, we'd nibbled
meticulously arranged turkey and tortilla rolls at the home of my
wealthiest friend. Nanette brought me a faux-leather Timex watch,
which I wore every day for the rest of the summer, and a framed picture of me playing in the sand at age three, accompanied by a card
about "building sandcastles."

As I tore the wrapping paper away from the photograph, I began to
realize Nanette and I have a lifelong bond. She took care of me from
the time I was just out of diapers, and the connection, though perhaps
a shade nostalgic, is real and enduring.

Nanette is the most tragic person I know. She hails from a large
Catholic Italian family, the Fragos, too few of whom are still alive.
Nanette's brother, a California Highway patrolman, was killed on duty
when Nanette was in her teens. Then the defining loss, the death of
Nanette's father when I was eight: He hung himself from a tree in his
own backyard. Nanette called my Grandpa Ben, who lived two blocks
away, to come cut Mr. Frago down.

There's more. Years later, after my father had died and my contact
with Nanette had become limited to her thoughtful Christmas presents (teddy bears, rocking-horse music boxes), Nanette's younger sis-

ter killed herself. Howard family myth has it she hung herself from the same tree as her father, though in fact she died many miles away. "You'd have thought they'd have cut that darn tree down," Grandma Mae likes to say with a rueful shake of her head every time she recounts the story.

And the curse lingers. Around the time my dad died, Nanette married again and eventually had two daughters. Then, after sixteen years of marriage, Nanette and her second husband, Don, separated, though Nanette hung on to hopes of patching things up. In 2002, Don was killed in a motorcycle crash while cruising the foothills above Merced. I sent flowers the day I heard, and Nanette sent back a thank-you card. She assured me she was doing fine, though it was "tough for the girls to adjust, as you know."

I kept Nanette by my side, neglecting all other guests that graduation night. We sat on the sectional sofa opening gifts and posing for photos with my mortarboard, letting her eight-year-old daughter, Vanessa, decorate her hair with the wrapping bows. Mom left us alone to catch up, without rancor; she and Nanette had never been hostile, even while Nanette was still married to my dad. It was Grandma Mae and Grandpa Ben's presence that made including Nanette feel knotted up and awkward. Mae and Ben hadn't expected Nanette to be there, of course, and I felt like a nervous young man bringing his fiancée home to finally meet the family. Did they understand the ties between us? Would they approve?

She looked great: hair still thick and lustrous black, figure still trim, eyes weighted by worry, even when she smiled, but unfailingly wide and friendly. "Your father would have been so proud to see you now," she said, but discreetly, as though she understood how much I wanted to hear the words and yet how difficult hearing them still was. She was the only person I wanted to speak those words, that night.

"I still go out to his grave every few months," she said, as my stomach tightened. The grave had become a kind of Holy Grail for me. I had no idea where within the cemetery it lay, and would never ask my grandparents to take me to it, out of fear that they might sense even the slightest trace of lingering pain, a pain I had decided they didn't want to see or talk about or even know I experienced. But

I felt that if I could find the grave, without them, the mystery of Dad's death would be made tangible, etched in a headstone and not just my imagination.

"Would you take me to it, his grave?" I said as the party circulated around us.

"Of course," Nanette said. "Whenever you want."

Nanette's home was like a dollhouse, trimmed in white and even smaller than the two-bedroom Nanette, Dad, and I had shared on Twenty-fifth Street. As I walked past the living room window, I spotted most of the furniture I had climbed on as a preschooler. There was the ocher and burgundy paisley couch, the matching side chair, the walnut and glass coffee table from ten years ago. Beneath the coffee table stood Nanette's musty old stuffed bobcat.

I knocked and heard footsteps on the hardwood floor. Nanette threw her arms open and hugged me. "Come on in," she said, flustered. "I was getting ready in the back room." As I entered, I saw that the back room was not more than six paces from the front room. This might well be the smallest house in all Merced County.

Nanette's husband was out for the afternoon, but her little girl, Vanessa, was with her (Marina would not be born for another four years), so we sat at the same dining room table I'd eaten dinner at as a child and drank iced tea to gear up for our pilgrimage. I asked to use the bathroom and noticed a framed copy of the photo of me building sandcastles, the picture she'd given me for graduation, hanging above Nanette's towel rack.

As we walked toward Nanette's car, I realized it was the same red Subaru wagon she and my dad had bought together more than a decade ago, though considerably worse for wear. The floorboard carpet was missing, and a trail of ants tracked up and down the door well as Nanette apologized profusely. She insisted I take the front seat even though I wanted Vanessa, so patient and quiet for an eight-year-old, to have it. Vanessa was the same age I had been when Nanette and Dad had divorced, an observation I barely let flicker across my consciousness.

We stopped by the Payless drugstore, where Nanette worked as a cashier, to equip ourselves with the help of her employee discount.

Nanette picked up a little straw hand broom and then steered me to an aisle of fake flowers to choose some graveside adornments. The blooms were all unbearably tacky, not about to fool anyone closer than twenty paces with their not-quite-silk buds and shiny green plastic stems. But they were curiously sweet in their gaudiness and heartbreaking in their earnestness. I passed over the orange- and blue-hued varieties and picked out a dozen in seminatural shades, and then Nanette insisted on paying for everything.

We parked the Subaru in the gravel roadside outside the cemetery and walked, Nanette and Vanessa hand in hand, up the tree-lined driveways. It was a large cemetery, and all the groups of plots looked alike, undistinguished clusters of indentations on the flat lawn, but Nanette walked straight to my dad's headstone. It was covered in dry grass clippings, which she lifted off in a clump like the lid to a pot. I took the hand brush and knelt down to sweep away the remaining layer of dirt and straw, trying, more than anything, to look busy and engaged, feeling fidgety and self-conscious now that this big moment had come.

The little square headstone read BELOVED HUSBAND. Neither I nor Nanette said anything about that.

Nanette's daughter hugged her thigh, patience fading fast, as I threaded the fake roses into the little well provided for them on the headstone. "*Who* are we visiting, Mom?" Vanessa asked, and Nanette gave that goofy, sweet, tension-diffusing laugh she has, a steady rhythm of five fast *huh*s.

"This is Rachel's dad," she said.

"And how come you know him, Mom?"

Nanette laughed again, embarrassed. "I was married to him, sweetie, before your dad. A long time ago."

The quiet and the tension and all the other facts of Dad's life left unsaid made me want to turn straight for the car, but I was grateful to be standing there with Nanette, knew I would later be glad I had done this. As for in the moment, there was nothing except the sweet smell of grass clippings, a ghostly hum of far-off freeway traffic proving the impossibility of silence, a hot wind across my bare legs and arms. There was no release or relief, no feeling I had come to the conclusion of something. If anything it felt, unexpectedly, like a tentative beginning.

Maybe that's why Nanette and I started talking about the murder over dinner at Perko's, as Vanessa colored her kid's menu. I don't remember how we got started on the subject, but I'm pretty sure Nanette gently led us into it, since I rarely had the guts back then to so much as whisper something about Dad's murder.

"I talked to some people at the Sheriff's Department a few years ago," she said. "They said Sherrie had a brother, who didn't get along with your dad. And they told me they think this brother did it." She meant Steve Serrano, though I would not hear this name until nearly a decade later.

I tried to dip my french fry nonchalantly, without trembling. The idea that someone—an ordinary someone like Nanette, or my grandparents, my uncles—could just talk to the Sheriff's Department was a revelation to me. I flashed to my grandparents' brief mentions of my dad, their even briefer asides on what "that thing" had done to him. So this relative of Sherrie's might have been "that thing"? It all seemed way too strange and melodramatic, and I didn't have the courage to ask Nanette for more information, or even to admit to myself that after all these years I wanted to know more.

After Nanette hugged me good-bye, I started toward the freeway but drove beneath the overpass instead of taking the on-ramp and headed to the house where my dad was stabbed. The sun was just starting to set. I found the house quickly, without asking directions, even though I hadn't seen it in eight years. Like every Merced house I ever lived in, it looked smaller than I remembered. And sinister. It was painted in the same colors Dad had chosen, a little dulled but decently kept. I managed to turn off the car engine, and to sit for a few minutes just remembering the night of the murder, the blood in the hallway, the way Bobby had picked up the weight-lifting glove—just registering a reality I felt my family always wanted me to forget. And then I turned the engine on again without so much as unlocking the car doors, and headed for the freeway.

I'd left the radio off, too flummoxed with basic tasks like finding the blinker switch and checking for cross-traffic to fidget with the tuner. But as the rows of paint-chipped migrant workers' homes and dingy laundry lines passed and the on-ramp deposited me onto the freeway, a feeling I'd never known before overtook me.

I watched the sun set through the windshield, the creeping darkness, and I felt eerily at peace. I had faced the reality of what had happened. It was real and now I was driving away from it, and as long as I kept driving, I would feel whole, settled.

Eventually I turned on the radio and let the disposable pop tunes swirl pleasantly around me. Something had changed. I thought, I could die right now without a twitch of panic or regret. I could never make it home, and that would be fine. I'd be ready to die.

At eighteen, I was prone to such melodramatic notions, which I had begun recording in my journals that same year. I also thought I was experiencing that clinical-sounding, talk-show-promoted, ever-elusive thing called closure. I thought this was my moment of closure and that some less-potent manifestation of this feeling would stay with me for the rest of my life.

BREAKDOWN: 1996

CIGARETTE BUTTS AND BEER CANS cluttered the gutters of Pasado Street. The last of the raucous Friday-night parties in Isla Vista, the college town attached to UC Santa Barbara, had died down an hour and a half ago. The thudding bass of the Beastie Boys and the reggae rhythms of Sublime, the squeals of drunken girls and the "Hey, dudes" of loaded frat brothers, had faded; the faint sound of the ocean, crashing against the cliffs just a few blocks away, filled the void. It was five a.m. I was twenty-one years old. And I was falling apart.

I leaned against my car, convulsing, snot running down my T-shirt, flailing my arms against the bug-splattered windshield in full melodramatic glory. I wasn't just crying anymore, or even sobbing—all that was warm-up.

I staggered back from the car, mopping up ribbons of mucus with my arm, and fell to the pavement as Eric lunged to catch me, sliding from his arms with each full-body shake. Flecks of asphalt dug into my calves. Eric grabbed under my armpits to pull me up and wrapped his arms around me. "It's okay, calm down," he whispered, stroking my shoulders, but my panting only grew heavier. My spasms crescendoed to epileptic proportions. I tried to shove Eric away, and slammed his thick upper arms with my fists, until he stepped back in consternation and I collapsed to the street again, not even feeling the asphalt, head tingling with what I could only hope was the onset of a blackout.

I cried for an hour and a half. I would have cried longer if I'd had

the strength. Instead, as the sun began to rise, I realized with due embarrassment that I had not died, would not die, that I would have to
hang my head and go home. I let Eric subdue me and hold me tight
enough to stop the shaking, let him walk me to the stoop of the house
he shared with three friends and sit with me on the top step, petting
my hair and rocking me. Dawn gave way to yet another day of Southern California sunshine. The green of the neighborhood's palm trees
popped like Kodachrome in the daylight, and the street's trash glared
in dirty contrast. The ocean waves kept crashing, but the birds began
to add their own grace notes. Eric helped me up and walked me back
to my car, kissing me on the crown of the head as I ducked into the driver's seat. I drove the mile and a half back to my apartment for a morning of sleep I never wanted to wake up from.

My entire infatuation with Eric is recorded in four journals, typed
pages of which I once delivered to his house in yet another failed bid
to shame him into becoming my bona fide boyfriend. Seven years later
I reread those journal pages, and let's just say they aren't anything I'd
thrust in people's faces now. The earliest entries are written in the
chirpy "dear diary" tone of a recent high school graduate. They're big
on words I once thought fancy, like *illuminated*. A positive response
from a date might be recorded as "I think he reciprocated my interest."
At the start of my sophomore year, I used *reciprocated* five times in five
months. The highfalutin words fall off as the school year wears on, the
sentences get longer and more complex, and the voice grows braver
and more candid. But whatever the quality of individual entries, the
detail still compels me. Those journals are a record of my failed obsession with Eric, but they're not really about unrequited love. What the
journals more accurately capture is my two-year slide into a nearly suicidal depression. All my past relations with men had been leading to
this juncture, but Eric was the ultimate trigger, intensely affectionate
one moment and utterly aloof the next. He precipitated this climax in
my sadness, no doubt, but he did not exactly cause it. After all those
years of trying to pretend my father's murder was firmly in the past, I
have to think I simply had it coming.

* * *

We both worked on the *Daily Nexus*, the college newspaper. I'd shot up the ranks in two months to assistant campus editor; Eric coedited the arts and entertainment section. We met at the California Intercollegiate Press Association competition for college journalists, shuttling between parties at the Irvine Marriott with beer in hand. Later that night after the other eight students sharing my room had fallen asleep, I snuck into the hallway to study for Elizabethan Lit, and Eric followed me. I'd locked my sights on him the night before, sizing him up over a group dinner at a Mexican restaurant festooned with serapes and sombreros. He was about six foot two, built like a thick teddy bear, and softspoken. He had close-cropped ash-brown hair, clear blue eyes, and tanned skin, and wore thick-framed glasses like Elvis Costello's. He had his own hip-hop group, and a radio show on the college station. I thought him an attainable target. I was clueless as to how hard I might fall.

I'd had serious boyfriends before and even been in love, more than once. I'd loved Scott in high school and had an intense summer fling after senior year with Stuart, the timpanist in the Blue Devils Drum and Bugle Corps. And then I'd moved to Santa Barbara for college, escaping the Central Valley and my lackluster high school career by winning a university-sponsored writing contest. I'd decided to forgo higher education for a career as a flag-team instructor—after all, my grades would barely get me into a bottom-rung college—when I saw the contest posted on a school bulletin board and entered on a whim. My earnest essay on Virginia Woolf won me a dean's petition into the University of California at Santa Barbara and a no-strings fellowship. I remember driving to Santa Barbara with Mom and Aunt Kathy on move-in day, cutting over from the barren I-5 to the seaside 101 and keeping my nose practically pressed to the window as cardboard-brown hills gave way to purple-flower-laden cliff sides and views of lush green mountains. *Thank you, God,* I thought, *for that ticket out.* A new life in paradise had arrived courtesy of either divine intervention or dumb luck.

Santa Barbara was a fantasyland of red tile roofs, endless ocean views, and gentle sunshine, but the first year of UCSB was hellish. I got straight As and found an instant rapport with my writing teachers, churning out several short stories each quarter. But my social life was a minefield. The student town adjacent to UCSB, Isla Vista, is one of the most notorious party zones in the country, and thanks to my years around Howdy's drinking and drugs, I was more suited for a monastery. I clung to my pert, proudly religious roommate, until she began making out with her deodorant-challenged boyfriend while I tried to sleep in my bunk bed above. We had planned to share off-campus university housing the next year, and by the time our friendship soured, I was in a panic that I could not survive another year in the dorms. So my mother did an extraordinary thing. She saw that I was fragile, and she blew her entire 401(k) to move herself and Emmet to Santa Barbara so that I could live with them.

We'd had a grand time sharing a leaky rental house three blocks from the beach. Our first night there, I slept with my bedroom window open to let the scent of jasmine and the ocean mist waft in. It was the first time in my life I'd felt safe before falling asleep. Merced, Sherrie, Dad's murder, and Howdy were 250 miles away, and I would never go back.

During that difficult first year at UCSB, intimidated by the slick kids from L.A. and newly fattened by the "freshmen fifteen," I'd opted for safety with a pimple-faced, nice guy named Forest. Forest was sweet but not bright. I reached for him like a baby blanket for a year and a half, obviously not in love, until my mother and Emmet moved from Fresno to Santa Barbara. Secure again with my family and fifteen pounds lighter, I dumped him and joined the school paper. I'd been testing my newly recovered allure on UCSB men for just two and a half months when I met Eric.

I called and asked him out. He said he had been "seeing someone," but it wasn't serious, and would I like to have dinner Friday. We ate at a restaurant on the beach and then walked around downtown Santa Barbara, talking about Vonnegut and Nabokov (he was an English major too), office politics at the newspaper, the hip-hop radio show he hosted on the college station. After a few more dates like this, and long nights making out, I was slayed. He was good in bed, but I didn't write that. I wrote that he was "mature"—my ultimate compliment, as though I had any maturity myself—"sweet, funny, cultured, sensitive, and tall," chastising myself for the shallowness of that final adjective and adding four exclamation points.

But the status of the other girl was still unclear. After a few weeks, we sat down for our big talk, and Eric said he and the other girl were just friends now. But clearly I was not his girlfriend. The next weekend he went home to San Diego; I counted the hours until his return. He promised to call from San Diego but didn't. When we sat down for another talk back outside the *Nexus* office, following an afternoon of cold exchanges, Eric's eyes watered. His parents were getting divorced. One of his closest friends was also dying from cancer, though he never talked to me about it. He had too much to deal with. He didn't want a girlfriend.

Still we went on a few more dates before the semester ended. He called in May, and we slept together, and when I asked what direction things were headed in, he told me he wanted "friendship with a twist." Bristling at that definition of our relationship, I swore off him. But just when I'd nearly shaken my longing for him, he'd call. In June, he met my mother and brother but acted standoffish the next day. The next week he came over for lunch and I broke down crying during sex.

The week after that he didn't call and I wrote, "I think this marks the end." UCSB was out for the summer. We'd both quit the *Nexus*. I now had an internship at the town's weekly paper and a job checking guests in at a red-tile-roofed boutique hotel. I was moving out of my family's house in Santa Barbara and into my own apartment with Suzanne, the former editor in chief of the *Daily Nexus*. I didn't know what Eric's plans were. We had no reason to hear from each other again.

But we did. Again and again, for the next year and a half. Sometimes I'd call and beg to see him. Sometimes when I'd try to move on, Eric would call me and ask to meet for coffee, and I'd tell myself I could go meet with him as "friends." We'd end up in bed, without fail, having sex that left me feeling incredibly empty.

How to explain what it was that addicted me to Eric? I think it had something to do with one of my recurring dreams. The action of this dream took place in various locales—the little house on Twenty-fifth Street, my grandparents' home, on the side of the 99 freeway. But the basic story was always the same. In it, I learned that my father had not died the night of the stabbing—he had survived. But all those years he'd let me believe he was dead because he didn't want to see me, a fact that became clear when I looked into his hard, indifferent eyes. He had never loved me as I had believed, as he had always fervently sworn. Every time I had that dream I would wake with a brand of sadness remarkably similar to the devastation I felt at Eric's rejection.

In my late twenties, when I began to think again about this dream and its connection to Eric, it all made sense. Why would I dream that my father hadn't actually loved me? Because if he had loved me as much as he swore, why didn't he take care of me and provide a safe, stable home? Like my father, Eric showed intense affection for me and then failed to follow through on it. And I was always left wondering why I hadn't been good enough. With Eric, I would redeem myself, prove myself worthy of the love my father had proclaimed but not delivered on. What hooked me on Eric, what made me progressively more determined to convince him that he loved me, was not the high, but the crash. His affection was as intense and unattainable as my dead father's. I sometimes felt like I might as well die if I could not secure it.

By that July after sophomore year, I was feeling a new kind of sadness. I was still stuck on Eric, though I had, once again, decided to have nothing to do with him. But now other feelings were entering the increasingly volatile mix. I wanted to write more and had signed up for extra short-story workshops that coming fall semester. I'd finished a few semifictional short stories about Howdy and, for the first time since that *Sassy* article, started to feel a compulsion to write about Dad's murder. The combination of obsessing over what had gone wrong with Eric and mulling over Dad's death put me on edge. I took long afternoon naps and walked mental circles. I worked alone at the Eagle Inn front desk, and sometimes hours would pass without a guest arriving or the phone ringing. I now hated being alone. I was afraid of my own thoughts and sadness, in need of distraction. I walked to the beach for relief, despairing when it was empty. Still I was determined to "set my mind straight and healthy again."

For the next few months I vacillated between writing Eric off and calling him. I cried at work when no one was around. I cried at home. I wrote about Howdy and Dad and worked seventy hours a week, mostly alone, at the inn, saving up for next year's tuition. Mom was no longer paying my school bills. She talked Grandma Mae and Grandpa Ben into giving me $500 toward expenses. The day I received the check in the mail, I cried. I wrote that I was not "one of their clan," that I was only a "link" to Dad, and "probably one they'd rather forget."

I moped through that summer and fall, dating dozens of guys and liking none of them. In December, Eric started calling, and I agreed to see him, writing floridly about the moment when he grabbed my hands across the table at Carrows. I told him about how sad I had been, how I'd been thinking more about my father and about Howdy. I slept with him, but even as I hoped the sex would magically change his feelings for me, I saw the dynamic between us all too clearly. "We only have our quasi-relationships," I wrote, "when he can depict me in emotional need and himself as the kind shoulder to cry on." The intensity of our reunions was inextricably bound to the inevitability of our breakups.

One March afternoon I walked into the lobby of the Eagle Inn shaking, keeping the water in my eyes from overflowing just long enough to take over the switchboard from the girl on duty and wave good-bye, wondering if she could see the mental state I was in as she handed over the hotel's master keys. I believed I was having an "absolute nervous breakdown," as I diagnosed it in my journal. The end of the quarter, that hazy in-between period lacking the structure I needed to hold myself together, had brought it on. "I don't want to live, and I don't think I could ever feel happy again," I wrote. I checked a few families into their rooms and took a handful of reservations, scanning the red-carpet hallways for visitors after the phones fell quiet. As soon as the lobby was clear, I called Eric. I sobbed on the phone with him for two hours, dragging the phone into the office's back closet, arriving guests be damned. Eric told me I needed psychiatric drugs. He told me I should see a therapist.

I dodged the real issue. I forced him to say he'd never feel "that way"—romantically—toward me again. The next night, after my roommate Suzanne had left for winter break, I begged Eric to come over. I had just gotten a laptop computer and, while cutting open the packaging, had begun stabbing the Styrofoam with a steak knife in a fit of anger. I left the steak knife standing there in the Styrofoam for Eric to see when he arrived. Once he got to the apartment I drank André mimosa straight from the bottle until I was sloshed, and then I slept with him. "Although I wouldn't admit it to myself, that's what I planned all along," I wrote the next day.

My mother had just decided to move Emmet back to Fresno, where the schools were better. It upset me to see them hightail it back to the valley when I'd felt so safe and removed from the past with them in Santa Barbara, but I had no control over it. I'd been having nightmares in which Howdy was hunting me down, trying to kill me. Just after my family moved, I promised myself never to talk to Eric again.

The evening of the breakdown started off innocently enough. Eric called asking if I'd like to come over and meet his friend from high school who was visiting for the weekend. "Sure," I said coolly, but my heart was jumping, thrilled by the sheer miracle that Eric had asked to see me after our torturous eighteen months of on-again, off-again pseudo-dating. "And he wants me to meet his friend from high school!" I said to my roommate, Suzanne, who could smell a bad scene brewing a mile away and could never resist watching. She invited herself along. We hopped into my sparkly red Dodge Neon and sped over, bottles of cheap wine clanking under the backseat.

Our giddiness drained the moment we walked in the door. Something was off about the party, and it had to do with our presence, as though we'd dragged shit in on the soles of our flip-flops. Eric and his roommates and friends, a roomful of mopey guys in baggy pants, lounged on their holey sofa and beanbags watching MTV and nursing Sam Adams beers. The look from Eric across the room told me at once the night would end badly. I had grown expert at analyzing his glances, discerning whether his blue eyes looked friendly and beckoning or, just as often, cold and aloof. Whatever impulse had prompted him to call me, it had deserted him during the half hour it'd taken Suzanne and me to touch up our makeup and race right over. He crossed in front of the television to usher us inside, grabbing our wine bottles but not offering a kiss on the cheek, walking us to the kitchen, where, I thought, we were out of the way.

Suzanne set to uncorking the wine with zeal. Eric introduced me to his old friend. "Hey," the friend said. "Hey," I said back. Eric declined to tell us more about each other, to start us chatting. Instead he stood with his arms crossed, waiting, I guessed, to see if I would take a glass of wine from Suzanne and start drinking, to see if I planned on hanging around. His desire for me to leave steeled me to stay. I took the wine. I gulped it down.

They needed more booze, Eric said. He and his friend would have to drive to the grocery store. He'd be back in a few. "I'll come along," I said.

"Sure," Eric said, shrugging.

The ugliness of the night ahead shone as bright as the grocery store fluorescents. Eric and his friend strolled the spirits aisle, ignoring me as I picked up bottles and shouted that maybe we should get some champagne, or how about wine coolers, or was that too silly? The look on Eric's face was frostier than the refrigerated beer case. He wanted me to go home. And so I would—but kicking and screaming.

Hours later, after all of Eric's friends and roommates had passed out or gone to sleep, long after Suzanne had caught a lift back to our apartment, way too long after it had become obvious that Eric wanted me gone, the crying started. Hours later I found myself flailing in the street, realizing in the pit of my stomach that what I was experiencing was not simply a case of college-age melodramatics that would pass on its own.

When school started again, I made an appointment with the college's mental health services. I was now feeling suicidal. I was taking a course on Milton's *Paradise Lost* that semester. During class introductions, our teaching assistant had asked us to give our names and then our own personal descriptions of hell. Other students led off with lines like "Hell is finals week" or "Hell is Las Vegas when you're broke," as I sat at my desk growing more and more agitated. I wanted to blurt out, "Hell is not wanting to be alive but not wanting to kill yourself either." Instead, when my turn came, I put on my old dependable smile and, mindful of my family's recent move back to the valley, said, "Hell is my hometown, Fresno, heaven is Santa Barbara, and purgatory is driving back on the 101 freeway." But my line about wanting to die was much more honest.

My course work was eerily feeding my depression. In a class on twentieth-century novels, we were asked to read Jean Rhys's *Voyage in the Dark,* about a twentysomething chorus girl who hopelessly throws herself at an aloof older man, bringing herself to emotional collapse. Somewhere in her hazy personal history, her father has died, and her family has abandoned her. Everyone else in class found the book too dark, the main character too desperate and inert to relate to. I read the book twice, engrossed, and stood as the lone voice in its defense during class discussion, until I began to fear the other students could see how closely I identified with Rhys's narrator.

Our next assignment was Sylvia Plath's *The Bell Jar,* a novel I had read in high school. This time the book took on a new life for me. It was based on Plath's own college depression. Her father had died when she was young. So had mine. Her mother didn't understand what she was going through. Neither did mine. Every description of her desire to die resonated with my own. I painted the book's pages in a patchwork of yellow and pink highlighter, marking favorite lines.

"You're very high-functioning," the slate-faced female psychologist said when I told her about Eric, and how I wanted to die, how I was still getting straight As and working full-time and running five miles a day. *High-functioning what?* was the question that lingered in my mind, and I thought I knew the answer. High-functioning depressive. High-functioning crazy person. The counselor told me my issues were too big for the UCSB mental health services to handle. I needed frequent, regular, long-term therapy. I'd have to find a psychologist out in the real world, quickly.

My mother set to finding me a provider from her health care plan as though she had anticipated this moment since the morning of my dad's murder. When I told her I needed her to find one faster, because I felt I wanted to die, she decided to drive to Santa Barbara for the weekend to save me from my own fragile state.

We tracked up and down State Street shopping that afternoon like sorority sisters on holiday, except that the effort to pretend that I was enjoying myself, to act like I was experiencing anything other than sheer despair, was crushing me. Later we checked into the uptown economy motel where Mom had made us a reservation. That night felt like the most dangerous of my life. Mom thought we'd make popcorn and watch a pay-per-view movie; I shook with fear that I would eventually have to give up my act, fall to the floor with sadness, curl up on the bathroom tile, and refuse to move. I told Mom I'd left my toothbrush in the car but walked instead to the strip mall next door to use the pay phone. I called Eric. "I need to talk to you," I said, voice wavering.

A long pause. And then quietly, tersely: "I've got friends over. I can't right now." I read the terseness as annoyance, uncaring. "Are you okay?" he said, but I decided the question was perfunctory, not heartfelt. I hung up.

I walked back to the hotel room and pretended to have found my toothbrush, unaware that Eric and one of his friends would soon be driving from one Santa Barbara hotel parking lot to another, searching for my car, afraid that if they didn't find me, I would hurt myself.

THERAPY

I WAS TWO MONTHS INTO THERAPY when the hallucination struck.

On the week of my twenty-first birthday I had selected a marriage, family, and child counselor at random from the list of mental health providers my mother's insurance company sent. My only requirement was that I not see a psychiatrist; I had resolved never to take psychoactive drugs. I felt that taking antidepressants was a fake way out, a cheap fix, and that needing drugs meant you were irredeemably broken. Less consciously, I didn't want to take prescription drugs because my years with Howdy had left me with a lifelong fear of mind-altering substances.

I had developed a deep commitment to beating the depression on my own terms. Just before the peak of my sadness, I had applied to spend my senior year abroad in London. In the midst of a semester's worth of crying fits, I'd smiled my way through an entrance interview and won an assignment to my top pick: University of London, King's College, right in the city's center. I would study Shakespeare with one of the world's top Shakespeare editors, on a campus just across the Thames from the newly reconstructed Globe Theatre. Students departed for their year abroad in late September. This became my post-depression deadline. I had to be of healthy mind again before September, or I would never make it through two semesters alone, in a strange country, and on a dangerously tight budget. And I would not be able to live with myself if, because of my own psychological weakness, I was forced to stay behind.

So every week, at first several times a week, I met with the therapist. She was fine-boned, fortyish, with heavy bags under her eyes, and mousy brown, feathered hair. I barely bothered to learn her name, because I did not entirely trust her. She spoke in soft, New Agey tones—instantly suspect. Because I had awful breathing problems—Suzanne would stare in fright each night as I lay in bed nearly hyperventilating, anxiety thwarting my attempts to draw just one full breath—the therapist suggested I attend yoga classes to "learn to breathe again." Yoga was just beginning to go mainstream, and I still thought of it as a woo-woo cult activity. Worse yet, the therapist chain-smoked. I'd walk up to her office, set off a garden porch at the back of a pink, three-story Victorian, and find her urgently sucking down skinny cigarettes in between appointments. Because of Howdy, I would guess, I had an irrational hot-button response to smokers. I could not trust them. Later, I even made my fiancé promise never, ever to touch even low-tar filters to lips.

But I didn't tell the therapist about my fear of smokers or my disdain toward yoga. I didn't realize at the time that trust between a patient and therapist is crucial; I just knew I wanted to be healthy and that she was the tool that could get me there. And so I told her what I knew or could remember of Dad's murder, and growing alienated from my grandparents, and living with Howdy after Dad was gone, and she gave me new perceptions of the situations that made me feel even more pitiful before they made me feel angry. "You had no one to protect you," she'd coo in her scratchy smoker's voice, and I'd shrunk at what I saw as a demeaning interpretation, then grow hot with rage toward—whom? Toward fate in general, it seemed, and so the objects of my quickly repressed wrath continually shifted.

One day we began concentrating on Sherrie, on what it was like to live with her those summers before Dad died. I started telling the therapist about the night of the murder, about how Sherrie had covered my and Bobby's eyes as Dad rolled by on the gurney. And then, maybe because of the way the slanting afternoon sun illuminated her leathery skin and the split ends of her hair, it hit me midsentence. This woman, the therapist, was Sherrie. She had tracked me down after all these years and posed as my therapist to kill me. In a flash, I knew it to be absolutely true. My whole body turned rigid, and my heart skipped several beats. I could only hope she hadn't noticed, because the one way out, I felt certain, was to keep talking, to hold her falsely empathetic stare until the session was over, until I could say thank you and shake her hand and escape the confines of her office. I continued to describe the murder night, how we'd gotten into the car and followed the ambulace to the hospital, but I was now narrating with Sherrie as my sole audience, so I downplayed suspicion, told things straight and factual with no indication of my feelings.

A cloud rolled over the sun outside the office window; the light on the therapist's craggy face faded. And then I knew, just as suddenly, that this woman before me was not Sherrie, that I had been seized by some strange fit of fear. Perhaps the therapist said something un-Sherrie-like to break the spell. I can't remember what. But though my heart still raced, I knew again that I was safe. I did not tell the therapist that moments ago I had felt certain she was my former stepmother.

There were many things I did not tell the therapist. My state was improving, perhaps boosted by some success writing arts stories for the local weekly newspaper, but I was still behaving strangely. I met a guy at a downtown bar and began sleeping with him; one night among the Wild Cat's red-leather booths he introduced me to a paunchy, balding Frenchman in his late twenties (or so he claimed) who produced soft-core porn movies. The Frenchman casually shouted over the bar's music that he was casting his latest production, and that I looked sweet, innocent, and real—much preferred, despite my modest B-cup, to the porn careerists he auditioned. He slipped me a dog-eared card.

I called. He told me in his lisping French accent that he could give me $500 for filming one scene having sex with him. It seemed like a lot of money at the time, when my $350 monthly rent kept me taking extra shifts at the Eagle Inn. I mockingly ran the idea of appearing in a porn movie past Suzanne, counting on her to confirm my instincts against doing it. She seemed titillated at the notion and joked that maybe I should, and tell her all about it. I called the porn producer, arranged a lunch date to talk terms, and began using Clearasil to combat the pimples on my camera-shy derriere.

The porn producer took me out to eat pasta and said I should come to his next filming session to watch a scene being taped and get a feel for what the role would involve. He walked me back to his BMW convertible and showed me black-and-white glossies of other women who had auditioned, posed naked on their knees in the sand or lounging with feather boas draped across their nipples. I agreed to attend the filming but backed out while driving to the set in Thousand Oaks the next weekend. I had spent the previous week of spring lectures checking out my college classmates, deciding which women were more attractive than I was, and realizing those women would never agree to be in porn films. Appearing in a porn flick, I decided, did not validate your attractiveness. But there was still the temptation of easy money. Not until I was driving south on the 101 freeway did I concede to myself that the effects upon my sense of identity would send me reeling into full depression again. A foray into the porn industry was not part of the "mentally sound by London departure" regimen.

Neither was any further contact with Eric, whom my therapist called "poison" to me. I didn't speak to him for the rest of the spring. Summer came, Suzanne moved out, and miraculously, my mother decided to move my brother back from the valley to Santa Barbara again; Emmet had missed the sun and sand and bombed out during his freshman year back in Fresno, while Mom complained of valley "culture shock." Emmet, Mom, and I shared a one-bedroom apartment two blocks from West Beach, on a street canopied by thirty-foot-tall, pink-flowering trees. With my family back and my sights set on London I could spend the next three months simply soaking in Santa Barbara's beauty, no longer dismayed by my past inability to feel any joy at the gorgeousness that surrounded me. The town's very air, its cool, sea-salt-tinged balminess, seemed to saturate my pores with healing properties. The insurance coverage ran out, and rather than pay for sessions out of pocket, I felt strong enough to discontinue therapy.

Which is about when Eric reached me at the Eagle Inn. I had one month left until my flight from LAX to Heathrow. Recoveries are never as tidy as storytellings would have them be; I would go in and out of therapy many more times. Meanwhile Eric and I had a final fling, taking long walks along the beach, holing up for hours in his dank Isla Vista bedroom. It was the closest Eric had ever ventured toward being my boyfriend, and it was possible only because I was leaving, because a certain end loomed near. Eric took me out to a fancy dinner two nights before my departure for one last rendezvous. I told Eric I loved him. He cried and said he loved me too. Maybe he felt he had to say it. Maybe he meant it. Maybe, in a strange and unsustainable way, it was true.

During the flight from L.A. to London I read, and reread, and read again, the magazine article that changed my life. Mom and I had stopped by one of the huge chain bookstores on the way to the airport to gear me up with reading material; I had lingered over the "cultural/current affairs" section of the periodicals racks because I was now fancying myself literary and had taken a late-blooming interest in magazines like the *New Yorker*. Just as I was about to start thumbing through *Harper's*, the cover of the September 1997 *Atlantic Monthly* leapt out at me. A GRIEF LIKE NO OTHER, it read in block capital letters. And below, five all-caps lines spanning the width of the page: HOW DO YOU RECOVER FROM THE DEATH OF A SON OR DAUGHTER? FOR THOUSANDS OF DISTRAUGHT AMERICANS, THE TERRIBLE ANSWER IS THAT YOU DON'T.

A few months earlier I would have passed the magazine over, unwilling to recognize myself in the headline. Now, standing in the bookstore, I seized upon it, showing the article to Mom. We flipped to the first page of the story. The byline was Eric Schlosser. The subhead read, "Americans are fascinated by murders and murderers but not by the families of the people who are killed—an amazingly numerous group, whose members can turn only to one another for sympathy and understanding." The single sentence captured the way I'd always flinched at popular murder games like Clue and murder musicals like *Chicago*, and the alienation, the fear of being branded a freak, I'd experienced. I headed straight for the cash register, and Mom paid.

The article made the twelve-hour flight to London seem considerably shorter, as my sense of self and what I had been through transformed while I crossed the Atlantic Ocean. The twenty-nine-page story described a support group called Parents of Murdered Children and narrated, in chilling detail, the murder of twenty-three-year-old Terri

Smith, outlining not so much how she had been killed (shot in the head by a paranoid-schizophrenic boyfriend) but the way that death had haunted her mother, who went on to lead a local POMC chapter. "The fear of murder has grown so enormous in the United States," Schlosser wrote, "that it leaves a taint, like the mark of Cain, on everyone murder touches." The article focused on parents, siblings, and friends of murder victims, paying scant attention to the effects upon children, but I too had always felt tainted. Now this article was showing me that I was not errant in my reaction, not weak and pitiful. In fact, there existed a reasonable basis for my lingering feeling of separation from "healthy" society. The article was illustrated with nearly a dozen snapshots of ordinary people from across the country who had been murdered, smiling wide on their wedding day, enjoying a beer in the backyard with pals. I looked at the photos up close, studying the details of their seventies- or eighties-era attire, peering at the faces, stunned by their randomness, their normality, their naive pre-murder joy. I looked at the friends of the victims, so blissfully unaware of the trauma about to befall them, and thought, "I'm one of them."

The story also explained the symptoms of post-traumatic stress disorder, a condition I had never heard of, which often affects war veterans, survivors of sexual abuse, and murder victims' next of kin. "People suffering from PTSD become 'stuck': they constantly relive the trauma in powerful detail and then organize their lives around avoiding anything that might provoke these terrible memories," Schlosser wrote. "They swing between vivid, almost lifelike re-creations of the trauma and total denial of it." This was me to a T. Someone who had witnessed the murder might experience nightmares and flashbacks. Me again.

Not until six years later did I buy several books on PTSD to see whether I might be able to affix an easy label to my experience. I matched my symptoms against the lists of diagnostic criteria. "Recurrent, distressing dreams." Check. "Acting or feeling as if the trauma were recurring (illusions, hallucinations, flashback episodes)." Check. "Efforts to avoid thoughts, feelings, or conversations that remind one of the trauma," "efforts to avoid activities, places, or people that arouse recollections," "feeling of detachment/estrangement from others." Check, check, and check.

Another symptom, the "exaggerated startle response," made me remember one mortifying night. I had always jumped or flinched much more easily than my friends and would take as long as twenty minutes to stop shaking if someone snuck up behind me. During my sophomore year at Santa Barbara, Mom had taken me and my then-boyfriend to the Knott's Berry Farm amusement park for Halloween, when the venue becomes Knott's Scary Farm, with fake spiderwebs hung everywhere and staff members in gory costumes jumping out at you from dark corners. This so unnerved me that I had to lie down crying on the bottom of the boat during the waterlog ride, where Freddy or Jason impersonators holding plastic knives ambushed you at every turn.

On the first day of my semester at King's College, I found my way through the sooty, labyrinthine British hallways to the library and photocopied the *Atlantic Monthly* murder article. I put it in a manila envelope addressed to my grandparents in Merced along with a note on yellow binder paper. "I thought you might want to read this article about the effects of murder," I wrote. "I believe I experienced many of the symptoms of post-traumatic stress disorder. Maybe you have too. Love, Rachel." Then I went on with my new life in London, the daily trials and tribulations of learning to ride the underground, pub crawling, and scampering through yet another onslaught of bone-chilling rain, making little contact with my grandparents.

London was difficult. And in a way that was the point. I was determined to have a healthy, mentally sound adulthood, and if I made it through England's cold, gray climes I would know that I'd grown strong enough to fend off depression no matter my circumstances. I had underestimated, though, just how tough London would be. My school was near lovely Covent Garden, but my student housing was in derelict Southwark, surrounded by rotting council estates. I made a handful of good friends to get me through, but my bank account was always overdrawn. My room was the size of a ship cabin, and just when I was beginning to make it homey, someone threw a brick through my window and stole my laptop computer. I never adjusted to the time zone and would fall asleep at four a.m. I never found a boyfriend and was plagued for months by the desire to call or e-mail Eric back in the

States. But only for one fleeting moment—as I stood contemplating a painting in the Tate Gallery, realizing how little I knew of art history and despairing of ever knowing enough to make anything of my life— did the old desire to die overcome me. And during all those dank months, when every day felt like a dire challenge, I saw a wealth of world-class dance and theater and art and took refuge in books, in the stimulation of my university courses.

When I came back to California eight months later, I felt like I was safe on the far bank of a wide river. The depressed, unhealthy Rachel lay on the other side of the swift current, waving at me across the ex-panse. I would never be that old me again; I would see the warning signs of another depression coming on and do whatever was necessary to battle it. So much had changed in a year of independence and harsh weather. I was no longer obsessed with Eric. I had begun to write, ten-tatively, about Dad, tiptoeing around upsetting scenes and wandering through digressions. But I had started to integrate the murder with my sense of identity.

I visited Grandma Mae and Grandpa Ben the summer after I re-turned from London, taking photos of me in front of Big Ben, Buck-ingham Palace, the National Gallery. After we'd passed the shots across the kitchen table, Mae got up to use the bathroom and Ben said, "We got the literature on murder you sent."

"Oh, good. I hope you found it useful," I said, but sheepishly, shuf-fling the photos back into their case to keep my hands and eyes busy. I assumed that Ben had brought the murder article up while Mae was out of earshot because he wanted to clear it out of the way, a piece of dirty business to get through quickly. In fact, I would realize later, at that time he would probably genuinely have liked to talk more. But I still wasn't ready. I concentrated on packing up the photos with un-characteristic fastidiousness, buying time for Mae to reenter. Finally she ambled back in, picking up the deck of Skip-Bo cards from the china hutch. Grandpa dealt and we played three rounds, without an-other word about the article I'd sent.

WHY I LOVE ROD STEWART

ONE AFTERNOON AFTER I HAD GRADUATED, as I searched for a dance review among the Santa Barbara Public Library's newspaper racks, a tall, smiling guy in a striped, button-down shirt asked if I knew where in the *Los Angeles Times* the Liz Smith column ran. I flipped to the inside of the entertainment section and showed Liz Smith's placement to him. He said thanks, and then, with a glimmer of suppressed pride, added, "I'm in it." I asked why he would be mentioned in a Liz Smith column; he said he'd just founded a magazine. He looked impressively young to me to be starting a magazine; it turned out he was twenty-nine and a Santa Barbara native. I was then twenty-two and writing for the *Santa Barbara Independent*, and I thought he might make a good "local entrepreneur" profile for the paper. I also thought he was handsome, with a lean frame, dark brows above hazel eyes, and a confident smile. We exchanged cards, and one interview, one article, and a few after-work drinks later we were dating.

Bill was completely unlike other guys I'd met in Santa Barbara, and I fell for him swiftly. Brazenly defying the standard beach-town attire of board shorts and flip-flops, he wore crisp trousers and well-shined loafers. He'd attended an Ivy League college and loved to talk about philosophy, analyzing the movie *Life Is Beautiful* through the lens of Schopenhauer the night we saw it together. He'd played classical piano seriously throughout high school and could teach me about music theory when he accompanied me to ballet performances. If the performance was awful, we'd make our intermission repartee the entertainment. We'd spend weekends brainstorming ideas for the country-western musical he wanted to write with his brother, or conceptualizing a flamenco version of *Riverdance*, which we titled *¡Duende!* And when, over drinks at a local dive bar, I told him about my father's murder, Bill didn't coddle me or exclaim, "Oh my God, how awful," but reacted with a cool intrigue, as though this were just one more facet of me, like my love of ballet or my disdain toward Fresno, to explore.

My dates with Bill had an urgency about them; in less than a month I would be relocating for a better journalism job, only three hours away, but since we had just started seeing each other, that seemed hopelessly distant, a premature test of our commitment. One night after we had dated for two weeks, he pulled me back to him, kissed my hand, and said, "I love you." I said, "I love you too," blushed, gave him a long kiss, and finally climbed into my car. As I drove away, I pushed a tape into the cassette deck, in a euphoric daze, not knowing what album I'd left in. A tinkling mandolin came on, followed by that unmistakable voice and a familiar opening verse. *Wake up, Maggie, I think I've got something to say to you.*

My brother, Emmet, had borrowed the car the night before and evidently left this cassette in it. Apparently it was a mix of favorite songs—Rod followed by Elton John, improbable choices for a high-school-aged punk-rock lover, but there they were, perhaps a gift from some seventies-loving girlfriend. "Maggie May" was the only Rod Stewart tune in the mix, but during the next week I played it over and over, singing along as loudly as I could and replaying in my mind the moment Bill said I love you.

I hadn't listened to Rod Stewart in many years. In fact, I had written him off as dated, washed-out, ridiculous. The turning point in that verdict came one night in high school, as Jennifer Cooper and I drove through the rural byways of Clovis to pick up Lisa Reid and head to Blackstone Avenue for a night of cruising and flirtation. The bombastic commercials on the radio ended. A strangely familiar, scratchy voice entered: *If I listened long enough, to you . . .* The gentle acoustic guitar joined in. *I'd find a way, to believe, that it's all true.* The gravelly singer was building to his indignant climax:

Knowing
That you lied, straight faced
While I cried.

I gazed through the window's glare at the frostbitten November fields surrounding Jennifer's neighborhood, drumming my fingers but not noticing the tune, thinking instead of the boys we'd lure to the nearest McDonald's before the evening was out. Then Jennifer snapped her blue eyes and blond ponytail to attention as though realizing she'd made a horrible mistake. She glanced at the tuner and rolled her eyes. "Cheeseball," she hissed.

Like a striking viper I reached for the knob to turn the station. I'd failed my duty as shotgun passenger to tend to the radio. It was a tricky position, one that required constantly second-guessing your own taste to suit the musical whims of others. I'd learned not to take dissent against my radio choices personally; hits by singers like Michael Bolton and Bryan Adams, overblown love songs I had little feeling for, were most likely to keep my friends happy. But that night, Jennifer's swift correction hurt. I couldn't identify why. I'd barely registered the offending tune and the singer belting it; it hadn't sounded that different, in tone or sentiment, from the kind of song that made Jennifer happy. But there was a sting in this condemnation, and it lingered.

That was the moment it began to dawn on me that among my peers, Rod Stewart was hopelessly passé. The song on the radio, I realized later, had been the new acoustic rendition of "Reason to Believe." Rod's *MTV Unplugged* CD had just been released, and while middle-aged men catapulted the album's singles up the charts, the aging rock star's renaissance was not about to sweep Central Valley high schools by storm. A few days after my wild night out with Jennifer (during which we'd burned through a tank of gas, withstood catcalls hurled at fifteen miles per hour by likely ex-convicts, and ultimately ordered Big Macs alone under the buzz of Mickey D's unflattering fluorescents), she blithely flipped past the *Unplugged* rerun on cable, but not before wrinkling her eyebrows at Rod's peroxide coiffure and leathery laugh lines. And then later that year came the hit movie *So I Married an Axe Murderer*, with the scene in which Mike Myers, playing a flub-faced

Scottish grandfather, belts out "Do Ya Think I'm Sexy" while wearing a kilt and squeezing out the instrumental on bagpipes. Rod Stewart was a joke. I wondered why I'd never realized this before, and why it bothered me to realize it then.

Because I hadn't really thought about Rod in years.

An invisible chasm stood between me and the Rod-saturated days of life with Dad. It's hard to say how it began, when the first fissure broke. Up until Dad's death, Rod's music had just been a fact of our existence, ever present, nothing a ten-year-old would reflect upon and attach significance to. And so after the murder I proceeded as though Rod's music had no special meaning to me, because it didn't, yet. Because I tried to avoid any sentimental recollection of my father, any acknowledged connection to his life that my mother or grandparents might pick up on and take as occasion for reminiscing, it would take years for me to reclaim Rod. Instead I thought and acted as though he were just another pop singer, another entry on the charts. When, two years after Dad died, the lovesick ballad "My Heart Can't Tell You No" entered heavy rotation on the Fresno stations, I recorded it on my mix tape and sang along—because I did that with all the hit songs, not because I thought Rod's music might mean anything to me.

Three years later, as I finished junior high, Rod released a new album, *Rhythm of My Heart*. The first hit single was "Forever Young," and every time I saw the video, with Rod singing to a sweet little red-headed boy while riding in the bed of a pickup, I felt a pang in some piece of me I couldn't pinpoint. It was a persistent little pang, but I ignored it the way you might not bother to swat at a fly. I didn't stop to contemplate why a video in which a fatherly Rod Stewart looks lovingly into the eyes of a nine- or ten-year-old child might stir uncomfortable longings in me. Instead I told myself I felt nothing. Fortunately my mother missed the subtle connection that my heart felt and my head denied. She bought the album on cassette and we played it in the car, singing along, never saying a word about Dad.

By the time Rod Stewart staged his *Unplugged* comeback the following year, I had already tossed *Rhythm of My Heart* upon the pile of other past mistakes, Falco and Debbie Gibson cassettes that had once made my foot tap but now made my face redden. The days of my father blasting "Hot Legs" as we cruised to the mall, or dancing with my feet on top of his to the strains of "You're in My Heart" on the turntable were long behind. And yet Jennifer Cooper's Rod-bashing had sparked something in me. Whereas before I had let Rod Stewart tunes float by, oblivious, I began to turn the station within a few bars if I were riding with Mom and one of his songs came on. If we were waiting in line at the grocery store and an old standard like "Maggie May" wafted overhead on the easy-listening programming, I began to wish the checkout clerk would scan the items faster.

The next year, when I was seventeen, I came across a dusty cassette in the bottom of an old shoebox I'd shoved to the back of my closet. Alone in my pink-wallpapered room, the door locked, I popped the tape in the cassette deck. A garbled version of my father's steady back-beat plodded in my ears as a now-long-forgotten family friend sang. *Wake up, Maggie, I think I got something to say to you* . . . It was an old demo tape by Dad's band. It should have become a cherished posses-sion, but I couldn't handle that yet. I never listened to it again. I taped hits off the radio over that irreplaceable cassette, and within a few months I had lost it.

Bill and I did not catapult straight toward happily ever after, and neither did I come to embrace Rod's discography overnight. Rod's songs from the late eighties and onward struck me as ridiculously sen-timental, overwrought, and contrived. But the songs I had shared with Dad, when I would happen upon them playing in, say, a mall or the dentist's office, still seemed to hold up. Nevertheless, in many of them I now heard dark and icky overtones I had missed as a child. "Tonight's the Night," I realized, was a ballad of sexual coercion. And "Do Ya Think I'm Sexy," although infectiously danceable, suddenly seemed obviously permeated by a tragic brand of arrogance.

Just as I resisted accepting Rod in his entirety, I was still holding back from facing the fullness of Dad's memory. Since college, I had begun to acknowledge Dad's absence, revisiting my photo album more frequently and even displaying in my dorm room a photo of him hold-ing me as a toddler. But I still had no words to explain why he had died, and as often as his image inspired love, it also filled me with a queasy knowledge that his murder had left me vulnerable and broken.

Just weeks after Bill said "I love you," I moved 150 miles south to Laguna Beach for an incredible arts journalism job at the *Orange County Register*. A small part of me dared to fantasize that Bill and I would continue seeing each other, but my more skeptical nature, always on the lookout for the first signs of breakup, assumed he would prove a sweet transitional fling. We'd see each other for a few weekends, and then he'd call less and less; he'd meet some gorgeous blonde in Santa Barbara, and I'd date some dopey surfer dude in Orange County and we would remember each other fondly.

But Bill managed to see me every weekend, even though, because the magazine start-up had fallen apart, he had no money and no car. He scraped together Amtrak fares and rode the train, and I spent all week at the office daydreaming about his return. One weekday night, walking around Laguna Beach alone, I stopped at the boardwalk and looked out at the ocean and felt a tingling surety. I thought, I can't believe I've found my future husband at age twenty-two. I can't believe I'm this lucky.

We'd been dating for about six months when Bill asked if he could move in with me. He would try to find a job in Orange County or L.A. I wanted nothing more, but I wanted it as the next step toward a secure future together, not because he had nowhere else to live. He assured me he wanted to move in for the right reasons, and with only a tinge of worry I set about preparing for his arrival. I cleaned my ocean-view, beach-shack apartment from top to bottom, rearranging the cardboard boxes and card tables that served as furniture. I went to the store and stocked up on Bill's favorite foods, hoarding cans of tuna. I told everyone at the *Register*'s arts section about the big move.

And then the night before his scheduled arrival, Bill called. "I have some news," he said with a strangely edgy cheerfulness. "I got a job. In San Francisco. It starts on Monday."

I felt the world change all around me, as it had when the doctor had walked into the waiting room that June morning and said my father was dead. A minute ago, life had been fine; now it would never be the same. The man who loved me was leaving me. After Dad's murder, I had always known that desertion could come swiftly and unexpectedly. I had let my guard down and my prophecy had become true.

I saw Bill off to San Francisco through three days of almost nonstop tears. I lost my appetite and ten pounds. I arrived at the office each morning with a face swollen from crying and tried to smile through my work. My colleagues treated me to fancy lunches, trying to cut through my shock, and then insisted I take a few days off to recover.

When Bill kept calling and even paid my airfare to visit every other weekend, I shifted from shock into emergency mode. I had to be with Bill, and I had to be with him in a way that was permanent, that meant he could not leave me again. I proposed that I move in with him in San Francisco, at first offering every false rationale I could clutch at: Orange County was too stifling, the dance scene in San Francisco was more vibrant, the journalism opportunities more exciting. When my campaign worked, and Bill began to get excited about the move, I progressed to phase two of my scheme. I was giving up an incredible job to be with him, with no prospects in the Bay Area. If he wanted me to come live with him, it would have to be as a step toward engagement. I hoped he might actually propose right then, but he didn't. So just after I had tendered my resignation at the *Register*, I called him from my car, teary with doubts, threatening not to come. "Just come," I finally got him to say. "Move up here, and we'll get engaged, and it will all work out."

He meant that we would get engaged eventually, not anytime soon, but after I moved to San Francisco I waved his words in his face as a false promise. Of course it was too much pressure. Within my well-established pattern of frequent breakups, I set a new record. Bill and I broke up dozens of times. Sometimes we broke up two or three times in one week, Bill at first sleeping on the floor, then at hotels and friends' houses, then in his own apartment while I kept the place we'd shared. The fundamental issue was always why he would not marry me. And yet he loved me. But not, it seemed to me, enough.

After I had lived with Bill for just over a year, I bought my first Rod Stewart CD, a greatest hits collection. I'd stumbled across Rod's lingering significance to me during an impromptu writing workshop assignment. Asked to imitate a Grace Paley story in which the narrator turns on the radio, I had my main character yearn to hear Rod Stewart. The odd choice intrigued me, and I decided I should give his tunes a spin, see what they brought back. My first Rod acquisition was a modest start, only nine of his most popular tunes, but they evoked memories I hadn't encountered in years. I closed my eyes as certain songs played, and there Dad and I were again, dancing around the tiny living room at the house on Twenty-fifth Street, my five-year-old heart filled with love and safety.

Incidentally, relations with Bill settled. He got his own place and I stopped nagging about marriage. We had four or five consecutive happy months together, and I thought, if this isn't good enough for him, I can't make him propose. I had joined a church and found a certain stability in it. Rather than threatening to break up, and doing so hoping he would run after me proclaiming undying love, I simply broke it off. For real. I moved to a new apartment. I didn't talk to him for months. I had loved him but I needed to move on from a relationship I feared would never offer me security. It was painful but I was strong enough for it now. And I was strong enough to start sorting through the reality of Dad's murder. I wrote about Dad, tentatively. I looked up old newspaper articles. I listened to more Rod Stewart.

By the time Bill called me, four months later, proposing marriage, I had taken the plunge with Rod and bought the four-CD boxed set, along with four other albums. I was at home in my memories of Dad, surrounding myself with them aurally every day, and writing them down.

I said no to Bill's proposal—how could I know that he truly wanted to marry me, that he wasn't simply saying whatever it took to get me back? But he persisted. For three months, calling me as a friend when I refused to date him, dropping off cards for me at my office at the *Examiner*, leaving quirky birthday presents—like a Brita water filter and a tiny potted violet—that proved how closely he'd been listening to what I wanted. One night I called him from New York, wanting to get back together, then had second thoughts when he picked me up at the airport. It was two a.m., and we slept in my bed that night as friends, barely touching. He began to describe a lunch he'd had with another girl a few days before, and I realized it had been a date. "That's great, you should be going on dates with other people," I said, glad he could not see the sadness on my face in the dark.

Bill rolled over and grabbed my shoulders, shaking them. "Don't you understand? It's you that I want."

That proclamation convinced me. When I finally assented, it was uncomfortable at first, and then shockingly harmonious. We never fought anymore. The time apart had made him see what he wanted, and he never wavered. I knew I would never have to test his love again.

Rod Stewart's music was just the background to all this, but music can be as powerful as smell or sight in evoking memory. And now when I listen to "Maggie May," I have two memories, equally strong. I see my father dancing with me on a Sunday morning. And I see Bill saying I love you for the first time. And this is why I love Rod Stewart.

HOWDY'S ABSOLUTION: SPRING 2002

WHEN I WAS TWENTY-FIVE, I chose to be baptized by the Episcopal Church. I'd been drawn to religion on and off throughout my life, despite being raised without any. My Grandma Dirks was some small-sectarian form of Protestant—I could never get straight exactly which—and though she kept copies of James Dobson's "Focus on the Family" pamphlets scattered throughout her house and attended her colorless little church in Atwater every Sunday, Mom and Emmet and I would join her only on Easter and the occasional Christmas. Mom kept her old study Bibles on the top shelf of our bookcase and bought a few volumes of children's Bible stories in case the urge struck either Emmet or me to peruse them. But she expressed a mild surprise, at best, when I asked to go to Presbyterian youth group with my junior high friend Michelle, and in her more philosophical moods she would say that she thought God was in nature, not in church, and that she was drawn to Buddhism. I didn't know anything about Buddhism, but I thought this vague attraction of hers deep and sophisticated.

While Bill and I were going through some heavy rounds of breakup, I started attending Grace Cathedral, on the top of Nob Hill in San Francisco. I knew the church was Episcopal, part of the worldwide Anglican Communion, and I knew from my senior year abroad in London, when I had visited many of the English cathedrals, that I was drawn to the sensuous beauty of the Anglican service. I loved the music and the liturgies, the stately set words, "world without end, amen." I loved the colors of the stained-glass windows and the smell of incense and the sounds of wall-shaking organs and whisper-soft boys' choirs. I knew the immediate response evoked within me was aesthetic, but this did not strike me as an illegitimate point of entry for spiritual contemplation. I was, by my early twenties, working as a dance critic, spending much of my time considering what made one work of art beautiful and meaningful, another hollow. To me the church's pageantry was one of the most profound works of art of all.

I also knew that many Catholic services were almost identical, in form and appearance, to the Anglican Eucharist, and for a while I hoped that when Bill proposed, I would then convert to Catholicism to satisfy his devout Catholic parents. But Bill was inclined neither toward engagement nor toward religion. He felt he'd had enough religion forced upon him growing up, and that he never wanted to return. At first this was a small disappointment, later a gift, a chance to seek a religious home myself rather than wait for one to befall me. We attended the Episcopal baptism of one of Bill's friends in Los Angeles, and I thought, I think I'll do that someday.

My outstanding reservations had to do not with practice, but belief: I wasn't sure I could brook a perfectly orthodox or literalistic understanding of Christianity. The philosophically minded Anglican Church proved a good home for me, and Grace Cathedral itself even better. The dean, Alan Jones, delivered charismatic sermons about the dangers of fundamentalism, the way in which literal interpretations robbed scripture of its richness, and the commonalities among the world's religions. His intellectual arguments could be erudite and highly nuanced, but the key message was always the same: love and forgiveness. I saw in these services another version of how certain kinds of truth lay far beyond the facts, beyond debates over when the world was created, beyond doubts over whether Jesus was, in a scientifically provable sense, resurrected. There were many different kinds of truth: poetic truths, metaphorical truths, narrative truths. The latter variety had taken on an urgent importance to me, as I struggled to understand Dad's death.

Bill and I broke up while I was preparing to be baptized, then got back together just before my baptism, then broke up again soon after.

The breakups did not devastate me as they had before. After one night of arguing with him, I climbed the steep block of Jones Street from my apartment to the cathedral. To the right of the cathedral's main doors, facing Huntington Park, is a stone labyrinth copied from one found on the floor of France's ancient Chartres Cathedral. It is a circle of lines paved into the concrete. It looks like a giant maze, but it isn't. There are no wrong turns, no decisions of direction to make, only many twists to follow as you walk to the center, then trace your steps back out. It was eleven p.m. and deserted, a nice evening outside, not as brisk as San Francisco can be. I started walking the labyrinth, filled with unease and fear and frustration as I wended my way toward the center. On my way out, I suddenly imagined my father waiting for me at the end, his arms held to envelop me in a hug, and when I was finished, I was filled with a sense that he was holding me. I returned home calm and at peace.

Other aspects of my adopted religion were not so soothing, at first. Around the time I decided to convert, Howdy began leaving me persistent phone messages, asking me to let him drive three hours to San Francisco and take me out to lunch. I knew he wanted to apologize to me, because he was working through his Alcoholics Anonymous steps and had reached the point at which he was supposed to reconcile with those he'd wronged. My mother and brother had already sat through their absolution sessions with him. And I knew my duty, laid out in my baptismal vows—"Seek and serve Christ in all persons"—and my Lord's Prayer—"as we forgive those who trespass against us." For months I balked. "I don't know that we'd have much to talk about," I told him once over the phone when he caught me at home. Gnawed by guilt, I considered seeking my priest's advice. But I knew what he would say, and I knew I had to meet with Howdy.

Howdy had to hobble the two blocks from our parking space to the restaurant, like a dog that needed to be put down. Aside from liver failure, which had made his once sportsmanlike face doughy and bloated, he had hepatitis C, which made his joints ache. At fifty-two, he was two years older than any male Cullen descendant in living memory, and he was weak. But more vivid than my pity toward his decrepitude and even my vengeful disgust was my old fear, that visceral awareness of his physical power and volatility that I'd learned as a child. I kept an arm's length between us. No matter how ill and ailing Howdy became, I would always feel intimidated by him.

We were given a too-small table nearest the bar, the last in a line of chic postage-stamp-sized tables. Howdy wore his standard ensemble: pointy-toed boots, jeans with a big silver buckle, and a red plaid flannel shirt. Techno music ricocheted off the exposed brick walls and steel-beam rafters, louder than I had counted on for a weekday lunch. I had chosen this ostentatiously hip Mission District restaurant, one of my favorites.

"At least you're getting a nice lunch out of it," Mom had said when I told her I'd finally agreed to meet him. She'd had her own absolution session with him about a year ago; Emmet had sat through his a few months later. This was all part of Howdy working his AA plan, coming to the ninth step of "making amends"; for years Mom and Emmet and I had resisted his requests.

But after we ordered, and Howdy pulled out a sheet of tattered yellow legal paper full of lists and scribbles, I considered asking our waitress to turn the thumping synthesizer beats down.

"So you quit the insurance business," I half-shouted, leaning across the table for his response. He was looking over his notes, as though making last-minute preparations for a Toastmasters meeting.

He lifted his head slowly. "That business was killing me." His voice was grumbly and low, as though he'd suffer a hernia if he tried to raise it.

I leaned in farther. "Emmet says you're in landscaping now."

"Yeah, big job last week, putting a pond in someone's backyard. I designed it myself, drew up plans, picked out the plants. You remember how I used to paint? Work with stained glass? I get to use my artistic side again."

He told me about how he picked up Mexican day laborers to do the planting and installing and gave them a small cut. "Pays good too. If I could just get the IRS out of the way. I'm working on that."

I knew his IRS woes well. Every time Emmet returned from a visit with his dad, he had some tale about money doled out from the trunk of the Town Car—no bank account.

"I tell you, Rachel, it's all about clean living," Howdy said. "See, I've got these back payments with the IRS all worked out, and with this landscaping money, I'm putting that aside and taking care of my debts . . ."

My skin was turning prickly with irritation. I considered pointing out to him that since his landscaping work was under the table, he was cheating the IRS out of yet more money. And noting that without a contractor's license, he was performing that work illegally. I held my tongue. Today was the first day of Lent, a fact I never would have known a year ago, before I began attending church. I had come here, I told myself, to forgive and not to criticize.

And even though I was fighting with every last reserve of indifference to be flip about this meeting, just a year ago I'd told Mom I would never meet with him, never call him back. In fact I'd told her that again just last month.

The food arrived: clam chowder for Howdy, who could no longer stomach anything spicy. He took a few slurps and pushed it aside as I picked up a slice of my goat-cheese-and-arugula pizza.

"Listen, I want to thank you for agreeing to meet with me," he said.

I shrugged and rubbed my arms to ward off the restaurant's overzealous air-conditioning. "You're the one who had to drive all the way in to San Francisco."

"No, really. You know I've been thinking over these things long and hard since I got clean. And I realized out of all the people I did wrong when I was using, what I did to you was worst."

I set my glass of water down.

"I mean, you were just a kid, no way to protect yourself." His arms were tight to his sides, clutching the yellow legal paper in front of him, and his eyes weren't looking into mine, but staring blankly at his lists as he wagged his head. "To hit you like that—I don't know, the only way I can explain it is cruelty."

"You hit me?" The information was so serious that my immediate reaction was disbelief—except that the idea that Howdy had hit me, after all my years of fearing him, was far too likely to be true. I did not remember a single incident of physical abuse and never would, though I could easily believe it, though later my mother would tell me of walk-

ing into my bedroom one morning when I was three and finding my
face bruised, and knowing that Howdy had done it.

"Well, yeah," Howdy said, in a way that read, *Well, duh*.

"You know what, I don't even remember it," I said, trying to act
light, but worried that I would start shaking. "And the other stuff, I
stopped being angry at you a long time ago." This was not entirely true.
Four years ago, to name just one instance, I'd started to jot down notes
about Howdy in my journal and suddenly began stabbing the page with
my pen. A significant part of me, when sufficiently stimulated by vivid
memory, would always be angry at Howdy. But what had really started
happening, a long time ago, is that I'd begun experiencing a kind of de-
tached amusement, a gee-whiz disbelief, at how Howdy had treated
me. And at the same time as I'd grown older and built my own life and
seen it coming along quite nicely, an almost satisfied pity for the way
Howdy had led his crept in. Finally the moments of pity had overtaken
the moments of anger, until I'd been left, as to this day, with a peculiar
fascination with the man.

That's why I could still, at this lunch, keep my voice nonchalant. I
was only partly bluffing, only partly shrugging it off out of pure embarrassment. Even as I sat there facing him, another growing part of
me needed to believe that none of this mattered now.

I wanted to explain this to him, because I hoped now he would understand it.

"You know, all the traumatic syndromes you gave me, they're not
bad ones to have," I joked. "Drugs, violence—there are worse aver-
sions. And cigarettes. I hate cigarettes—actually I have this neurotic
thing about cigarettes. Do you know if I'm going out with a guy—and
it doesn't matter how nice and sweet he is—if I see him smoke a cigarette, he's instantly evil in my eyes?"

I'd often marveled that my mind could take all the screaming and
drugs and, if I could now count something I didn't remember, violence
and concentrate their effects into such a relatively harmless and ubiqui-
tous symbol as the cigarette. I am fearfully obsessed with them—with
the idea of smoking them, with the idea of seeing anyone I love smoking
them or even hearing that they have smoked them. When Bill snuck a
cigarette on a night out with friends, it occasioned one of our breakups.

Howdy laughed, understanding the connection. "Like Satan incarnate? Is that what I was, Satan incarnate?"

We'd both started laughing, Howdy with relish, I with unease. "I used that on a woman in my AA group once, just to freak her out," he said. "You know how in AA we're supposed to appeal to a higher power, but we can call that higher power anything we want? So at the meetings I used to say my prayer to Satan, and she would just flip."

I almost choked on my pizza as two business-attired women slid into the next table over, inches away. "Listen, I mean it, I don't know how to explain it except cruelty," Howdy said. "And what you've got to understand, what people don't understand, is that you're not yourself when you're not clean. You're the disease."

The women scanned their menus in silence as I considered a prudent change in topic. But I'd grown tired of keeping things hushed from the supposedly normal people all around me, and tired of being ashamed. Let them eavesdrop, if they wished.

"So exactly when did you go clean? What did it for you?"

"I tell you, Rachel, it's some story."

I asked him to tell it. He reached back ten years and told of cocaine and then more cocaine and then heroin and then ending up crashed out alone on a bloodstained mattress somewhere on Fresno's ratty Motel Drive. He spoke of "the disease" and lost hope and topped his story with a scene: Howdy standing before a cracked mirror, with a handgun in his mouth.

In the second half of his tale he found hope and an AA sponsor. "The thing is," he said, "for all those years I couldn't feel anything." His voice was gruff even as he said this, and I wondered if he could feel anything now, if he was clinically capable of it, if he ever would. But I could see that he wanted to. "I knew I was hurting people," he said. "But I didn't even understand what it felt like to be hurt. I didn't get it. It didn't mean a thing to me." Silently I doubted that he really had feelings now, for anyone other than himself. Just a few weeks earlier he'd been nasty to my brother. I stared at him with cynicism. He was apologizing to me for his sake, not for mine, so that he could check off the next step of his program. He was meeting with me because he was supposed to feel guilty, not because he did, I felt sure—though he swore otherwise. "I tell you, Rachel, it's only in the last few years that I've started to have any feelings," he said. "And they're weird. But one of the first feelings I had was regret about what I did to you."

"So you really were heartless." The cynical part of me had taken over. The confirmation of his cruelty felt rich, and I was tempted to get smug about it. "Do you think you're a—what's the word Mom used?— a sociopath?"

Howdy stopped flipping through his wad of bills and looked up from the check, dead into my eyes. "Of course I'm a sociopath," he said with a grin, and shook his head as though disbelieving my naïveté.

We drove back to my place down derelict Sixth Street, passing addicts and a cartel of crack dealers. I knew that's what they were because I'd seen them rustle up their shirts or down their pants to pull out little wads of white powder every day—the *Examiner* offices where I worked were on that corner, as I pointed out to Howdy. The scenery dovetailed nicely with our conversation: Howdy now wanted to tell me all about his recovery, and I wanted him to tell me all about his drugs. In detail, if possible. Just because I'd decided to forgive his drug-fueled abuse didn't mean I couldn't try to chronicle it in exactitude. "So you were off the heroin the whole time you were with my mom, right? So what were you doing, was it really just the pot. . . . ?"

"Oh, no, no," he corrected me. "Cocaine too. I was shooting it because it was more intense that way. I had a routine. At the end there with you guys, you remember I would make sure your brother was in bed after your mom went to work and then shut myself in my room? See, I would shoot a gram of cocaine—"

"Is that a lot?"

"Yeah, it's a lot. And then I would drink a pint of whiskey. And then I would just lie there and feel my heart beating like crazy and hope that it would kill me. Because I knew in the morning your mom would come home and I would have to be sober again."

"Hmmm."

"I should write a book about my life. I'm serious."

"If you ever need help with it, you know who to call." He asked me if I'd read some writer I'd never heard of, and Gabriel García Márquez's

One Hundred Years of Solitude, and I lied and said yes as he stopped at my street corner.

Throughout lunch I'd imagined myself bolting from his car to my apartment, eager to have our meeting and my obligatory acceptance of his apologies over and done with, but I sat for a moment with the rain softly drumming and the engine humming. Perhaps it was the terrible satisfaction of finally seeing this man who had so threatened me rendered old and ill and impotent. But mixed in was genuine concern. I wanted to stay; I was warming to him. When you've spent that many years with someone, even if you've spent most of that time hating him, you have a connection. I looked at his face, so rough and tired, his eyes so hardened. Even his smiles looked mean and hateful. And I felt I wanted to stay with him, inside this warm car, to just sit alongside him. I thought, maybe his apology is deep and sincere, maybe it isn't. But I accept it. And for the first time possibly since I'd met the man, I wanted him to get better, to be healthy and safe.

"Listen, if there's anything I can ever help you out with, I really mean it, you have my number," he wheezed as I stepped out of the Lincoln Town Car into a light rain.

"Thanks," I said. For an instant I could picture myself calling him. He pulled down the street and I stepped inside.

Mom called me that night with a sarcastic drawl in her voice. "So how did it go?" She said Howdy had called her that afternoon, right after he got home to Fresno. He was worried about the Tenderloin neighborhood around my office, the one I walked through every day to work, full of dealers and hopeless users. "Guess he knows what they're capable of," Mom said.

He wanted to make sure I was safe.

part
four

THE DETECTIVES:
AUGUST 2002

I CALLED THE DETECTIVES from my desk at the arts and entertainment section of the *San Francisco Examiner*, demanding information in the most authoritative tone I could muster. "I'm following up on a letter I sent requesting documents under the Freedom of Information Act," I told the sergeant matter-of-factly, trying to follow the script one of my fellow reporters on the crime beat had suggested. "My father was killed in your . . . your *jurisdiction*, in 1986." Journalism had trained me to cold-call people and request information with total confidence. But anything regarding my father's murder still turned me tentative and mousy.

"I'd like to help you out," an unfazed voice said. "But I don't know what you're entitled to under the Freedom of Information Act. Do you?"

"Well, no, I don't, actually, but a police report is public record and that entitles . . . ," I stammered on, but my voice admitted defeat.

"What's your father's name?" the detective asked, and I quit back-pedaling to tell him.

"Stan Howard?" he said, pausing as though struck by a distant memory. "Ah—I know that case."

"You do?" I shrank inside my cubicle, certain that my face had gone pale.

"Sure—a case like that you never forget."

"Really?"

"You're his daughter? So you must have been pretty young . . ."

"I was ten," I said almost giddily. Here I was after all these years, the traumatized little girl, getting the acknowledgment I deserved.

"Listen, if you want to come into the station, we could sit down and just *tell* you what we can about the case."

The idea was so new and strange that it took me a moment to accept. Exhilaration pulsed through my veins as I fumbled for a pen to write down the appointment. "So I'll see you next Monday, one o'clock," I said.

"Looking forward to it," the detective said.

It had taken me sixteen years to work up to that phone call. Little did I realize that everything from my childhood had dovetailed to bring me to that moment.

At age forty-seven, my mother had just met Frank, a Southern-tongued Tennessee native with an affinity for slightly off-color jokes and stiletto heels, which he was trying to convince my five-foot-ten mother to wear. Eventually I'd come to appreciate his roguish Southern charm—and the sincerity of his love for my mother—but at the time everything was moving way too fast. Since her divorce from Howdy, Mom had never had a serious boyfriend, because she didn't want to subject her children to another man, and because she didn't trust her taste in love interests. I too feared a Howdy redux. I heard alarms sound when, three months into their relationship, Mom traded in her high-mileage Mercedes for the extended-cab truck Frank had always wanted, a truck Frank drove while Mom took his beat-up pickup to work.

Then came the bomb: Mom was selling her condominium in Santa Barbara—immediately—to buy a house back in Merced. Mom and Frank would use the house as their home base. In the meantime they'd hit the road for a few years of sojourns, Frank quitting his job to follow Mom from one traveling nursing gig to another.

Frank's sudden omnipresence spooked me, but the news about leaving Santa Barbara for Merced sent me into crisis. Santa Barbara was more than my adopted hometown. It was the place where I'd begun to find a new life, one freed from constant reminders of my father's murder and Howdy's guardianship.

Mom had stayed in Santa Barbara during my senior year abroad in London, and after I graduated college she bought the condominium. Though I'd followed Bill to San Francisco, I envisioned returning one day. Mom and Emmet and I would all live in Santa Barbara together again, leading a sunny existence that had nothing to do with the lives we'd known in the valley.

But Emmet had grown up and joined the army, and now Mom was moving back to the valley voluntarily. "I can't believe you're doing this," I snarled after semirational pleas had failed. "You're making the biggest mistake of your life," I screamed at her, and often hung up the phone in sudden anger. I snickered openly at Frank's Confederate flags and corny jokes, convinced that Mom was recklessly inflicting irreparable damage on all our lives.

But after a few months the sense of crisis faded. For one thing, it was around this time that Bill and I got engaged, and I felt a new security in our commitment. Bill and I were moving into the future. Mom's return to Merced would not unravel the supposed progress of my life, not suck me back to the past. The idea of returning to Merced no longer struck me with terror. And yet a distaste for the town, something stronger than an aversion, lingered. I knew it had to do with my father, and that I needed to face it. And so I decided to visit Mom's new house in Merced to meet with the detectives on my father's case.

The Merced County Sheriff's Department was housed in a colorless 1960s block of concrete canopied by trees. Next to it stood cheap portable buildings, like the ones at overcrowded schools, which functioned as county courts. As I approached the main office, inmates in bright orange jail suits and handcuffs trudged along the portables' ramps, one unshaven defendant apparently just leaving a hearing, another going in. So that was what justice looked like: a badly groomed man in fluorescent pants shuffling into a clapboard building, none of the glamour of a courtroom docudrama. I wondered if living through such a scene would have brought some satisfaction to my family, if a trial could have united us and allowed us to move on. But I couldn't picture it. My imagination went blank. It was no use speculating; it would in overwhelming likelihood never be our reality.

I'd pictured a trim, thirtysomething cop, hair neatly coiffed like a 1950s officer on neighborhood walking rounds—or at least someone in uniform. The sergeant, Rick Marshall, who met me at the entrance to the county jail was fat in a jolly way, his polo shirt coming untucked, his gray hair curly and unkempt. I liked him.

He greeted me with a wink and took me to a windowless office on the second floor with a little waiting room and a secretary sitting at a desk. Off to the side were two smaller rooms with signs that said IN-TERVIEW and another sign you could slide to indicate IN PROGRESS. We went in and waited for the detective's partner, Larry Parsley, a darker, leaner man with cowboy boots and slicked-back hair.

Parsley closed the door behind him. In his hands he held a fat gray binder. Written on the spine in Magic Marker were the words *Howard, Stanley P.* I looked at it and I thought, Hand me that. That is what I need: all there is to know about Dad's murder organized and paper-clipped into place, held between my two hands.

He pulled a photo out of the binder and handed it to me. "You recognize these folks?"

It was a picture of Dad, Sherrie, me, and Bobby. There was a Christmas tree in the corner of the shot, which meant the photo was taken either a year and a half or six months before he died. I bolted upright. This was the first time I had seen Sherrie or Bobby, in person or in photos, in sixteen years.

"That's me," I said, pointing. "And that's my dad's wife Sherrie. And that's her son, Bobby."

"Awww, that *is* you!" Detective Marshall said, as if genuinely charmed by my nine-year-old smile. I liked him even more. But it was clear he wasn't running the show. Parsley shot him a stern look and then faced me dead-on.

"So what kind of information have you come here to share with us?" he said.

I blinked, unable to comprehend. I'd come to have the *detectives* share information with *me*. I'd come to have them hand me the conversational equivalent of that binder, a file I could store away and call on whenever I needed to tell the story of why my father had died. Perhaps they wouldn't tell me who had killed him. But they would give me some key fact—maybe even several—that would make my face light up with instantaneous understanding. Some fact that would turn what I knew about my father's death into more than a random assortment of peculiar details and half-processed memories that sat stored away in my consciousness like old rolls of film, waiting for someone to develop them.

"Well, I don't know," I said. "I thought—well, it's been so long since my dad died, and I was so young when it happened, and no one in my family talks about it, so I was hoping . . ."

Marshall leaned in toward me kindly, but Parsley wasn't softening. "If you have some questions about the case, we can do our best to tell you what we're able," Marshall said.

"Well, I don't know *anything*," I said. "I heard a few things, about a relative of Sherrie's . . . a brother?"

"That's right," Parsley said. "Did you ever meet that person?"

"No, I didn't."

Parsley gave a swift glance to Marshall, checking in. "Were you there when your dad was killed?"

I nodded my head compliantly, but I was miffed—shouldn't these guys already *know* that I was there? Did they ever bother to know that? Or had it just been buried in that gray binder for more than a decade? "I had just come to stay with him for the summer," I said.

"So you might not have ever seen this person, if you'd just been visiting on the weekends," Parsley said.

I nodded again, but held his gaze. He seemed to search my eyes for a second, then looked over at Marshall and gave a tiny raise of his eyebrows: the green light, I thought.

"The guy goes by the name of Steve Serrano," Parsley said. The idea of a brother was familiar to me only from my conversation with Nanette eight years ago, and a few mystifying comments from my grandparents. The name was completely new.

"Evidently your dad didn't like him much," Parsley went on. "He doesn't live that far from here. We asked him to come in and talk with us. He refused. So we told him we were considering him a suspect. He said you just go ahead and do that, but I'm not talking to you.

"The strange thing," Parsley said, as if there were just one strange thing, "was how quiet this case has been. Nobody talking. Usually, case like this, somebody talks, some kind of rumor comes down the prison pipeline. That's what we're looking for, someone's big mouth. A murder case isn't closed until it's solved, you know."

I did know that, but I also knew a case like my dad's could be as good as closed, and that this was a line the detectives used to give people like me false hope. It was the wrong line to use on me. I'd never dreamed of seeing "someone pay" the way relatives of murder victims are supposed to. I wanted sense, not comeuppance, and I didn't believe the two were bound. But I understood the necessity of this inept attempt at consolation. What rankled me was the detectives' stance, leaning in but not too close, arms crossed. Did they think I had come here to demand justice after all these years, to blame them for not nailing the killer? But what had I come here for? And if I didn't know, how could they possibly give it to me?

"What about her?" I said, pointing at Sherrie in the photo.

"You know, we heard from her again, a few years ago . . . How many years ago was that?"

Marshall shrugged. "Five years ago?"

"She said she wanted us to look at the case again," Parsley continued. "So we did some more investigation at that time."

My chest felt as though it had been hit by a two-by-four. The idea that Sherrie was still out there, still interested in the case . . . why? Maybe she really had nothing to do with it. Maybe she wanted it solved too. My stomach twisted with the idea that I had blamed her, wrongly, all these years, if only in my mind and memory. I felt a surge of pity for her. But something else too.

"She was a very strange woman," I said. "I mean, kind of scary." There was no "kind of" about it—she had scared the hell out of me. But what did I know? So what if she had been a strange woman, if she had intimidated me and shouted at my mother. Did that make it right to blame her for a murder? "Did she say why she wanted you to look at the case again?"

Parsley looked ready to say something, but Marshall cut him off absentmindedly. "It wasn't five years ago. It was more like ten years."

Parsley looked annoyed. If he did know why Sherrie had wanted the case looked at again, he wasn't going to tell me, and if he didn't, he wasn't going to speculate. I wanted to share every bad recollection I'd ever had of her, to tell them about the lingerie shopping trips, about the hard stare in her eyes when my dad left the room and she called me a brat, about the dream I had, days before Dad's death, that she poisoned my cereal. A dozen vivid scenes played through my mind while I held my mouth silent. My impressions weren't any kind of evidence, just unflattering memories. And why should the detectives want to hear them? I hadn't come in here to implicate her. I had come here because I didn't know where else to start.

"If you have any more questions for us . . . ," Parsley said.

A glaze must have washed over my eyes. I had *hundreds* of questions. I'd waltzed in here so stupidly, thinking my only bar to truth had been my own fear. Still, I threw something out there. "Is it true"—I paused—"that the knife was taken out of our kitchen?"

"We have evidence to suggest that may be true," Parsley said.

And then I knew the detectives didn't have truth for me. They had evidence, and not enough of it, and taken together, even filed tidily into that binder, it did not add up to truth. We were done.

"I guess that's it," I said. "Except, can I get a copy of that picture? I don't have any photos of her or her son, and it would mean a lot to me."

"You know what?" Parsley said with a wink. "You can have it. I'll go make a photocopy and you can take the original."

His pompadour hair glided out of the room atop his heavy boots. Alone with Marshall, I felt momentarily uneasy, pressed to make conversation, but the tension passed. This was the nice guy. I could talk to him.

"She really was a strange woman, you know," I said shyly, guiltily. "She'd do things like—well, like right after the funeral, she took me and her boy back to the house."

Marshall's gray eyebrows perked up a bit, and his arms uncrossed. "No kidding?"

"And right before he was killed, maybe a few weeks before, they had a fight. My dad took her into the back room and we heard her crying, and we had to run to the neighbor's to call the police on him." I wasn't certain on the timing; they could have had this fight a year before his death. But Marshall, obviously acquainted with only the barest facts of Dad's case, couldn't set me straight.

"Hmmm." It wasn't quite dismissive. He sounded genuinely curious, if only for my sake and not the case's. I dreaded Parsley's return. I had a feeling that if he stayed away long enough, I could nudge Marshall into really talking with me, into hearing out my memories. What purpose this would serve I did not know, and yet I wanted the exchange badly.

But the door opened and Parsley handed me the photograph. "Thanks so much," I said. "It really means a lot to me. And thanks for your time." I meant it, though I felt cast aside.

"Hey, listen," Marshall said, speaking to Parsley. "Did you know about some kind of fight between her and him, domestic violence incident, right before . . ."

Parsley slipped his photocopy of the picture he'd given me into the gray binder and slammed it shut. "Yep, it's in here."

Marshall saw me down the back stairwell and out the building's side door, making small talk about my career as a dance critic and his niece's ballet recital, telling me that if I had any other questions or ever needed to talk about the case again, to call him. He handed me his card, his voice echoing off the concrete walls. "I hope you got what you came here for," he said.

"Thanks, I think I did, just to hear some things from you guys," I said as I stepped out of the overly air-conditioned sheriff's offices and into the Sahara-like August afternoon. I shook his hand with gratitude. But what I told him was only partially true. I felt more restless and unsettled about the murder than ever. Sherrie had wanted the case investigated again. Why would she want that if she had been involved? Perhaps all these years she'd wanted answers just as badly as I had?

I crossed the street to my car like a somnambulist, hardly feeling my steps. Maybe Sherrie never was who I thought she was. I sat in the driver's seat with the engine off and the windows rolled up, the hot air eddying around me like a sauna, and stared at the photograph. Bobby's hair was longer than I remembered. My dad looked dorkier than I remembered, his hair as puffy as his leather bomber jacket. And Sherrie didn't appear as wicked as I'd imagined. At first glance, she looked simply like a prettier-than-average woman, lean, with luscious full lips. I knew a closer look would show another side. But I didn't want to look closer yet.

I wanted to go to the house where everything had happened, so I set the photo aside and drove to our old home out in the boonies. The drive felt short, and not at all frightening. I parked on the same side of the street as the old house, though not right in front of it, and stepped out of the car without hesitation. I felt calm and rational. I wanted to look at everything now for what it really was, to hold it in my mind as simple statements of fact. This was the house where my father was killed. He'd been killed here sixteen years ago. No one was here to hurt me now.

The street hadn't changed—not a single new home or shed or barn had gone up to make the strip of five houses feel more like a real neighborhood than a slice of lower-middle-class twilight zone. The big straw field behind our old house was now filled with rows of some kind of low-lying, leafy green crop, maybe spinach. I'd brought a cheap disposable camera with me, and I walked in front of the house, taking pictures. The house was painted in different colors now, with a truck in the driveway, but it was essentially the same.

The afternoon was blindingly hot and bright, and something about the immense sunlight, the scorching warmth, emboldened me. I decided to knock on the house's front door, explain to the owners that I'd once lived there, and ask if I could look around and take some pictures. I took my time standing in the dirt roadside hatching my strategy. I'd say nothing about the murder. It was silly of me to think that anyone around here would know about what had happened sixteen years ago anyway.

I knocked and rang the doorbell and knocked again, but no one answered. I lingered at the doorway, flashing back to age ten, waiting for Dad to shepherd me to the car. When the memory grew too strong, I pulled myself back from it, determined to stay firmly in the here and now.

Walking around the edge of the property again, haphazardly aiming my camera, I noticed a man next door, hosing down his driveway as chickens scattered out of the water's way. Mariachi music wafted from his garage. He was dark brown, Mexican, and wore a white cowboy hat and mustache. He looked as if he'd like to know what I was up to taking all those pictures, and I couldn't blame him, so I decided to say hello.

"How're you doing?" I said, walking toward him, and he smiled back, lowering his hose.

"I used to live here," I said, pointing to the house. "So I was just looking around, for memory's sake."

"How long ago you live here?" he said, tilting his head.

"Oh, jeez." I started to chip a hole in the lawn with my shoe and shielded my forehead with my hand to look back up. "Sixteen years ago."

He narrowed his eyes as though trying to place my face. "You live here back when the incident happened?"

I tensed, but the man seemed friendly if tentative. "You mean the murder?" I said. "Yeah. Yeah, I did."

"Oh, I see. When was that—'85?"

"Nineteen eighty-six," And then, because he was peering at me as though trying to calculate: "I was ten."

He laid his hose on the lawn. A hen walked between us, with a bunch of chicks skittering behind, and I bent down in hopes they might come near me. The neighbor and I stood nine or ten feet apart, half-shouting at each other above the mariachi tunes. I took a few steps forward. "How are you related?" he said.

"You mean to the man who was murdered? I'm his daughter."

"Ohhhhh." He took a step toward me.

"Another man, nice old man, used to live in your house when I lived here," I said, trying to change the subject and act casual. "And this field—it used to be empty. There was a horse back there, that we used to go play with."

"Yeah, I bought the house and the field a few years ago," the man said.

"Looks like you've got a nice crop," I said stupidly.

The man walked over and turned off his hose, then walked back toward me and looked up thoughtfully. "I remember that night," he said in his mild Mexican accent. "The night it happened. It was a weird night."

I didn't need to encourage him. For some strange reason, he was eager to talk.

"See, I used to live in that house over there." He pointed across the field. "And at four in the morning, see, I'm washing out my ice chest, 'cause we're getting ready to drive to Reno, you know?"

I didn't know. It struck me as certifiably weird to be washing out an ice chest at four a.m. But I didn't want to derail the conversation.

"So I look up and there's lights, bright lights, all shining on me," he says. "The cops. They were out looking for the guy, the guy who did it. So they want to know what I'm doing out at four in the morning, but I tell them, about going to Tahoe, so finally they let me go."

"Weird." I meant everything he had told me, but he took me just to mean the police search, which suited me fine. As strange as his story was, he relayed it in an easygoing way that made me trust him. And after what I'd just learned about Sherrie wanting to reinvestigate the case, I wasn't sure I could trust my suspicions anymore, anyway.

"The people who live in that house now," I said, "do they know what happened there?"

"Yeah, they know. It's all right."

"Well, thanks. Thanks for talking with me." I felt more gratitude for him than I had for the detectives. He'd shared his memory with me willingly, unguardedly. He'd made my father's murder real in a way that a mountain's worth of disconnected facts couldn't.

We stood together looking out across the field, not talking, more mariachi music blaring from the garage. The sun was shining so hard, it felt like it would burn a hole right down the part in my hair. The heat felt wonderful. A hot wind blew between us. Whether because of the intense sunshine or my relief in coming out here and feeling safe, knowing that I could face what I'd wanted to for so long, I filled with a gentle happiness. We said good-bye and I got back in the car to drive to Mom's new place.

But back in real life, back at Mom's new house, I was on edge again, and surly.

"How did it go?" Mom asked, and as I tried to explain what the detectives had shared with me, and how much they *hadn't*, Frank entered the room and cut in.

"The important thing," he said in his Southern twang, "was did you find some closure?"

I took in a sharp breath and forced myself to look away, filled with shame and anger. Maybe on talk shows people confronted their pasts in video montages and dabbed their eyes with Kleenex and left the set with their once-broken lives instantly made whole, *case closed*. And I suppose I had thought some moment of resolution like that, minus the theme music, might happen for me with the detectives. But the word *closure*, the expectation that you could stage a finale to half a lifetime of confusion, and then at the end of an hour's meeting leave shut tight and self-contained, like a book—the whole idea horrified me. I didn't know with whom I felt more irritated: the detectives for not making this miraculous moment happen, or myself for having the naïveté to imagine I could just talk to them and see all the facts of Dad's murder snap neatly into place, like evidence in a binder.

Like the detectives, Mom and Frank wanted to know if I'd gotten what I'd come for. I gathered all my self-restraint and smiled weakly at Frank. "That's a complicated question," I said.

Frank saw not only the smile but the irrepressible glare in my eyes and retreated to the kitchen. Mom looked at the photograph the detectives had given me. "She looks a lot better than I remembered," she said.

It was true. Sherrie wasn't smiling, but she looked lean and pretty, dressed conservatively in a T-shirt and hooded, zip-up sweatshirt. Her hair was long and straight. But if you looked closer, the pretty-girl image started falling apart. Her lips were strangely puffy. And strangest of all were her eyes. The eyebrows were creepily thin, like those of older women who wax off every last facial hair and then draw their features back on. Those drawn-on eyebrows seemed to relay a deeper variety of deception. When you looked closer, there was something off, something phony about her altogether.

The detectives hadn't given me closure. What I'd been seeking, though I had not known it, was an opening. Sherrie was out there, and she was a real, living person.

*   *   *

A week later, I woke from a dream, frightened. In the dream I was sitting across a table from Sherrie. We were making small talk. I was terrified, unable to take my eyes off her for fear of meeting bodily harm. I woke in a sweat but with a strange sensation of triumph. As sleep receded, the fear drained from my blood, and a new conviction took its place. I had to talk with Sherrie.

THE CRIME REPORT

MY MEMORY IS FALLIBLE. The crime report proves it.

After meeting with the detectives, after realizing that looking close and hard at my father's murder would not snap some fragile thread in me, I became fixated on collecting black-and-white, documentary "facts." I couldn't tell whether I had undertaken this because I wanted to know who had killed my father. Certainly that was the dominant course of action that seemed melodramatically appropriate to the relative of a murder victim such as myself, the story of delayed justice played out in mystery novels and television shows. I felt I should have a thirst for justice, and yet I didn't. There was something else I wanted, and I couldn't put my finger on it. All I knew was that I urgently needed to assemble whatever information about the murder I could.

So I asked Marshall for the report as sweetly and politely as possible; he took three weeks to call me back and then informed me, with a falsely chummy demeanor, that he wouldn't release it. His reasoning was practical, if difficult to accept: If too many details in the report get out, Marshall said, inmates all over California might start calling with false tips, using descriptions from the report to make their snitching sound legit, in hopes of retaliating against enemies or lightening their sentences. And the understaffed Merced County Sheriff's Department might end up trekking all over the state checking out dead-end leads.

So the coroner's report was all I could hope for. That document was still within my rights. A honey-voiced secretary at the coroner's office

directed me, with refreshing efficiency, to send a self-addressed envelope along with my request. Four days later the papers landed in my
mailbox—but with a bonus. Folded alongside the autopsy and toxicol-
ogy screen was a vivid if maddeningly brief typed description of the
murder scene, discreetly headed "crime report."

I read the papers alone in my studio apartment over dinner. And
then I read them again and again and again, until a headache forced
me to try to sleep.

*At approximately 0330 hours on 6-22-86, I was dispatched to a
stabbing at 631 E. Gerard Ave., Merced. Myself and Sgt. Rainwater arrived on the scene and we noticed a young male juvenile staring at us from a window in front of the residence.*

*As we approached the front door, we found it was locked, and
the house was dark. We knocked on the door and identified ourselves as Merced County Sheriff's Dept., and after approximately 15 to 30 seconds, I heard somebody screaming "I'm
coming, I'm coming." Sherrie Howard opened the door and
screamed, "He's in the bathroom." Sgt. Rainwater and myself
did not know whether the suspect was still on the scene. When
we entered the residence I noticed that the sliding glass door
leading from the dining room to the backyard was open. Sgt.
Rainwater and myself proceeded to the rear of the residence in an
attempt to find the victim. There was blood splattered all over
the hallway and in the bathroom located off the master bedroom.
We found the victim lying nude on a white throw rug lying in his
bedroom. Blood was splattered on the curtains and on several
piles of clothes all over the bedroom. Sgt. Rainwater directed me
to apply direct pressure on the victim's neck. We did not move the
victim as we did not know the exact location of the cut and there
was no visible signs of anymore bleeding. Sgt. Rainwater had dis-
patch notify Riggs Ambulance to respond Code 3 and also have
a Detective respond to the scene. While I was applying the direct
pressure, Sgt. Rainwater searched the rest of the house and did
not find a suspect.*

Riggs Ambulance Personnel arrived at the scene and took over

working on the victim. At this time we attempted to get a state-
ment from Sherrie Howard, and she was in an extremely hysteri-
cal condition. All she could remember is that it was a possibly
large man with a beanie cap on and a plaid shirt. While I was as-
sisting Riggs Personnel, Sgt. Rainwater went with the Canine
Unit of the Merced Police Dept. to attempt to locate the suspect.
The victim was then transported by Riggs to MCMC. Det.
Walthour arrived on the scene and we briefed him as to what
Sherrie Howard had told us and what we had noticed when we
arrived.

    No further action taken by this officer at this time.

The crime report largely corroborated what I remembered. But the
points where the report and my memory differed felt like vast canyons
that I might plummet into, that might send me reeling in self-doubt.

She was in an extremely hysterical condition. I didn't remember
Sherrie as hysterical. Surely that reflects some kind of bias on my part,
I thought as I read the report for the tenth time, carrying it from the
table to the desk to the couch and then to the bed as if reading it in
every possible location would make it real. Surely that denial of her
hysteria reflected my desire to build her up into the picture of a
bizarrely calm, controlling murderess.

A young male juvenile staring at us from a window. Bobby must have
been looking out from my bedroom, nearest the front door. I didn't remember that either. I remembered the house dark, the back sliding-
glass door open during the hot night, sitting together on the sofa and
picking up Dad's weight-lifting gloves. I remembered the paramedics
coming through, and Sherrie rushing to cover our eyes, but not the
deputies' arrival. Bobby and I must have waited in my bedroom until
the deputies arrived, and then sat on the sofa considering Dad's gloves
in the time between the deputies' inspection of the house and the arrival of the paramedics. But about the volume of blood in the report I
had no doubt. I remembered the blood too well, as though seeing it
again for the first time.

    Now I knew just how bad Dad's wound was. Now I had the autopsy.

The murderer stabbed my father on the left side of his neck, an inch and a half below his earlobe. The wound was one inch long and a quarter inch wide—a straight jab. It tore through the thyroid cartilage, and through the esophagus, and then through the larynx and the vocal cords. It sliced open the carotid artery and it hit the jugular too. It almost sliced right through the carotid: *Approximately ²⁄₃ of the wall is transected with the two ends held together by the remaining strip of intact arterial wall.*

We found the victim lying nude on a white throw rug. The crime report records the time of Sherrie's 911 call as 3:34 A.M., and the coroner's report records the time of death as 4:22. In truth, he was probably dead on arrival, under cardiac arrest within minutes of the stabbing. Still, he made a last gasp. He sprang from bed and chased the man who had killed him. He came back to his bedroom and collapsed naked in a pool of his own blood.

Records like this play a nasty trick on you. They dole out enough detail to make your loved one seem more real than he has in years. The coroner's report told me my father's height was five foot ten inches, his weight 170 pounds. Under "distinguishing marks or scars," it noted the little tattoo of a single rose on his upper right chest, the tattoo I so clearly remembered snuggling my face against during late-morning sleep-ins as a little girl. More than any photograph, the cold, hard facts on paper made Dad real again. And that felt like a gift.

The flip side is that the records also make the gruesomeness of what he suffered more real than ever. *We found the victim lying nude on a white throw rug.* Bare and bleeding and clutching your throat—there are worse ways to die, but none that I can feel on my own skin, that I can see with my own eyes. Reading those words, I wanted to go back to that night, to cover my father with a sheet, to hold him and tell him I loved him.

I had two bad dreams that night—or at least two that I remember. The first one was new. In it, my mother and my aunt Kathy were staying with me in the house where my father was killed. Then they told me that they had to leave to live in their own houses again, and that I would have to stay in the house where Dad was murdered, alone. My reaction was sheer terror. When I woke up, I decided the dream was an obvious metaphor for having to "live within" Dad's story as I struggled to make sense of it.

But it was the second dream that lingered longest in my mind, the familiar dream that Dad hadn't died after the stabbing but simply hadn't wanted to see me all these years.

As with every other time I'd had this dream, I woke up crying.

LOVE AND SYMPATHY:
FEBRUARY 2003

I STOOD OUTSIDE MY GRANDPARENTS' DOOR one foggy Merced morning, relieved to find the family room's vertical blinds drawn shut. The valley air was cold and damp, but I was in no hurry to knock.

If the blinds were closed, Mae and Ben hadn't seen me walk up the brick path that led through their tidy front yard, and I could stand at the door for a moment and gather my courage. Or I could turn around, retreat to Mom's house, call and explain that I didn't have time to stop by after all. They were expecting a routine visit, one of those tours of familial duty grandchildren have to give when they're in town. But I had come to Merced specifically to see them, and I had dreaded it all week. I had to try to talk openly with them, to see if it was possible, about the murder.

Sixteen years had passed since Dad's death. We'd been silent about it for so long that I figured the topic was too painful for anyone on my dad's side of the family to discuss amongst themselves, let alone with me. I'd sit in my apartment at night flipping through my solitary photo album of Dad, overwhelmed with questions and curiosities, but then I'd think of Grandpa Ben's close-lipped demeanor and Grandma Mae's loudmouth theatrics. He'd glower and she'd bellow. I imagined being driven from their home in shame, undoing years of slow and steady work toward feeling comfortable in their company again.

I'd been working to fit in again with the Howard clan for at least six years, placing strategic phone calls, sending occasional cards, and showing up in Merced most Christmas Eves. I'd sometimes taken along significant others to buffer my discomfort. Now I had a fiancé to hold the floor, to fill in dangerous silences with silly jokes when I felt a threatening topic looming. With Bill by my side I had started seeing Mae and Ben more often. But still I feared an explosion between us. In part this fear was born of a desire to hide my own persistent pain over Dad's murder. And the hazard of broaching Dad's death was very real, though the true danger was not Mae and Ben's anger, but my own.

The anger had burst through just six months earlier, at Mae and Ben's fiftieth wedding anniversary. Mae and Ben had organized a big family reunion at Lake Tahoe, and Bill and I had been assigned to share their cabin. The night we arrived, just before bed, Mae said she remembered something she'd been meaning to tell me.

"Darndest thing," she said. "Nanette's husband, what's his name— last name Ontis. He died. Motorcycle crash up in the foothills."

I was dumbstruck. I had met Nanette's husband Don only a handful of times, but I was flooded with concern for Nanette. How could yet another tragedy like this befall her? And her two daughters—I knew too well what it was like to lose a father.

"My God. When did this happen?" I said, as Grandpa Ben stepped into the room.

Three weeks earlier, it turned out. And my grandparents hadn't called to let me know. It wasn't as if they hadn't realized I would care, either. "I told you not to tell her tonight," Ben said, shaking his head at Mae like a teacher at a wayward pupil. He looked at me, stern. "Don't go making a big deal out of this and ruining the weekend."

This set my eyes ablaze. This was the unstated central tenet of my grandparents' code of behavior that had for so many years intimidated and confounded me: Strong emotions were not to be indulged. To show deep sadness or concern was to be melodramatic. I had sensed this from the moment I had watched Ben step outside to cry over Dad's death, alone. And I had kept my feelings about Dad's loss hidden because of it.

"Nanette's a tough old broad," Mae said. She meant it to console me, but it only hardened my disgust at what I saw as callousness. "She'll be fine. And her kids will get Social Security. What is that, Benny, something like five hundred or six hundred dollars a month?"

It was all I could do to stay seated. The discussion was not just about my supposed overreaction to Nanette's bereavement anymore; the discussion was now about me. Was that how they had thought of me after Dad died, doing just fine with my $500-a-month Social Security? "I know how much Social Security is," I said, glaring. And then Bill put his arm around me and I decided to shut up. We turned out the lights shortly after that, not talking, each jab of the sofa bed's steel frame only stoking my agitation.

I woke up the next morning still furious, cursing under my breath as Mae and Ben left to take the youngest cousins on a pony ride. But that afternoon I found the missing piece I needed to calm my anger. Just before Mae and Ben's big anniversary dinner, I flipped through the photo album they'd brought. Black-and-white shots from the fifties showed Mae, in horn-rimmed glasses and apron, with three strapping kids. These were my father's older siblings, Dana, Dennis, and Ric. Scanning their faces, how much they looked alike, I remembered what I'd always known but rarely considered: They were my father's half-siblings.

Mae's first husband had been killed in a car crash. She'd met Ben Howard after he'd enlisted in the air force, through her sister in Kansas City; they'd become pen pals and spent a weekend together in California. Ben quickly asked her to marry him. He was seven years younger than she and lonely, and he liked her long legs. She had her three children travel out by train. They hit it off with their new dad and never questioned him, and he treated the kids as his own. They moved to various air force bases in California, and then overseas to be stationed in England, and finally settled in Merced, near Castle Air Force Base. My dad and his younger brother, Brad, arrived along the way.

I'd known the story. But that weekend at Lake Tahoe was the first time it occurred to me that Mae had lost her first husband, that his death must have been horrifically difficult for her. It was the first time I realized that she had faced great pain long before losing my dad, her son Stan, and that pain had shaped her stiff-upper-lip worldview: Just keep pressing on. My grandfather, for his part, was a born stoic, and so they fit well together. And their shared perspective, that life is difficult and that we must simply keep going without self-pity, that we must look out for number one, kicked into high gear after my father was killed. It helped them keep their sanity.

The children and grandchildren and great-grandchildren of Mae and Ben Howard came together for a lovely dinner overlooking the lake that evening. Grandpa Ben made jokes about how Grandma Mae still had sexy legs. I marveled that they'd stayed happy together through so many years and one potentially devastating shared, unresolved loss, their son's murder, and I felt happy for them.

But driving home with Bill the next day, the anger returned. "It's all insensitive at best, callous at worst, right?" I demanded, as Bill navigated our rental car around the Sierra Nevada's hairpin turns. "I mean, about the child support. Did they think that way about me?" Indignant questions overcame me: Why had they never asked me if I was doing all right after Dad died? Why had they never said "This must be hard for you" or "We're here for you if you need anything"?

Bill, to whom I'd felt so grateful for his buffering, was only haplessly worsening my state. "They look out for themselves," he said, but he didn't sound derisive. "Maybe that's what they needed to do. They lost their son. That's a tough thing. People freak out over that kind of thing, divorce, commit suicide, slide into depressions. They look genuinely happy."

He was saying all the things that had struck me last night, after flipping through the photo album. They were all true, but I hadn't fully absorbed them yet. I gave up my argument and stared at the winding road, arms tightly crossed in protest. But as the green forest retreated, as my grip on my elbows loosened, I remembered the photo album, Grandma Mae's dead first husband, the fact that perhaps nothing could be harder than losing a child. I was still angry, but I felt a growing love and sympathy too.

And I knew that in the end love and sympathy would always win out.

That weekend in Tahoe was still fresh in mind months later as I knocked on Mae and Ben's door, on a mission to talk about Dad's death. I thought of the portrait hanging just across from the foyer, Dad rendered in oils from the shoulders up, looking especially broad-chested, gold necklace glinting and mischievous smile gleaming. Grandma had commissioned that portrait when I was in junior high, as a tribute to Dad's memory. It had become the bane of my relations with Mae and Ben, standing sentry over the entrance and daring me to deny my grief every time I visited.

Grandma had assembled a photo album for the portraitist to give her an idea of Dad's "spirit" and passed the album on to me once the painting was done. Most of the photos were of Dad, but a solid third or so were of me, from birth until the year Dad died. "I put so many pictures of ya 'cause you always were the greatest love of his life," Mae had said. It was a sweet sentiment, but back then it had made me recoil with shame and embarrassment, too afraid to acknowledge my love for Dad, or my grief.

It took a while, that February morning, for Mae to shuffle to the front door. "Benny, look who's here!" she shouted, and I hurried through the foyer and past the portrait.

Mae and Ben were in the midst of their usual routine: sitting across the kitchen table from each other filling out crosswords, clipping coupons, and playing Skip-Bo. I blew on a cup of Lipton as Mae rambled on about Cousin Jillian's softball team and trailed Grandpa to the living room when he felt a need to stir the fire in the wood-burning stove. But he never traveled farther than Mae's earshot. I let one chance after another to broach the subject float awkwardly by. "So whatcha been doing?" Grandpa asked as he flipped through the paper.

"Nothing," I said, eyes averted.

"Nothing?" he chuckled. "Huh, nothing." He was onto me. He turned to his page and started meticulously extracting an advertisement for tube socks, folding the edges before tearing.

I burned my tongue on the tea. I glanced at the microwave clock and saw my window of opportunity shutting. I stared as Mae turned back to her subject du jour, bladder irritation. At seventy-nine years old, she had been diagnosed with cancer of the bladder and had just finished her last round of hormone-injection therapy. If that failed, she'd need to have her bladder removed, but her doctor felt an operation at her age was risky. "And when I pee I have to fill the toilet with Clorox before I flush so that my medicine won't get into the sewer, see?" she explained. Even though I was concerned for her health, I cut her off, and not just because I'd heard enough about her urinary routine.

I blurted it out: "I'm writing about Dad's murder."

"No kidding," Grandpa Ben said.

"Well, I'll be," Mae said. They weren't glowering or bellowing.

"You don't mind?"

"Nah, why should I mind?" Grandpa Ben asked. "I never did anything wrong."

At that moment, my face flushed with relief, I started to believe that he had a point.

We talked for three hours. Grandpa Ben would start to remember something from just after the murder, and then Grandma Mae would interrupt his telling with some tangent. "Hey, I'm talking," Grandpa would snap.

"Oh, all right, don't be such a horse's bottom," Mae would fire back. They each wanted to get in their piece, like the passersby who hold up "Hi Mom!" signs for the nightly news cameras. And I realized at that moment that they'd obviously wanted to talk with me about the murder for years. Their attempts had been clumsy, but I'd been the one to turn them down, casting my eyes on the floor, quickly changing the topic, visiting less frequently. Now that I was ready, they were thrilled to oblige.

We didn't talk much about the facts of the murder. The detectives hadn't interviewed them in any great depth. But as I had slowly come to suspect, they had never liked Sherrie, and it didn't take long after Dad's death for them to want her gone forever.

"See, we had your uncle Ric's friend helping out, whatchee's name, Tom," Mae said. "And soon's we turn around, Sherrie and Tom are hugging and kissing, lovers."

Ben dropped his head. "They'd turn back up at the house real late, after cleaning, and I'd hear them partying and carrying on in the den," he said. "And in the morning I'd come out and find all my good liquor gone."

"You see," Mae said, "Tom was into bad stuff back then. But he's cleaned up now, nice wife and kids. He was a good guy in a bad spot."

A week of living with Sherrie under those conditions, Mae said, felt like six months. After just seven days of her drinking and running around town with Tom, Mae told Ben she couldn't take it anymore, couldn't move on with that woman living in their house. The ink had barely dried on the *Merced Sun-Star*'s final Howard-murder update when Mae and Ben turned Sherrie and Bobby out on the streets and never saw either of them again.

We seemed to have reached a dead end. Except there was someone other than Sherrie who I wanted to hear about, in detail. "What was my Dad like?" I asked. Until I said it, I hadn't realized that he was almost more mysterious to me than his third and final wife.

Grandma heaved herself up from the chair and trudged into the den, opening a cabinet in the bookcase and lugging out a tall, edge-battered cardboard box. I took it from her arms and carried it to the kitchen table. It was full of old photographs floating loose like last month's newspapers. "I've been trying to get all the grandkids to come over here and grab what they want out of this box," Grandma said. "Take as much as you like. I've got too much junk piling up."

We started extracting stacks of photos to file through as Grandpa returned from another round of stoking the fire. Underneath the first layer of photos lay a sepia-toned eight-by-ten. I took it out and gasped with delight. "Check it out!" I said, moving it to the center of the table. It was a shot of Dad's wedding to Nanette, stamped *Nov. 1979* on the back. Everyone—my aunts and uncles and grandparents—stood in a wobbly line with their arms wrapped around each other's shoulders. Nanette's lace dress draped to the floor, and her long brown hair bore a crown of red roses, but Dad was obviously the star of this show. He wore a white tuxedo with extrawide contrast lapels, and an idiot-savant smile.

Ben stood toward the edge of the photo. "Get a load of that striped tie!" I said, pointing at his car-salesman getup. He picked up the photo between his thumb and forefinger and gazed at it thoughtfully. A grin crept across his lips.

"That was some tuxedo," he said, shaking his head at Dad's fashion statement. But from the concentration in his eyes I could tell he was studying Dad's face, not his clothing.

"He looks like he was a handful," I said. "Was he your most difficult kid?"

"Well—" Grandpa Ben said, but Mae cut him off.

"You betcha! He always told me, 'Mom, I don't never want to be a teenager, because they're ornery and nothing but trouble.' He was the most lovable kid. Everyone loved him till he got to be a teenager, which he never wanted to be."

So my father's immaturity hadn't just been a product of my imagination. He'd never wanted to grow up, and he hadn't.

He squeaked through grammar school and tested off the charts in verbal skills, Grandma and Grandpa said, but when high school rolled around, he could barely sit still for test-taking. He grew his thick, wavy hair to his shoulders, against dress code. When the principal threatened to dismiss him, he went to live with his older sister, Dana, twenty miles away rather than get a haircut.

I picked up an old picture of Dad standing in front of his Dodge pickup, wearing his cap and gown with Grandma Mae smiling next to him, tickled by sheer surprise. "I told him I'd believe he was actually graduating when they put the diploma in his hand," Ben said.

But the diploma came. Gainful employment didn't, even with my mother and a baby to support. That's where the janitorial business came in. "I was *not* going to have anyone in my family on welfare," Grandpa Ben said. "And the one thing I knew how to do was clean up." So he helped Dad and Uncle Brad start Howard's Janitorial Service and in effect became their boss, one who would never fire them.

"Your mom wanted more than to be the wife of a janitor, and I guess I don't blame her," Grandpa Ben said. It was the only sympathetic thing I'd heard him say about Mom in years, and it sounded sincere.

Grandma Mae looked up from the photo of her and Dad and jumped back in. "You know, I don't know if Stan really loved any of his wives, but he sure did love you," Mae said, squinting at me. "He was just crazy 'bout you."

Grandma Mae had said this to me before. She'd said it to me half a dozen times over the years, catching me red-faced and shameful in front of other relatives, or alone and on the spot, trapped. She'd said it the day she'd given me the photo album she'd assembled for Dad's portrait. I hadn't ever really heard it or dared to think how much she meant it. I'd thought of it as a paltry stand-in for the things she hadn't said that I'd always wanted to hear, things like "We're here for you" or "That must have been hard for you."

This declaration of Dad's love was what she had to offer instead. For the first time I felt that I could take it rather than leave it.

But Mae was not one for sentimental pauses. "I've got to use the potty," she said, struggling up from her chair. That left me alone with Grandpa Ben, who rose to place his dishes in the sink and put some distance between us. Without Mae present to buffer us, I didn't really have anything to say to him. The room turned so quiet that we could hear the fire crackling in the den. He chuckled nervously. "You sure are looking skinny," he said. I said thanks but floundered for anything to add. It didn't matter. I just wanted to stand alone with him, no matter how uncomfortably. I hadn't loved Grandpa Ben for a decade. I'd thought of him as someone I ought to love, someone I would try to love. Now, after hearing how my dad gave him hell, how he worked so hard to help Dad keep his life together, I understood his deep affection for my father, and I felt my own love toward Grandpa again because of it.

We heard the toilet flush and Grandma Mae came blustering back into the room. We resumed our places around the kitchen table, Mae rifling through another stack of photographs. She took out one of Dad dancing with Grandma at his wedding.

"He didn't know how to dance but he faked it just for me," she said. "He could convince people he knew anything.

"And you know," she said, as if just remembering, "right after he died, I saw his ghost, plain as day. Remember, Benny? I fell right out of the bed."

"Yeah, I still have dreams," Grandpa said. "We'll be at some grocery store trying to wax the floors and it's not going right. It's so real, those dreams. He says, 'Don't worry, Dad, I'm all right.'"

"I think I'll see him again," Grandma Mae said as I slid a pile of photos into a manila envelope and tucked my notebook into my purse. "We'll have a dance."

Ben stayed in the kitchen as Mae walked me to the door. Had Grandpa followed, I would have had to rush through the foyer, past Dad's painting; I was still fearful of showing much emotion around him. We had broken through to each other, but the awkwardness would take years to dissolve, if it ever did. But with Mae I felt a new boldness. I stayed in the foyer to hug her and took a look—not a long one, but not a surreptitious one either—at Dad's smiling face before stepping back into the fog.

COLD TRAIL

THERE IT WAS AGAIN: my father's face, on the front page of the *Merced Sun-Star*, staring out with a serious air in grainy black and white. The photo surprised me—I'd hoped for a three-paragraph news brief and an obituary, at best. But I recognized the shot at once, both from seventeen years ago, when a framed enlargement of the image had stood on display during the funeral party, and also from just half an hour ago, when Grandma Mae and Grandpa Ben and I had sat at their kitchen table, digging through old photos in an effort to reconstruct the major facts of Dad's life. In the original three-by-five, beneath the newspaper crop, Dad was holding a pair of European-cut underwear he'd received as a Christmas gift from Nanette. Whoever took the shot had obviously caught Dad off-guard—he held his lips parted as though about to say something, not smiling but still handsome, incapable with his thick black hair and confident eyes of taking a truly bad picture. Still, the unposed position, the mug-shot-like bewilderment—you knew it was the hastily selected photo of a dead man.

'FAMILY MAN' KILLED IN STABBING. A jolt of pride ran through me as I squinted at the microfiche machine's screen. My dad had made the front page, above the fold, as they say in the newspaper industry. I surveyed the orange-walled confines of the Merced Public Library, wondering if anyone on the sparsely populated second floor was seeing what I was, registering the small thrill. Two previous news items had proved disappointing, as anticipated. The day after the murder, the headline MERCED MAN STABBED TO DEATH had run on the *Sun-Star*'s third page, beneath a puff piece about locals trying out for the new *Fresno* TV miniseries. An item on the facing page listed the week's top pop hits: Patti LaBelle's "On My Own" and Madonna's "Live to Tell" dominated familiar tunes from Billy Ocean, Whitney Houston, and Simply Red, each playing through my mind as I scanned the titles. The juxtaposition amused me, but also insulted the importance of Stan Howard's life. Now it seemed his case had simply been waiting for the limelight.

The periodicals librarian peeked over my shoulder. "You found him," she said, as though gratified to see her years of filing efforts finally utilized.

"I did." Shame and excitement—even some excitement at my own shame—ran through me, and I was glad to have someone to share it with. I'd liked this matronly librarian with her frizzy red hair from the moment I'd walked up to her counter and slapped down my driver's license as collateral for the microfiche. She'd offered to let me use the phone for free when I'd realized my wallet was nearly empty, and that I had no money for photocopies; my grandmother, I said, could bring me quarters if it turned out I needed any. The news items were short enough to write down: address of incident, detective on the case, time of death, "no other details of the case were available." But this front-page story I needed in its entirety. I wanted to frame it.

"Do you want to make a copy?" she said. I thought I heard a tenderness creep into her voice. She'd read the last name on my driver's license and helped me search for articles on "Stan Howard." Now that the headline was screaming "murdered," surely she had realized the dead man was my father.

"About using your phone . . . ," I said, but the librarian waved me off.

"Nah, a few copies is no big deal," she said. Sympathy, I thought, had its benefits.

I printed the front page, the 1970s equipment wheezing and sputtering as the librarian retreated to her desk.

"It just seemed so senseless." The quote was from Sherrie.

"It was just an ordinary Saturday night for the family of Stan and Sherrie Howard," the article began. "He was a real homebody," Sherrie told the reporter, who described our evening spent at the stock car races, followed by dinner, a movie, and murder. The article grasped at any tidbit that would paint the picture of a happy home: the couple's recent first anniversary, Dad's service as a Cub Scout master at Weaver Elementary, where Bobby went to school. It referred to Bobby as "Robert Howard." It misspelled my name "Rachael" and inaccurately described me as a fourth-grader at Weaver. It made Bobby sound sweet and pathetic. "At least Dad got to see my honor roll," he told the reporter. No one else—not my grandparents, not me, not any of Dad's brothers—was quoted.

But the details of Dad's case were intact. A "serrated blade of a steak knife" was removed from Dad's throat. The intruder most likely entered through the back sliding-glass door, and took the knife from a kitchen drawer. Sherrie provided an elaborate theory for the intrusion, explaining that Dad's truck had not been parked in front of the house that night. "Maybe whoever it was thought the children and I were home alone. He was quite a man," she told the paper.

Police dogs had picked up the scent of someone who had run through the empty field behind our house, but quickly lost the trail. The newspaper quickly lost the trail too, I discovered as I forwarded the microfiche.

Another article ran on the front page the next day, sans photo. DEATH IS SURROUNDED BY MYSTERY it proclaimed. This time the *Sun-Star* quoted the detective on the case. "We still haven't come up with anything," Sergeant Hector Garibay reported. Investigators had "combed the area, canvassed the neighborhood, and conducted numerous interviews." That was the sum total of his update.

Another quick flash-forward through the microfiche revealed that by Thursday, Stan Howard had been relegated to page three. STILL NO SUSPECT IN HOMICIDE CASE the follow-up lamely declared. "It looks like it's going to be weeks and weeks of hard work for all of us," Garibay said, offering a cliff-hanger final line.

Except in truth the story was over. An obituary had already run. Another obituary had run correcting the mistakes in the first one. This dead-end update would be the last time Stanley Paul Howard ever made the paper.

I tucked Dad's front-page story inside my folder, careful not to fold any edges or leave the top of the page hanging out. But I no longer wanted to frame it. My misspelled name, the "happy home shattered" myth, the stereotype of the bereaved widow, Sherrie's boasting over my father's intimidating masculinity: None of it squared with my memory. This didn't shock me, because I'd worked as a journalist the last five years, knew from experience if not personal practice the way reality got manufactured into cliché. A reporter molds the incident to the stock story at hand. But had there ever been any truth to that cliché? Had Sherrie really believed that we were the happy family torn apart by tragedy?

I was overcome by a sensation of being watched, fearing that my thoughts could be heard out loud or read on my face. Even the guy filling out a crossword three desks down looked suspicious. Without thinking, I turned the knob to rewind the microfiche—and wound it forward rather than backward, whipping it through the spool that had connected the two reels. The librarian clucked and shook her frizzy, braided hair when she saw what I'd done.

"I'll have to rewind that by hand," she said as I offered fawning apologies. "It takes forever." She sighed but smiled, like a mother only lightly irritated at having to clean up her toddler's spilled milk.

"Thanks so much," I said, and left her there, wrapping the film on the spool and preserving the cliché of Stan Howard's murder for whatever phantom researcher cared to look it up.

RIC'S DIAGNOSIS

AFTER VISITING THE LIBRARY I decided to see my uncle Ric.

Ric lived in a 1980s tract home about six blocks from Mom's new place. I'd been there once, twelve years ago, when he married his second wife, Debbie, in his backyard. The house had seemed bigger then, but it was still classy by Merced standards, with clusters of birch trees and rocks imported from the foothills, the ultimate valley landscape status symbol, arranged in miniature groves in the front yard. Debbie had financed it by pulling down $80,000 a year as a loan officer. That was high-rolling money for Merced, and Ric was proud of his spouse's breadwinning abilities. He was still managing the Madera Savemart, putting in two more years to collect his pension. His life had found new meaning with Debbie. Ric was tall and wide, with beady, dark eyes and Afro-curly hair. Debbie was slim, with close-cropped hair and a plain but attractive, always makeup-free face. She was coaching club softball and sending teenagers on scholarship to the best colleges. She was going to wait until Ric hit retirement and then go back to school to coach university-level.

We sat at Ric's kitchen table as the NCAA basketball play-offs blared on the TV. Ric was eager to talk, to lay out a theory about my dad he was burning to share.

"He was what you would call now attention deficit disorder," he said. He said he only knew this because Debbie's eighteen-year-old son, Dustin, had ADD, and he'd watched him struggle with it for the last decade.

Ric had done all the reading on the disorder and felt firm in his posthumous diagnosis. Dad had all the classic symptoms: lack of concentration, outgoing demeanor, complete inability to comprehend consequences or see a longer-term picture.

"Stan didn't have anything he was going to plan for in life," Ric said. "And when ADD folks like something, they like it too much. He got into things and took them to the extreme. You know, he took up weight lifting and within a few months he was buffed. He lived for the moment. You don't run off to Reno and get married at a moment's notice again and again if you're right in the head."

I had to agree with Ric on that last point. And ADD explained a lot of things. It fit neatly with the nervous habit of rocking back and forth Mae and Ben said Dad had. It fit with his utter unsuitability for employment. Ric had thought out his ADD theory to the last symptom, and the case was compelling. It didn't erase the pain I'd felt when Dad had shunted me to Mae and Ben's back in second grade, or when he'd seemed oblivious to Bobby's and my needs that summer before he died. But it gave a deeper reason for the failures, one more comforting than the thought that he hadn't really loved me.

Like your classic ADD kid, Dad had fought hard and made up sheepishly, Ric said. One high school morning when Mae was trying to get Dad up for school, Ric heard him shout, "Shut up and stop being such a bitch." When Ric walked in to defend Mae's honor, Dad threw an alarm clock at his head, so Ric punched him in the nose. They were sworn enemies for all of eight hours, until Dad came home from school and said, "You clocked me pretty good. I'm sorry."

Ric's theories as to who killed Dad and why didn't hold up as well as the ADD profiling. But like Mae and Ben, he felt certain of one thing: Things started going wrong when Dad divorced Nanette.

"It had to be the sex," Ric said of Dad's involvement with Sherrie. "Although she wasn't a good-looking lady at all. But she was so flirtatious." She'd push conversation into inappropriate realms. One day Ric had visited Dad's new house, and Sherrie had dropped a pair of her underwear on the floor while taking clothes out of the dryer. She dangled her lace thong in Ric's face, just as she'd done to me that day shopping at Mervyn's.

Dad was just a drug dabbler, Ric claimed. Dad had never smoked marijuana because he couldn't stand to lose control of his thoughts; when the brothers would go fishing together, Dennis and Brad would end up in "the pot boat" and Stan and Ric on "the alcohol boat."

But Ric and Dad had both gotten into cocaine recreationally. "We'd do a little on bowling night or Sunday afternoon," Ric said. It wasn't a daily indulgence for Dad, who didn't have enough money to support a regular habit, and the way Ric remembered things, the drug use had trailed off by the time Dad was killed.

Our talk was quick and to the point, but friendly. Ric spoke as though he had thought all this through and edited himself to the key points. We'd only been sitting together for twenty minutes or so when I said, "What do you think happened that night?"

"I think someone came into his bedroom for his wallet—he always left it on his nightstand, you know," Ric said. "And then Stan woke up and they stabbed him." That didn't make sense to me given what I now knew about the wound. It had to be hard to get a straight, deep jab like that, and probably near impossible during a hand-to-hand grapple. In my mind, whoever walked into that bedroom did so with intent to kill.

But I didn't dispute Ric's speculation. I hadn't come back to Merced thinking that my relatives held the answer, that they'd simply hidden it from me all these years. I knew they were as baffled as I was, and I just wanted to hear about their frustration, and share in it.

Half-time commercials roared in the background, only underlining the quality of momentary silence between us. And then Ric rolled up his sleeve to reveal a chalk-white, flabby biceps—and in the center of the mild cellulite, a tiny, perfect red rose.

"Oh my God," I said. I recognized it instantly. It was a duplicate of Dad's tattoo, the tattoo on his chest I used to snuggle my cheek against.

"Just like your dad's," Ric said, patting his arm. "I got it on the tenth anniversary of his death. Put it there so I wouldn't forget, so that I hop out of the shower every morning and see this and think of him. It's all about remembrance. It's not sadness anymore."

"I love it," I said.

"Your uncle Brad's got one too. Same rose. And my boy Dustin. And your cousin Jonathan. Your uncle Dennis wanted to get one, but he's too scared of needles."

"I really love it," I said, peering closer at the rose's smooth blue outline and scarlet petals. I meant it. I was touched by the way my family had come together to mark Dad's life. But I was disappointed too. Why was I just now seeing this rose? Why did my younger cousin Jonathan, who barely knew my father, who'd seen him for a few hours on Christmas Eve as a preschooler, have a copy of his rose tattoo when this was the first I'd heard of their group memorial? But, as I packed up my purse and the final basketball buzzer rang, I chose gratitude over jealousy and alienation. I chose to keep myself out of it, to look with appreciation upon Uncle Ric's love for Dad, and to look away from the angering thought that I hadn't been asked to share in it.

Ric walked me outside to my car and hugged me before I climbed in. I wanted to ask him why he hadn't thought to show me the tattoo before. I said "Thanks" and "See you soon" instead. The thought that perhaps next time I could ask him, without recrimination—the very assumption that there would be a next time of talking openly about Dad—provided some consolation.

I drove back to San Francisco feeling strangely whole and settled, the way I had felt at age eighteen when Nanette had taken me to Dad's grave. But the feeling would linger longer this time. And I wouldn't need another eight years to take next steps, to build upon it. I'd come back to Merced when I felt I was ready to hear more about Dad and his murder—which would, it turned out, be only a matter of months.

HOMECOMING

I'D NEVER THOUGHT OF THE VALLEY as a land of scenic vistas, but from the train window every view looked positively pastoral. Unlike the freeway, which pushes past brown fields and peeling billboards, Amtrak's rail shoots through the prettiest part of central California, bucolic horse pastures and cattle ranches with split-rail fences, creeks lined by giant elms. Even as we slowed to stop at the Stockton station, the sight of vagabonds urinating on graffiti-covered fences seemed a minor eyesore when followed by glimpses of the well-shaded downtown park and then, as we trudged away from the platform, two more hours of green orchards and sunshine. I had chosen the ideal time to return to the valley, late May, when the meadows' mustard seed and purple lupine were in full flower and the grasses had not yet yellowed, when temperatures still hovered in the upper seventies. But I hadn't taken the train for the views. Driving was the obvious and preferred way to reach Merced for my immediate purpose: a second rendezvous with the Sheriff's Department. I had other items on my agenda, true; over the course of a week I hoped to talk with more members of my family and with Nanette, to gather as much information as possible about how Dad died. The real plan, though, the true reason I'd taken the train, was much more daunting.

Inside a FedEx envelope filled with pictures of Dad, coroner's records, and old newspaper articles, I carried a yellow slip of paper with Sherrie's current phone number and address. A semiretired private detective, a good friend of a friend, had tracked her down for me three months earlier, eyeing me up and down on his San Francisco doorstep before consenting to run her name through the databases.

"You don't look like you're out for vigilante justice," he concluded, and within days called me back with the scoop. She'd remarried and now lived in one of the tiny farming towns less than an hour from Merced. He gave me her phone number and her address and refused to accept any payment for his help.

I'd tucked the number away for a while and then carried it around with me for weeks, debating daily how and when I ought to use it. I knew I had to call. And I knew I had to call from Merced, so that I could casually ask to see her. I decided I wouldn't tell her I was writing about Dad's death; I would simply claim I'd been thinking about her all these years, and wondering how she'd been, which was true in fact if not in sentiment. My gut told me she'd play it cool and sweet and agree to see me. I wouldn't interrogate her—I was far too afraid of her. But perhaps, under the pretenses of a happy reunion, she would talk about the murder and offer her accounting of what had happened. And perhaps in hearing her talk, looking into her eyes, I would be able to divine whether she was lying, and how much she had to hide.

The plan seemed sound enough when I mulled it over or described it to friends, but when I pictured myself picking up the phone and actually dialing the numbers, my heart froze. I'd have to call her alone, but I couldn't meet her by myself. Besides, my mother, who had begun having nightmares about Sherrie since I'd hatched the reunion scheme, demanded that I take someone, as protection. The unpleasant duty fell to an obliging Bill, but he couldn't leave work for an entire week while I finished the rest of my research and built up the nerve to make the big call. So I would ride the train. When—and truly, if—I called Sherrie and arranged the encounter, he would drive to Merced. We'd face Sherrie together.

My mission was a nerve-wracking one, but I felt wonderfully at peace during the journey to Merced. The sensation was not the self-protective feeling of detachment that I'd known growing up. This was a deeper comfort, one without the nasty side effects of nervous tics and bad dreams. Something had clicked in me during the last three months, since I'd begun talking openly with Mae and Ben about the murder. Now that I had their support, new revelations couldn't hurt me. And Merced itself, once so threatening with all the memories it held, suddenly seemed positively welcoming.

My mother was at that moment living in Los Angeles with her new husband, about to head to a traveling-nurse gig in Miami. I was staying in the Merced house she owned and shared with her mother, my grandma Dirks. Grandma picked me up at the station and I dropped her off at the Senior Center for afternoon bingo and cruised around town, getting my bearings. Merced was on the verge of big change. The water tower downtown now read, in black block letters, HOME OF UC MERCED. In three years, if construction went according to schedule, a sprawling new University of California campus would rise about six miles northeast of downtown, on the shores of Lake Yosemite. I knew the college was either the city's economic salvation or moral downfall, depending upon whom you talked to. Mae and Ben looked forward to a wealth of new jobs and booming property values—which I knew, after the purchase last year of Mom's new Merced home base, had already started rising. Nanette, however, spoke despairingly of the new campus and how it would ruin "the character" of little Merced forever.

Most of the city, though, had been gearing up for years for the new UC era. My circuitous drive—the town was compact enough to canvass in just over an hour—took me past the mammoth new Costco, and that inevitable symbol of a small town that has betrayed its own soul, the just built Wal-Mart. Way over on Olive Avenue, on the north side of the city, I stopped for a latte and stared in wonder at the thriving Starbucks. Mom and Frank liked to run in for coffee when they were in town, and a few months ago, they said, they'd struck up an interesting conversation with a sociology professor. He was in Merced to research small-town demographics, and the new Starbucks made a fascinating case study. It shouldn't have worked, he said—the people of Merced just don't buy luxuries, don't go out for meals that cost more than $10 or dream of shopping anywhere other than Target and Sears. But here they were, clamoring for $5 Frappuccinos. Amazing.

In the heart of Merced, though, the area near downtown where I had spent my preschool days, astonishingly little had changed. The rose garden two blocks from the tiny brown house on Twenty-fifth Street was bright with blooms as though taunting the harsh temperatures that would hit come June. On my bedroom window at the old house I spotted the rainbow sticker I had affixed there twenty-three years ago. Applegate Park was freshly mown. Bear Creek had reached its high-water point. The ash trees lining the civic center's streets had grown imperceptibly taller. I chose a shady spot in front of the Sheriff's Department, five minutes late for my appointment.

The receptionist behind the bulletproof glass called Sergeant Marshall to say his appointment had arrived and directed me to walk out of the building and around the corner to the sergeant's new office. Marshall was waiting for me at the front door, arms crossed high on his chest above his round belly. He uncrossed them and pumped my hand vigorously.

The moment I stepped inside, this meeting with Marshall became an utterly different experience from the terse face-off with the detectives I'd bungled nine months earlier. The new office, a brick one-story, appeared to be a converted apartment. Marshall introduced me to a cheerful secretary who sat in what I guessed would have been the unit's living room. A ceiling fan hung from a flocked cathedral ceiling, chopping the overhead light with a strobe effect, but other than the bars of shadow, everything was homey. "What can I do for you today?" Marshall said like a chipper shop owner, showing me to his back bedroom office. A trio of Thomas Kinkade prints, paintings of cozy cottages twinkling among fuchsia-flowered landscapes, adorned the main wall. A leather-holstered walkie-talkie lay on the middle of the desk. "Can I get you a beverage? Ice tea, Dr Pepper, diet 7UP?"

"7UP's great," I said, pulling out a notepad and making myself comfortable in the mauve upholstered office chair. Marshall reached over to a minirefrigerator and cracked open the soda can. "Thanks," I said casually. I felt at ease, and not just because of the cozy surroundings. I'd brought a lengthy list of questions. I'd take as long as I needed this time. And Marshall would be more cooperative. A few weeks ago I'd called him to say I was writing a book about my dad's murder, and I needed to confirm details with him. I was no longer naive enough to think he'd take me gently in hand and tell me everything I wanted to know. But I guessed he'd be on good behavior in case the contents of our meeting might one day see print.

"I looked up those crime stats you asked for," he said, handing me a page of notes. Static crackled on the walkie-talkie. Marshall held up a finger as if to say "one second," winking a blue eye behind his wire-framed glasses. "Talk to me, whaddya got."

"We've got suspect number four here," the voice on the walkie-talkie said. "We're bringing him down to headquarters."

"So what do you need me for?" Marshall said.

"Just checking in to see I've got proper authorization."

"Authorization? Shouldn't you be calling your wife about that?" Sergeant Marshall the joker was in top form. "Breaking and entering out in Snelling, four intruders," he said to me. "Got three of them right away, then we go back to the scene of the capture to get the GPS co-ordinates and find guy number four hiding in the creek." On his desk facing me was a framed Viagra box and a Magic 8 ball, which he caught me looking at. "Friend of mine gave me that. Said it'd help us improve the way we make decisions around here." He chuckled.

"So this is just your office?" I said. "You the head honcho? What happened to Detective Parsley?"

"Parsley, that stooge! He's retired, he's off riding his horse. I'm sergeant of the major crimes division now, thirteen detectives under me."

"Glad to know I've gone straight to the top."

"That's right. Now what can I do you for?" Marshall lifted a big gray binder, Dad's case file, and laid it open on his desk, just a few tantalizing inches from me.

"Like I said on the phone, I need to double-check some rumors I've heard about my dad's case with you."

"I'll tell you what I can. Just shoot."

I started in at the top of my list. Bobby's interview, the absence of fingerprints, the unidentified hair. We checked them off, one by one. I asked him to tell me the results of Sherrie's polygraph, and he flipped through the file. "We've got several polygraphs in here," he said, thumbing. "I don't see one on her, though."

I wanted to grab the binder and search for it myself. If a polygraph on her wasn't there, if a polygraph had in fact never been taken, it was a pretty big slipup on the detectives' part. But I was also intrigued by the idea of other polygraphs. "Who are the other ones on?"

"That Diaz guy."

I gave Marshall a puzzled look.

"The guy they picked up over on Fifty-ninth Street?" he said.

I kept up the puzzlement.

"Maybe you don't know about that. They picked him up walking along Fifty-ninth Street at three thirty a.m., blood on his hand. He said he'd been in a fight. We brought in his friends and they corroborated his story, though you never do know with shady characters, the way they can concoct stories."

"Was this guy a serious suspect?"

Marshall stopped and looked me dead-on. "Parsley told you, last time we met, just who he believes did it." I knew exactly what he was talking about: Sherrie's brother.

"Did you ever meet that guy, the brother?"

"Sure, we interviewed him a few times. His alibi wasn't too strong."

"What was he like?"

"He's a street guy. Not big, though. Let me see." Marshall turned to his computer screen and started typing. "He's got a record, other small stuff. I'll look him up." He turned from the screen and folded his hands. "Parsley never forgot what he said last time we interviewed him. We said, if you don't come down to the station for a polygraph, we're going to have to keep you on our list of suspects. And he looked at us hard, and he goes, 'You just keep me on that list.' " Marshall said the last line in low, harsh tones for full menacing effect. And yet he offered no evidence.

The walkie-talkie cackled. "Talk to me," Marshall said. The voice on the walkie-talkie said he'd taken weapons into evidence. As he talked, I peeked over the desk at the open case file. Bobby's fingerprints were on the left page. He'd signed his name "Robert Howard." My fingerprints were on the right. Marshall signed off the walkie-talkie with a cheap shot at the detective's Eastern European heritage.

"I'd really like to flip through that case file," I said, narrowing my eyes mischievously. "Maybe you could just go through it and tell me what's in there."

"Not much you don't know. This whole section here, this is finger-prints." Marshall rifled through. "And this is the evidence log."

"Can you tell me what's in the evidence log?" He ran his finger down the page's column, reading it out to me.

"Pillowcase. Blue jeans. Knife. Photos. Curtains. Rug. Blanket. Hair samples." He flipped a few more pages. "And the autopsy photos. I don't want you to see those."

"Autopsy photos? What do they show?" I really wanted, at that moment, to see everything. I felt strong. I could take it.

But Marshall wasn't budging. "You don't want to remember your dad that way. This"—he held up the picture of Bobby, me, Dad, and Sherrie, the photocopy of it Parsley had made when we last met—"this is what you want to remember." It struck me as a melodramatic flourish he'd grown well practiced at.

"But it isn't what I want to remember." I pointed at Sherrie. "Not with her."

Marshall went uncharacteristically quiet and still for a moment. "How things going for you up in San Francisco? San Francisco. Now there's some crime for you."

"No kidding." I told him about the newspaper office I'd worked at on Sixth and Market, the most crime-infested street corner in the city, about the crack deals I'd see go down daily, the handful of times I'd been assaulted on the sidewalk, never seriously. He looked surprised, not at the stories, but at the fact that I was telling them.

"So you're a tough one," he said. I could feel that I'd changed in his eyes, and I liked it. I hoped now he'd tell me more, but it didn't seem there was that much more to tell. I asked him what kind of evidence had been preserved, and he said he'd check out the evidence box and call me with a detailed accounting. I told him I wanted to talk with Hector Garibay, the original detective assigned to the case. He looked him up and tried the number in the computer—it was Garibay's old work number. He said he knew where he lived, near Merced, and that he'd go out there and ask if he'd be willing to talk with me. He wrote down a little to-do list with these items and a few other requests and wrote my number at the top. I doubted that he'd get any of the requests done quickly, but I felt some satisfaction that he was now at least playing at helping me.

"Can I just ask you?" I said. "I know you get a lot of cases these days, obvious drug deals and gang situations, that are hard to solve because no one talks." Marshall nodded and described a few for me, drive-by shootings and such. "But among your unsolved cases, doesn't this have to be one of the weirdest?"

Marshall waited a beat. "Yes, it is. It doesn't fit the mold of anything." I leaned forward as though pleading, secretly hoping that the very mystery of the case might inspire Marshall to investigate it again. But it didn't. The walkie-talkie crackled. I let Marshall get it and then said, "I better let you get back to work."

He walked me to the front door. I didn't feel defeated as I had at the end of our meeting nine months earlier. Marshall was of limited use to me, but he no longer intimidated me. If I needed more facts after this meeting, I would call and ask for them, politely but firmly. If I had a question Marshall could answer, he would. He couldn't answer the one question that stuck foremost in my mind, though. He couldn't tell me if Sherrie had been in on it, either before the murder or after.

"Take care of yourself, kid," Marshall said, and watched me walk to my car. I started the engine and looked at the clock. We'd been talking for more than two hours.

I called Bill from Merced that night. "It's funny, I feel so peaceful here this time," I said. "I'm feeling fearless. I think it's time to call her."

"If you're in the zone," he said, but he sounded hesitant. After all the stories I'd told him, he wasn't looking forward to reestablishing connections with Sherrie. But, like my mother, he understood that it was something I needed to do, that I wouldn't move on until I had. "Good luck," he said.

The moment we hung up, I dug out Sherrie's number and sat with the cordless phone in hand. I couldn't get myself to dial. I imagined stunned silence on the other end, and then a deep, grinding voice, snarling insults and death threats. I snapped back to reality, to the smooth-talker I'd always known Sherrie to be. She'd treat me kindly, even if her sweetness was a sham. It was 7:22. I would call at eight. I opened my notebook and went over my script—tell her you're visiting Merced, you've been thinking of her, all these years . . . Eight o'clock chimed on the living room clock. My hand still wouldn't dial. Five minutes passed, frozen. I felt this heavy sense that the phone call would be irreversible, that the moment she answered, I'd never be able to return to my former state of ignorance. Then it struck me that it was already too late. I'd been moving toward this moment for seventeen years. I could not go forward in my life without facing this woman. I dialed the phone.

It rang twice, and I began to worry about whether I ought to leave a message. Then on the third ring—"Hello?"

It was a deep woman's voice, standoffish, as though uncertain of who could be calling.

"Hi, I'm trying to reach Sherrie . . ."

"This is Sherrie."

"This is Rachel Howard, Stan Howard's daughter . . ."

"Oh my God," she said quietly. She paused. And then louder and faster: "Oh my God. I can't believe it. Oh my God, how are you?" The voice had turned soft and sweet. "Wow. Rachel."

"I know, can you believe it?" I was so relieved at the warmth in her voice that I found it easier than anticipated to carry out my happy re-union scenario. We exchanged more *Oh my Gods*, like long-lost high school classmates.

"I've been waiting for you to call. All these years . . ." Her voice cracked.

"I hope you don't mind, I looked you up in the directory."

"No, of course I don't mind. I knew you would call one day. Oh my God."

"How are you?"

"Pretty good," Sherrie said. "I'm married again, you know, and we farm two hundred acres out here in the country."

"And how is Bobby?"

"Oh, Robert," she said, pronouncing the name flatly. "Robert's fine. He's in Merced. He's got a job now delivering milk. He's got a little girl, six years old."

"Wow."

"You still blonde?"

"No, I'm brunette now."

"Brunette, huh. It's just that the other day I was looking at old pictures . . ." She started sniffling, then out and out crying.

"I'm sorry," I said, feeling a bit guilty over my false sympathy. I was in shock just like her, but miles away from tears or nostalgia. I just wanted to keep her talking. "It's all right."

"You guys wanted to go to the stock car races . . ." She cried harder this time.

"That's right, I remember."

"I've been waiting a long time for you to call. Mae was so weird. I've only talked to her one time, you know, when she called wanting to change the headstone." I remembered that episode well. I wondered if Sherrie would bring up the strange phone call she and I had shared then, or if I should interject it, but she kept going. "You know, I just felt I couldn't let them do that. It was like they were trying to say I never loved him or something." She started crying again. "I miss him, I really do."

"I do too." But I was not about to start crying with her, though her display of emotion was disarming. I was enjoying our talk, finding it easy to go on. I was wondering if she'd never been as ugly as I'd remembered, or if maybe she'd changed.

"I'm in Merced visiting relatives," I said. "And I was wondering if I could come out and see you, in person."

"Of course. I'd love to see you. When can you make it?"

I chose Tuesday, noon. I asked to bring along my fiancé. She said she'd love to meet him. I had her give me directions.

"How's your mom?" she asked when the meeting was set. I told her my mother was traveling the country with her new husband. "I'm so glad to hear she's happy," Sherrie said. I marveled at the response. She had always openly despised my mother. But I didn't question it, partly because I wanted to keep Sherrie on perfectly nonconfrontational footing, and partly—it surprised me to realize it—because I was considering whether Sherrie could somehow, during all those years, have morphed into a nice person.

I asked if Bobby would mind if I called him. She willingly supplied his phone number. "He had a rough patch there," she said. "But I think a guy really doesn't become a man until twenty-five, you know? I think your dad was that way. He had his days running around. I was just glad I met him after all that stuff in his life."

This analysis stumped me. My dad had never been dependable, but he hadn't exactly turned into Ward Cleaver by the time he met her. But Sherrie said it as though she really believed it.

"It'll be great to see you," I said. I gave her my cell phone number in case she needed to get ahold of me. I hesitated, but decided it seemed natural and less suspicious to freely give her a contact number.

"Can't wait to see you," she said, and hung up.

I called Bill immediately. "She was . . . *so nice.*"

"You're kidding."

"Do you think maybe she's changed?" I considered my own question for a moment. A little voice in the back of my mind was speaking out against it. "I mean, some of the stuff she said didn't quite add up . . . but she was so *sweet.*"

Bill and I traded more astonishments. I hung up thinking that it was possible Sherrie had changed, whether she'd had any knowledge of the crime or not. Differences in our accounts were small ones, matters of omission and interpretation, not fabrication. Bobby and I had not asked to go to the stock car races—they'd simply dropped us off there, and the fact that they'd left us unattended was a glaring omission. Another omission: She'd always hated my mother. But perhaps even if her retelling had been selective, had her tears been real?

I reached my mother on her cell phone in Los Angeles and asked her that very question. She was taken aback to hear of Sherrie's warm reception. "Maybe she *has* cleaned up and changed her life, maybe she regrets the way she acted back then," my mother said, but halfheartedly. "What else did she say?" I said Sherrie had asked about her and said she was happy to hear that she was doing well. "You're kidding." Mom's benefit of the doubt had already stretched thin. At that moment it snapped. "She hated me," she said. "She's full of shit. What else did she say?"

We ran down the list of possible half-truths. I told her Sherrie had said she'd been waiting for me to call. "Rachel!" Mom said. "That's a line of crap. Remember that time she called, when you were in high school?" I said I did, a little sheepishly, embarrassed by how easily I'd been taken in by Sherrie's cooing. I told her Sherrie had asked if I was still blonde and had broken down crying. "She wasn't looking at old pictures!" Mom said. "Do you know all the nasty things she said to me? She can turn on the charm. But you still remember what she was like. Trust your memory, Rachel. Be careful."

It was nearly midnight when I said good-bye to Mom. The master bedroom I was staying in had French doors leading to the backyard; I locked both the screen doors and the inner dead-bolt, but neither measure gave much comfort. I turned on the bedside lamp so that I wouldn't have to cross a dark room to switch off the overhead light. Already nightmare scenarios were running through my mind: Sherrie climbing through the bathroom window, easily popping off the screen, knife in hand. I turned out the lamp thinking I could simply pull the covers overhead for security, but I'd miscalculated. The air-conditioning wasn't turned up high enough; the room was stuffy. I couldn't bring myself to walk down the long hallway to change the thermostat; I couldn't do anything except huddle in a corner of the bed beneath the comforter, sealing myself off from intruders. I kept the blankets overhead and sweated myself to sleep.

THE QUIET UNCLE

THE NEXT MORNING I MADE THE MISTAKE of telling Grandma Mae I'd
spoken to Sherrie. We were waiting for Uncle Ric and his wife, Debbie,
to arrive in their limited-edition Eddie Bauer Ford Explorer and drive
us all up to my uncle Brad's house in the foothills of Coarsegold, where
Grandpa Ben had spent the night before. We'd barbecue steaks and
help Brad finish a shelter for his new horse. Of course I had two mo-
tives in going along—visiting family and talking to Brad about Dad's
murder—and I felt a tinge of guilt over my second agenda, which
Mae's absentminded blabbing only made more acute. "Listen, Rachel
talked to Sherrie last night," Mae said as we cruised toward the freeway,
drawing it out sensationally. "And she's going out to see her on Tuesday." The car fell silent.

"No kidding," Ric finally said flatly, as Debbie resumed reading
her paperback copy of *Atkins for Life* without comment. What else
was there to say about this woman they all wished would have just
crawled somewhere and died? Mae asked Debbie to look up the
recipe for low-carb cauliflower "potato" salad, and the discussion
ended.

A few months earlier my mortification would have been paralyzing,
not only because of the taboo aura surrounding the murder, but more
powerfully because of my feeling of estrangement from the Howard
clan. That we were headed to visit Uncle Brad, the most intimidating
of the Howards, would have compounded it. Unlike the other aunts

and uncles, who shared a different father, Brad was Grandpa Ben's son, Dad's full-blooded brother. He was taller and his face was narrower, but he shared Dad's thick black hair and pale coloring, so that, looking into his face, I was always aware that I was talking to someone who had loved Dad as much as I had, who'd been just as struck, if not more, by his death. And Brad was hard to read. Dad had been chatty and outgoing, an incorrigible talker, but his little brother was so painfully shy that he'd maintained an imaginary friend, Charlie the Clown, into his early teens. Even now, getting him to make more than small talk about safe topics like sports or the price of gas required concerted conversational effort.

But I couldn't pass on talking with him. Among the brothers and sisters, he was closest to Dad. He'd worked with him for the janitorial service from the beginning, cleaning together five nights a week, six p.m. to four a.m. He was the only member of the family who had still been seeing Dad regularly right before the murder. And he had spent more time than any of the other Howards with Sherrie, the new object of my obsession.

I hoped Mae wouldn't go on about my scheduled meeting with Sherrie once we reached Brad's house and intensify the awkwardness of my mission. But if she did, I could handle it. I had reason to believe that Brad, the most aloof of the clan, would warm to me. Six weeks earlier I'd mailed him a package. I'd been listening to my Rod Stewart boxed set over and over recently, counting on it to stir up old memories. But I'd lost the fourth album in the collection, the volume that contained hits from the crucial final years before Dad's death. That CD was so important to me that I bought the entire set again to replace it, then considered what to do with the three duplicate CDs. I remembered the life-size cardboard cutout of Rod that I'd spotted in Brad's garage a few Thanksgivings ago and decided to ship him the extra albums with a short note.

Two weeks later a Hallmark card arrived in my mailbox. The return label read "Brad Howard," but I guessed Brad's wife, Lisa, had sent it. So I froze with surprise when I opened the card to find an entire page of writing in Brad's hand:

Hey Rachel!

I was so excited when I received your package. I've been listen-ing to the CDs everyday and thinking about you. We've made our reservations for the weekend of your wedding. It looks like most of the Howard clan will be there. (Party time!) I can't wait. Since I'm in a Rod Stewart mood I'll end this note with . . . "You're in my heart!"

Love ya,
Uncle Brad

This effusiveness was a side of Brad I'd never seen before, and I hoped I'd see more of it during the day's visit. We made our way down the winding road to Brad's property and pulled into the driveway of a small one-story house. It was set on ten acres of rolling wildflowers and oak trees, with clear-sky views of the Sierra Nevadas. The sun was bright but the mountain air was cool. Brad hugged me as I entered the sliding-glass door, but the hesitation in his approach told me he was still good old reticent Brad. He didn't mention the CDs or the card he'd sent.

The house was buzzing with activity to make up for Brad's quiet. Brad's daughter Jillian was primping for her senior prom that evening, and his wife, Lisa, ever the busy homemaker, was going crazy figuring out how to get her to her hair and makeup appointments. Brad's son Zach had just returned from a baseball game, while ten-year-old Megan plunked down in front of the pay-per-view movie they'd recorded the night before. A convenient, quiet moment to approach Brad about the murder wasn't going to just open up as I had envisioned.

So I spent the day surreptitiously tracking Brad's movements, help-ing him and Ben finish the horse shelter, lingering in the kitchen as they marinated the steaks. Hours passed without a break. Ben and Brad cracked open beers and settled in for the Giants game. I looked at the kitchen clock—three p.m.—and saw the day slipping by. I feigned in-terest in the game, listing names of the players I knew. I waited until I felt the coast was clear. "Listen, I hate to ruin your Saturday afternoon, but I was wondering if I could talk to you about my dad," I said.

"I guess so," Brad said, keeping his eyes on the game. He had the slurred speech of a high school sophomore. "I don't know, though, I've gotta run Zach over to his friends in half an hour. We'll have to wait till after dinner." I had a bad feeling the right time after dinner would never arrive. We turned back to the baseball game.

And then during the commercial break, Brad twiddled his beer bottle and stretched his legs. "Makes me sick, that family, hate to even think about them." Of course I knew which family he spoke of.

Grandpa Ben cocked his head without looking away from the game. "I suppose we could file a civil suit," he said. "Where you just go after them for money."

We debated the merits of a civil suit, the lowered burden of proof, what kind of good it would do us. I got the feeling that none of us really had any desire to sue—we were just filling up silence. And I knew that we didn't have enough evidence to sue, and that none of us had any intention to.

"We could put up a billboard, with a big reward," Brad said. "You think those work?"

"Don't know," Ben said.

"I'd pitch in to offer a reward," I said strangely cheerily, eager to be part of the gang.

"How much do you think a good reward is?" Brad asked. "Twenty thousand dollars?"

"You got to put up at least twenty-five," Grandpa Ben said.

"We could put up fifty. That's a big reward," I said.

They considered that a moment and turned back to the game. The Giants were up against Atlanta, one-zip.

The day was a Howard-family idyll of ESPN, home improvements, and Budweiser. Jillian returned in her strapless formal and her glitter eye makeup, and Ric, Debbie, Mae, Ben, and I supplied the peanut gallery comments as she and her boyfriend posed for photos. The steaks were thick and juicy, and all the new Atkins-diet converts laid off the bread. Ric served up fresh strawberries for dessert, showing off his new instant whipped-cream maker. We drank two bottles of wine. And then Mae and Ben got up to head back home, and still I hadn't talked with Brad.

"You coming with us, sweetie, or you want to wait and go with Ric?" Mae said.

I was caught. "We're going to head back pretty soon too," Ric said, and as my face paled, Lisa clued in on the situation.

"Brad!" she said. "You still haven't talked with her? You gotta do that before she goes!" And she ushered the two of us onto the back porch.

I asked Brad to tell me what he could remember about right before the murder. "Your Dad was crazy about fishing," he said. Sweet, but not a promising start.

But with a little prodding, he opened up. I tried leading questions: "What did you think of Sherrie? Did Dad seem happy with her?" As he'd made clear during the baseball game, Brad was not a fan of Sherrie's. "It was just a few months before they got married," he said. "It was just stupid."

"What happened after Dad met Sherrie?" I said. "Did he change?"

"Yeah. He got more stressed-out. And he got flaky." He and Brad would split up cleaning jobs, and Dad would take Sherrie along. They'd complete their rounds sloppily, so that the janitorial service's customers complained. Dad started buying into pyramid schemes and falling for sweepstakes scams. He was always telling Brad about the Caribbean vacations and giant-screen TVs that were coming his way, and how he was going to spread the wealth. He started buying veritable showrooms full of furniture at Sherrie's behest. Financially, he was stretching it.

And then Brad brought up the incident that had lodged most firmly in my mind: the day of the fight. Like Mae and Ben, he couldn't pin down when it happened, before the marriage or after. "I guess I blocked out a lot of stuff I didn't want to remember," he said. I wished he could understand just how much I sympathized. His right eye twitched with nervousness exactly as mine had right after Dad was killed, exactly as Grandma Mae's eye still did sometimes when she talked about Dad.

"Do you remember much from the morning of the murder?" I said.

Brad dropped his head, then lifted a hand to shade his face from the sun. "He'd done so much fooling around after high school—he rolled his VW van, you know. So when I got the call, four a.m., I thought, Stan's in another predicament; it's serious but not that serious. And when we got to the hospital, Dad told me it was all over. He'd seen the ambulance folks pulling up with him, just standing there looking." Brad paused and looked out toward the mountains.

Brad said that he started to wonder whether Sherrie's family could have been involved after he started working as a prison guard in Chowchilla. He'd ask the inmates if they knew anything about this Steve Serrano, but he could never know if the inmates were just playing mind games on him. He called the detectives with his hunch: "The detectives were cold. I thought they were arrogant." They told Brad that Sherrie's brother had had a shaky alibi. But they were curt. They'd never interviewed Brad after the murder and didn't sound as if they wanted to two years later.

"I'm sorry I can't tell you more," he said. "Like I said, I think I blocked a lot of this stuff out. I stopped asking the inmates about him a couple years ago."

I wanted to tell him how sorry I was to make him think about things he'd rather not, but I sensed that telling him that would only make him more uncomfortable. "Thanks for your help," I said. "It really is a big help." And we walked back inside like a teacher and student who'd just been having cross words out in the hallway.

Ric and Debbie had been waiting for me to finish. We piled into the Ford Explorer and drove home, in silence, as darkness fell across the golden hills.

SON AND FATHER

THE NEXT DAY, MAY 11, was Mother's Day, and coincidentally my father's birthday. I'd never been good at observing either. Mom wasn't big into commercial holidays and always asked that I not send her any gifts, a request I all too happily complied with, calling to say hi instead. As for my father's memory, it had never been something that I marked on his birthday or on Father's Day, special occasions set aside for forced contemplation. Instead, as a child, I had tried my hardest not to think too much about Dad, conveniently forgetting the date of his birth. Slowly, through my late teens and twenties, I had come to think about Dad several times a day, every day, but his birthday held no particular significance for me.

Nevertheless Dad's birthday just happened to be the day Grandpa Ben had agreed to take me to the grave. This was clearly a task he was undertaking because he knew he should, for my sake. He was out running errands when I showed up, ready for the drive to the cemetery, and when he walked back into the house, he looked disappointed, as though he'd hoped I'd forget the promise he'd made me. "Your grandma and I went out there just last weekend and cleaned it up," he explained.

"If you'd rather not go today, you could give me directions," I said, digging in my purse for a pen to write them down.

But Grandpa Ben grabbed his sunglasses and headed toward the door. "We better go now. I'm supposed to pick Brad's car up from the shop before five."

I drove the Corolla I'd borrowed from Grandma Dirks. The route was only about five miles, but I knew it would feel like fifty with stoic Ben in the car: through the cow pastures to the east of their neighborhood, over the white wooden bridge that crossed the train tracks, along the street just off Marthella Avenue, the site of Mae and Ben's old home. I talked about my wedding, which was coming up that September, to cut the tension. I wasn't planning-obsessed like the stereotypical bride, but I'd found the happy topic a convenient one for killing silence with my family. "I'm so glad everyone from Merced will make it. I know they're going to love Santa Barbara," I said.

"Yep," he said, barely holding up his end. He sat with his tanned hands folded in his lap, looking absently out the window. "It'll be real nice."

I decided to move on to more substantial subjects. "Have you and Grandma already bought that plot you were talking about?" A few years ago, a few years after Sherrie had called me about the headstone, Mae and Ben had told me they had a new plan for Dad's resting place: not only would they change the headstone, but they'd move him to a new plot next to the one they were buying for themselves. But they'd never called me to follow up on it, and I wondered if perhaps they didn't need my next-of-kin approval after all.

"No, we're going to do that soon, though," Ben said. "We need to move on it because the cemetery's filling up quick."

We drove beneath the freeway overpass, which is where I always lost my bearings. Ben directed me to turn left toward the hospital—the one where Dad had died, though he didn't say that. We crossed another set of train tracks and turned again and I regained my sense of direction. We were on a two-lane road with no gutters and no sidewalks. At the bend up ahead, I knew, stood the funeral parlor. A crowd of diminutive people in black stood outside the little square building, the children among them kicking at rocks on the roadside. "A funeral on a Sunday, strange," Ben said. He searched the faces. "Hmongs. Maybe they have funerals on Sundays."

"I need your help again. This is where I get lost." I had no idea which cemetery entrance to turn into. I had last visited the grave, with Nanette, nearly nine years ago. Counting the funeral, this would be only my third visit to Dad's grave. I wondered if Ben realized that.

"Turn in up there where the sign says OFFICE," he said. "Now it's not too far up here. Pull up next to this shed." I stopped the car and we stepped out onto the shady lane. "Okay, you see that tall headstone over there?" At the end of a row of flat indentations on the lawn stood a three-foot-high marker. "It's about in line with that."

We walked down the row, peering at the little stone markers. "Here," Grandpa said.

The stone was clean. Half a dozen peach silk flowers stood in the vase. "We brought those out here, last week," Grandpa said. They weren't as gaudy as the fake purple and blue blooms on some of the nearby plots.

The plots were packed together, an inch or less between them. I surveyed their markings. Most of them were austere, just a name and date of birth and death, perhaps a cross or a few flowers carved along the border. Dad's headstone was carved so that his name lay among the pages of an open book that formed the edging.

"Pretty," I said, pointing at the flowers. Grandpa Ben looked up at the sky as though he wanted to trudge straight back to the car. But I couldn't let him just yet. I knew he wasn't unfeeling, as I had always feared when I was younger. Back then, too focused on hiding the emotions on my own face, I never looked into his. Today I did, at his thin, straight lips and sharp foxlike expression, his lock of sun-blond hair falling on top of his forehead, so lightly wrinkled for a man his age. His blue-gray eyes were now focusing on the distance. And they were watering. It could have been the glare of the sun, but I suspected otherwise. At any rate, he cast his gaze back down on the ground and his eyes went dry again, no threat of tears.

"Nineteen fifty-four," he said, looking at the stone. "So he would have been forty-nine today. Huh, forty-nine. Can't picture it."

I couldn't see Dad as middle-aged either, though I'd tried many times. "He wouldn't have been happy about heading toward fifty." I felt stupid after I said it. How did I know what Dad would or wouldn't have been feeling in his middle age, any better than his own father? But I needed to say something, to make Ben laugh, to crack some kind of connection between us. "He'd still be fit," I said, but Ben remained silent.

He was staring at the writing on the stone, BELOVED HUSBAND. Those capital letters seemed to echo between us, but neither of us could bring ourselves to acknowledge them. "When you get the new plot, what will you have the headstone say?" I asked. I'd always assumed they'd simply write BELOVED SON; the unspoken exclusion of my relation to Dad hurt a bit, but it would still be an improvement, I told myself, over HUSBAND. And I'd always felt, still did as I stood there with Ben, that I'd never had a legitimate claim on my father. I had been so young; I had remembered so little. Who was I to assert my own attachment to him?

"I suppose," Ben said, as if just reconsidering it, "we'll have it say BELOVED SON AND FATHER." I smiled. I saw Ben smile too, although he didn't look at me. It was a promise. I felt he would keep it.

We walked back to the car slowly, Ben kicking at piles of grass clippings. "Do you still need my signature to move the plot?" I said.

"Yep."

"Then send me the papers as soon as you're ready to do it, and I'll sign them right away."

Nanette's Faith

Nanette had set aside two hours to talk with me before reporting for her evening shift at Rite Aid, and she pulled her red Ford pickup into the driveway of her tiny house at one thirty on the nose. We hugged hastily; we had spent half of the day before together and exchanged our gushing greetings then. For Mother's Day, Nanette had invited me along to a holiday brunch of runny eggs at the Itlo-American lodge with the whole Frago clan: Nanette and her daughters; her sister Paula and her children; her brother, Don; and her mother, Rose. Rose was now eighty and living in a retirement home, though she looked healthy with her soft red-brown hair and freshly pressed white blouse. Her round shoulders stooped badly above her cane, but her innocent smile was still irrepressible. "Do you remember the candle you gave me when you were four?" she asked giddily. I couldn't recall it. "I'll show you after breakfast," Rose said with a wink. "I kept it all these years."

Nanette was cleaning up Rose's old house and moving in, but the place had to be virtually gutted. We stopped by after brunch and Nanette showed me how she'd pulled up the musty fifty-year-old carpets and regrouted the moldy bathroom. The kitchen was still cracked and leaky and stank of stagnant water, but Nanette would tackle that later. And from the window of Nanette's future guest room, the room she had slept in as a child, you could still see the backyard tree that her father had hung himself from. In her future bedroom, the room that had once been her sister's, a chair in the corner held Nanette's high school portrait and, in front of it, the candle I had given Rose as a little girl, which Rose pointed to with a giddiness even her stooped condition couldn't contain.

After touring the house we all caravanned over to the city's massive new Catholic church to attend mass with Rose. When Marina, Nanette's five-year-old, grew restless, I offered to walk her outside, and we spent an hour hunting for ladybugs among the church's roses and in its grand new fountain. The weather had been sunny but not too hot, eighty degrees, and the whole afternoon had been pleasant. I was glad for that, now that I was meeting with Nanette alone and asking her to recount unpleasant things.

Nanette walked me through the backyard so that she could feed her new pet, an Australian cow dog that one of Nanette's coworkers had rescued from a house of drug dealers. The dealers had crudely cropped the dog's ears so that all that remained were grotesque holes on the top of her gray-speckled head. It struck me as just the kind of needy creature Nanette would take in, and it struck me as just like Nanette not to turn cross or say so much as a harsh word when the dog jumped all over her black polyester work slacks.

Inside the tiny house, Nanette offered me a glass of iced tea and we settled into the plush purple living room sofas that had finally replaced the furniture I'd known at the Twenty-fifth Street house. Steady sunshine warmed us through the window, which looked out upon a smooth lawn and a split-rail fence. "I'm going to miss this little place," Nanette said wistfully. "But Vanessa's going to live with us while she goes to community college, Marina's getting older, and we just need more space."

Nanette's life was in the middle of enormous change. In a few months she'd be moving to her first new home in sixteen years, even if Rose's place was actually her old home and only five blocks away. Her oldest girl, Vanessa, would be a senior in high school next year. And of course Nanette had lost her husband Don only eight months ago. A vase of lilies and a HAPPY MOTHER'S DAY balloon sat on her kitchen table, a gift from an admirer she'd dated a few times. "I don't know," she said, considering the gift. "I think I need to be by myself for a while."

She sounded content with that, and I was relieved to hear it. When I'd visited her during Christmastime, five months earlier, she'd seemed deeply fragile and unhappy, snappish, not herself, for understandable reasons. "I just wonder if I'll ever be married again," she'd said after we'd dropped Marina off at preschool. She sounded despondent, and I worried that it might take years for her to recover from Don's death, that she might never regain her natural sweetness. But during this trip she'd acted hopeful and optimistic, excited about moving into Rose's, and full of laughter, her old self. And she looked good, her eyes wrinkled but shining. She was more resilient than I'd ever given her credit for.

Nanette pulled out a packet of old photos she'd assembled for my visit, all happy shots of me and her and Dad, grinning family circa 1980. I felt a pang of panic that Nanette had prepared for a smiling trip down memory lane when I wanted to know, in as much detail as possible, what had gone wrong between her and Dad. But she made clear soon enough that she would not hold back. She'd met him at the county fair, she said. They married quickly. For the first four years we'd been a happy family, just as I'd remembered. They'd worked hard, saved money, and fixed up the house. They'd been trying to have children, but Nanette had so little body fat because of her running regimen with Dad that she'd missed her periods and been unable to conceive. "And then 1984 was the year everything fell apart," Nanette said. Her father had killed himself the spring before, and, yes, she'd had a hard time getting over it. And then the clincher.

"I found them in bed together," Nanette said. She meant, of course, Dad and Sherrie.

I knew Nanette was incapable of lying, but I'd never seen this spill-it-all side of her. I was going to get the full story; she wanted to tell it as badly as I wanted to hear it. And as Nanette recounted it, the story of her divorce from Dad was much more dramatic and heart-wrenching than I'd ever guessed, a year-and-a-half saga of good versus evil, commitment versus quick fix.

It started with what I knew or had already guessed. When Nanette's father killed himself, it struck her a hard blow. And Dad didn't stay the course. As she mourned, he stayed out longer and grew colder. The big new house, the flashy new Nissan 280Zx—Nanette had indulged Dad, hoping to appease him.

What I didn't know was that Nanette never gave up on the marriage. When Dad finally moved out of the new house, Nanette never doubted they'd fix things between them over time. She saw separation as a step toward reconciliation, not divorce. They continued to see each other, and Nanette believed that they were working toward a full reunion. And then one day she dropped by Dad's new apartment and found him having sex with Sherrie.

I could see every detail of the scene in my mind, down to Dad's mouth gaping with surprise and even some pleasure at the glamour of the scandal unfolding, a little boy with his hand caught in the cookie jar. I could see Sherrie's perky, naked breasts and hard gaze, and Nanette standing in the doorway, her unflagging trust devastated. My lip curled with disgust. "It was awful," Nanette admitted. "I think there was just this sexual kind of spell she had on him, from the beginning. And I just felt like, you know, your Dad and I had sex, good sex"—she blushed—"but I don't know, she was something else." Nanette flapped her hand and rolled her eyes. "I couldn't compete."

The discovery left Nanette's self-confidence dashed. But still she didn't file for divorce. Instead Dad went back and forth between Nanette and Sherrie for months. He told Nanette he was through with Sherrie, and they started dating again, working at saving the marriage. Then Nanette stopped by and found Dad and Sherrie in bed a *second* time. Even this did not deal the final blow to her belief in marriage as a holy sacrament, never to be broken. Her faith knew no bounds, and so neither did her forgiveness. "As long as he left her, I still thought there was nothing we couldn't work past together," she said.

Evidently Dad thought otherwise. He and Sherrie moved in together. Mae and Ben embraced the new woman, going along with whatever suited Dad's whim. "I really felt they pushed me aside," Nanette said with disappointment but not a hint of malice, and I felt newly impressed that she still kept on good terms with my grandparents, even dropping by to see them every few months. "I think marriage is hard work and as his parents they should have encouraged him to stick it out," she said. But Dad and Sherrie were moving forward with Mae and Ben's blessing. After they bought a house together, Nanette realized she had no choice but to file for divorce. Dad married the day the divorce was finalized.

I'd never known that Dad had gone back and forth between Nanette and Sherrie for months, and the fresh information cast a new light on the day I had remembered so vividly—the day of the drunken fight. I asked Nanette if she would talk about that day for me, the evening she had come over to Mae and Ben's house and told me that she and Dad were going to work things out. I hoped she could help me figure out when that fight had happened, before the marriage or after. She couldn't, because she had no idea which day I was talking about. "But I remember it so clearly," I said. "My dad had been drunk that morning, and he came back and shut himself in the bedroom with Sherrie—we had to call the cops on him. They took him back to my grandparents'. And I came out and found you on the doorstep, and I was just so happy and relieved to see you, and I gave you a big hug."

But she had no recollection of it. "I came over to your grandparents? Your dad must have called me . . ."

"That makes sense," I said. "And my grandparents remember it too. They say you and Dad drove up to Sacramento for a week to patch things up."

"We never stayed in Sacramento together," she said, finger pressed to the side of her cheek. "Huh, I don't remember any of that."

I knew she wasn't faking her lack of recall, because she'd been so candid about everything else. The day of that reunion, I figured, could simply have been one of half a dozen times they'd attempted getting back together, each incident now indistinguishable in her mind.

The back-and-forth carried on until Dad's death, she said. A few months before Dad died, some neighbors of Nanette's, friends of Dad's, said they had spoken to him. He'd told them he'd made a mistake and wished he'd never left Nanette. He wanted to get away from Sherrie, they said. Nanette was already remarried and had just had a baby. She couldn't go back to Stan now but hoped that he might leave Sherrie and they might resolve the past, as friends. And she hoped she'd be able to see me again; after Dad moved in with Sherrie, they forbade her to contact me. But of course Dad never did leave Sherrie, and a few months later he was dead.

"I always felt she was an evil force," Nanette said, the furrows around her eyes deepening. "Let's just say there was something . . . very unchristian about her."

That, it turned out, was putting it mildly. Nanette still remembered many of the nasty things that Sherrie had said to her, insults that made soap opera catfights sound tame. Once when Dad had left Nanette for Sherrie again, Sherrie hissed, "You snooze, you lose." Another time they'd started yelling at each other in the driveway of Rose's house. "You should go kill yourself like your father did," Sherrie spewed.

"She looked like a black widow," Nanette said, remembering Sherrie at the funeral. Like my mother, Nanette had held her suspicions from the moment she heard of Dad's death, when her mother, Rose, brought over a copy of the *Merced Sun-Star* and showed her the article about the murder. Nanette was so afraid of Sherrie that when the Sheriff's Department asked to interview Nanette, she asked that they meet her at Applegate Park. "I thought she'd had something to do with it," she said. She didn't want Sherrie to see her at the station and know that she had talked.

Much more haunting than her fear of Sherrie, though, was Nanette's pain over the unseemly demise of her marriage to my father. It was a story she felt she was still replaying, I learned after I asked whether Dad had used drugs. He'd gotten into cocaine, Nanette said, while they were separated, just after he met Sherrie. "I have pictures where you can see it in his face," she said. She didn't know whether he had ever quit, or when. "Your dad was a partyer, you know," she said apologetically. "I guess I have a pattern of choosing that kind of guy, or maybe they choose me, for stability, I don't know. Because Don was a partyer, too."

I'd met her second husband a handful of times and thought him nice enough, a bit gruff, with a beer belly, but he seemed like a gentle bruiser, a big bulldog. I hadn't known much about their separation a year earlier, which Nanette now told me had happened after Don had bought a piece of property in Cathy's Valley, an hour and a half away in the foothills. He began staying up there for days at a time, and when he'd come home, he'd act cold and angry toward Nanette. Nanette told herself they were going through a rough patch, holding out hope for reunion even after they'd officially separated, coaxing him into trying couples' therapy. And then last September he'd been struck and killed while riding his motorcycle, intoxicated. At his funeral, a woman in her twenties introduced herself to Nanette as Don's girlfriend. He'd been seeing her for months before he died and had spent his last night with her. He'd told Nanette he was staying in Cathy's Valley that weekend to attend a chili cook-off. Nanette had never guessed there'd been another woman in the picture.

Nanette sank into the sofa, bowing her head. "I don't know," she said. "I have to figure it out, this pattern I have, with men. I mean, am I too boring, or not fun enough?"

"No," I said. "Of course not. You're lots of fun. And you're beautiful. Way more beautiful than Sherrie ever was." Disappointment at my dad welled within me. How could he have been so careless with this kind and trusting woman? I wished he were still alive, so I could chastise him. Jeez, Dad, I'd tell him. How could you have been so foolish?

The other obvious question, of course, was how could Nanette have been so trusting? Twice? But I felt that question was horribly unfair. Her only fault had been to live exactly to the Christian code of feeling and conduct she'd been raised in. What she saw as a right and honest way of living was in fact a radical and dangerous way of conducting yourself in a world where others lied and cheated. But always, she forgave. Of course, she could have seen that my father and Don were not people she could give her trusting heart to. But to blame her for believing in those men—for believing in my dad? I could not do it.

I remembered what my mother and my grandma Mae had both said when I'd mentioned I was going to visit Nanette. "I hope she'll stay single for a while," my mother had said. "I hope she keeps away from men," Mae had said. "She's got bad luck with them." I'd agreed with each of them at the moment, but sitting there with Nanette, I changed my mind. I didn't want her to become defiantly self-sufficient after all. As I gathered up my things to leave and hugged Nanette good-bye, I hoped instead that she'd meet someone she could believe in, someone who would make good on her faith. I hoped she'd never turn cynical or suspicious, that her immense trust would instead be rewarded. It was possible, and she'd earned it.

Nanette called me that night at my mother's house, after she'd finished her shift at Rite Aid. "I've been thinking about our talk this afternoon," she said as Marina begged for chocolate milk in the background. My heart sank. I'd gotten this kind of call before, as a journalist, when interview subjects who'd spoken a little too candidly asked to strike several topics of conversation from the article I was writing. Often I'd struck those quotes on my own—I was an arts writer, not a tabloid reporter or gossip columnist. But if I felt the quotes were legitimate to the piece and I wanted to hard-line it, the strict answer was that they'd been speaking on the record at the time, and they'd known it. I would never use such a policy with Nanette, though. The rules of journalism did not apply to our relationship. Whatever protection she wanted, I would provide.

I took in a deep breath as I prepared for Nanette to list the comments she'd made that had gone too far, revealed too much. But she didn't. "I was just trying to remember as much as I could after you left," she said. "I figured out the date that my father killed himself, if you need it. And I thought of some other things . . ." She wasn't calling to retract information, but to offer me more. I grabbed a pen and a notepad and took notes for ten minutes as she unloaded her thoughts.

"Listen," I said when she was finished. "I hope this hasn't been too painful for you. I mean, I'm sorry to bring up sad things from the past."

"No, it's all right," she said. "I hadn't thought about a lot of these things, and I think it's good to now. I mean, I think it's a good thing, what you're doing."

She understood what I was trying to do, the account of what had happened all those years ago that I needed to reach. She understood completely. She trusted me the way she trusted all of humanity, fundamentally. I wanted to deserve her trust.

Bobby's Bad Times

After Nanette hung up, I kept the phone in my hand. I had been hesitant to call Tom, the friend of Uncle Ric's who had taken up with Sherrie right after Dad died. But now I felt I had nothing to lose. I turned to the page in my notebook where I had written down the number the operator had given me and dialed.

"Tom senior or junior?" a grandmotherly voice asked. "Because Tom senior passed away a few years ago."

"I'm looking for the Tom who was a friend of my uncle Ric Breth," I said. "I'm Ric's niece."

"Okeydokey." The woman didn't waste a moment asking what I wanted, but gave me Tom's home phone and his cell phone, just in case I had difficulty reaching him. I called his home right away and left a message. He called right back. He knew, of course, what I was calling about. And yet he was perfectly friendly.

"I'm not real proud of that period in my life," he said. "But I'll tell you what I can."

Tom had been in his heavy cocaine years when my dad died, when he began helping out with cleaning jobs for the janitorial service. Sherrie latched onto him. "I was being standoffish," he said. "She was—I won't say throwing herself—but being very suggestive."

The detectives tracked them, spying from store windows while they worked, announcing their presence only if they were spotted. After my grandparents kicked Sherrie out, she and Tom moved in together. He was using fiendishly—"That was *my* demon." Six months after they began living together, Tom entered rehab, and a month after he got out, they broke up. A few weeks later Sherrie met Tom's sister's ex-husband, whom she would marry. Tom had had no contact with her for more than fifteen years.

I felt terrible making this obviously good-hearted guy dredge up a past he'd rather forget. "I hear you have a really nice family now," I said, clumsily fishing for a way to make him feel better.

"I'm sorry I can't tell you more," he said. "I was pretty strung out at that time. But if you have any other questions, just give me a call."

About an hour later, the phone rang again. "Hello—who is this?" an angry woman's voice said.

"This is Rachel, Rachel Howard."

"Why are you calling my house?"

"I'm sorry?"

"I've got caller ID, and it says you called my house four times today." She read out Grandma Dirks's number. I understood immediately. I'd tried the number Sherrie had given me for Bobby a few nights before and left a message on a machine answered by a mechanical voice. I had no way of knowing if I'd gotten the right number, so I'd called a few times again, hanging up when the robot woman came on. This night was my last opportunity to catch Bobby before I headed back to the city; I figured I still had a chance of seeing him that evening or the next morning.

"Ohhh," I said as it hit me. "It's okay. I've been trying to reach Robert. Is he there? I used to be his stepsister."

The attack in the woman's voice melted into embarrassment. "I'm sorry. I just saw four calls, and I never seen your number before, you know? Hold on, I'll get him." She sounded young and unsure of herself. There was scratching as she set the phone down, and the sounds of television and a babbling child.

"Hello?" The voice was unmistakably Bobby's.

"Robert?" The name sounded wrong on my tongue. "It's Rachel, Rachel Howard."

"Hey!" He sounded mildly energized, like a teenager giving a friend a high-five. "My mom told me you might call." He talked like an inner-city twelve-year-old, tripping over each consonant. "I sometimes wondered what happened to you." As he said it, I pictured a smile of nostalgia on his face, a face that was still nine years old in my mind.

"I'm doing great," I said. "Actuall, I'm getting married."

"No kidding."

"How are things with you?"

I could just about see him shuffling his feet on the other end of the line. "Maybe my mom told you, I got into some trouble." He gave a little laugh.

"She mentioned. But she didn't say what happened."

"Ah, I got into some drugs and bad stuff. They put me into prison for check fraud. Served nineteen months. They let me out two weeks ago."

"Wow. I'm sorry—but I'm glad to hear you're out. And your mom says you're doing well now."

"Yeah, I got a job driving a milk truck now, see. And a little girl. She probably told you that. Six years old."

"I heard. That's great. I'm sure your daughter is beautiful."

"Yeah, and I'm hoping to go back to school now. To work in electric repair. You go to college?"

I told him I graduated from UC Santa Barbara. "Uh, I dropped out of school at thirteen," he said.

I wanted to say "My God." Instead I just said, "Oh." He said he'd moved around a lot after that—the story wasn't clear to me. But he'd moved back in with his mom later and gotten a GED. And then the trouble started.

"Well, all that's behind you now," I said.

"Yeah," he said, but he didn't sound convinced of it. "Hey, what do you look like now?"

I told him I was brunette now, healthy, five foot six. "How tall are you?" I said.

"I'm six feet. That's funny." He laughed to himself. "Your dad always used to say, 'Bet you a thousand dollars you'll be five foot six.' 'Cause my dad was short, see?"

"Funny. He was a joker." I paused. "That was a scary night, at the house." I was testing. I wanted to see how he'd react to talking about the murder, whether it sounded as though he might have something to hide, or—even better—whether he had insights he'd been itching to share.

"Hell, yeah," he said. "I couldn't sleep with the light off for like forever!"

It didn't sound like he had any inside information. But I still wanted to see him. I couldn't say I felt a rekindling of feeling for him. He'd been a good kid, when we'd lived together, but I'd been too blinded by rivalry to ever develop sibling affection. What I felt was a helpless pity, and I hated catching myself with that condescending emotion.

"I'd like to see you," I said. "Are you around in the morning tomorrow?"

"I go in to work at four a.m."

So I wouldn't be able to see him that night or the next, not without the visit seeming forced and totally unnatural. I told him I'd call next time I was in town. I told him to take good care of himself and his family. I wondered if I would ever see him, and I hung up.

SHERRIE'S STORY

"IF SHE OFFERS YOU KOOL-AID, don't drink it," Bill said as we drove west on the two-lane highway to one of the valley's tiny farming towns. Up ahead a Cal Trans team was working on the intersection; a line of cars and big rigs a dozen vehicles deep had formed waiting to cross, and as we took our place at the end of the traffic, I worried again that we would be late for our noontime meeting with Sherrie.

I laughed at Bill's advice. "Isn't that a great phrase?" I said. " 'Don't drink the Kool-Aid.' " We were happy to be together, ribbing each other as usual. But earlier that day had been another story. Bill had driven from San Francisco and arrived in Merced at one thirty that morning, and instead of acting grateful once we got up the next day, I'd barked at him. He was taking his sweet time getting ready, dillydal-lying over the newspaper at Starbucks, when I wanted to give us two hours to make the forty-five-minute drive to Sherrie's, just in case. And he was wisecracking left and right, imagining our much-anticipated en-counter as some kind of *Saturday Night Live* sketch. "Wouldn't it be funny if we both showed up wearing neck braces?" He raised his hand as though to stab his neck. "Just in case."

"Stop it!" I fumed as we climbed into the van Bill had borrowed from his best friend. I raised my hand to slap him, and not entirely in jest. "This is *serious* to me."

"Don't you think it's serious to me too? After all I've heard? I'm not looking forward to this. I'm just handling it differently."

I'd sat glaring at him, but then started to think he was right. No use turning ourselves into nervous wrecks for the big face-to-face, working up an acute attack of jitters to show Sherrie our true feelings. And so we joked our way toward Sherrie's town, Bill taking cheap shots at the drab country scenery and me defending it, surprised by the nascent protectionism I felt for my native landscape, until we saw the sign— POPULATION 3,900—and the new McDonald's at the corner. We turned where Sherrie had instructed, past the meatpacking building, looking for the last house on the road. The houses, it turned out, were two or three miles apart from one another, freestanding among some of this country's most fertile and uninspiring dirt. "That's it!" I said. "Fence made of wagon wheels, just like she said." I cooed over the cute cows in the front yard as we pulled down the tree-lined gravel driveway. We stopped in front of a little blue-and-white one-story with a swing on its porch and took a deep breath together before knocking.

Sherrie had not gained two hundred pounds as my grandparents had told me they'd heard. She did not look like a tramp, or white trash. She opened the door smiling, arms held wide for a hug, and I swallowed my fears and stepped inside her embrace without skipping a beat. As we patted each other's back, I felt the outline of a substantial bra, not the skimpy lingerie I'd known her to wear, but a practical Maidenform like my mother's.

"Oh my God!" she said, and stepped back from me, bracing my shoulders, to take all of me in. I was scanning her too. She wore a turquoise-and-white-striped shirt and denim capri pants with white leather sandals. She'd gained maybe thirty pounds since her skinny days with my father. Her hair was shoulder-length with square bangs, dyed that unmistakable shade of middle-aged, bleach-out-the-gray blond. Her eyebrows were lighter and more natural, not creepily pencil thin as they had been seventeen years ago, and her skin, though still leathery and wrinkled in a spiderweb pattern around her bright blue eyes, had taken on a healthy farmer's-wife tan. In physique, in grooming, and in attire, she looked like any fortysomething, middle-aged mom—like my own mom, in fact.

"Look at you!" she said. "So tall! And he's tall too!" She hugged Bill. "Come on in, come in."

The house was dark and cool inside. The low ceiling was flocked, and the windows were covered in heavy drapes, parted halfway. Wallpaper trim patterned with blue flowers and mauve ribbons ran along the top of the textured walls. The carpet was obviously freshly vacuumed, though the room smelled of stale cigarette smoke. The house was clean and had a grandmotherly vibe about it, with groupings of picture frames arranged atop walnut furniture. A large television stood to the right of the door, playing a rerun of some eighties sitcom. Sherrie turned the set's volume down to a low mumble, the laugh track fading to white noise, and Bill and I took a seat on the oversize sofa.

"Can I get you guys something to drink?" Sherrie said, bustling around a corner into what I presumed was her kitchen. "Iced tea, lemonade?"

"Water would be great, thanks," I said as Bill shot me a what-the-hell-are-you-doing? look.

"We've got well water out here," Sherrie apologized, rushing back into the living room. "So it's hard water, and it might taste a little funny to you."

"That's okay," I said as Sherrie hurried back to the kitchen. Bill kicked my foot and knotted his forehead. I felt a twinge of panic. Hadn't we discussed this in the car? But hadn't it been a joke? As ridiculous as it was, I honestly felt a tad scared—and Bill's concern, though overblown, appeared genuine.

"How about you, Bill?" Sherrie said. "I've got 7UP and diet Dr Pepper in cans."

"I'll have 7UP," Bill said, looking pointedly at me. Of course, I realized, go for the canned beverage.

"You know what, I'll have soda too," I said. "Dr Pepper's great." Bill nodded at my cooperation, easing back into the sofa as we heard the soda cans pop.

Sherrie returned with plastic highballs for each of us. "This is a great place," I said.

"Here, let me give you the tour," Sherrie said, and we followed her into the dining room, around the corner, and into a large white-tiled kitchen. The house was bigger than it looked, Sherrie explained. She pointed to the far side of the kitchen, where a dark hallway led to three guest bedrooms and a bath. We followed her out a sliding-glass door into the backyard, which held a kidney-shaped, built-in pool. Sherrie's two dogs jumped on us and licked our hands. Sherrie pointed to a big aluminum structure just beyond the fence. "That's our new shed we're building, right there." She sighed. "You know, when you're a farmer's wife, you're always the last to get improvements. I've been asking for new kitchen tile for years, but the shed takes priority. Always building on the farm, and it takes me a decade of begging to get new windows or carpet. The farm always comes first." I remembered all the pricey home improvements she'd talked my dad into funding during their year of marriage. Evidently she'd found a new husband to rein in her spending. I felt my eye begin to twitch and my hands go shaky. I wasn't going to be able to keep up my act. But as if sensing my tension, Bill cut in.

"What do you guys farm back there?" The field behind the house seemed to stretch to the vanishing point.

"Sugar beets, mostly. Sometimes cotton, and soybeans." Sherrie explained how her husband had owned a large dairy and sold it last year, and by the time she was done giving us the lay of the land, my eye had stopped twitching and my hands were steady.

We stepped back inside the kitchen and Sherrie stopped as though newly struck by the shock of us together, seventeen years later, in her home. Although she didn't really seem shocked or surprised at all. There was a coolness to all her reactions. It was as though she were working off a script she'd been studying for years, and I was there playing my part alongside, but being fed my lines one at a time. That was the only explanation I could think of for the sudden way she launched into an apparently random story.

"You know the story of how your dad and I met, don't you?"

"No," I said, though I'd heard from several sources they'd met at the bar on the Merced Mall. "No, I don't know the story, but I'd love to hear it."

"*Well,*" she said, smiling at Bill, "you see, my friend and I had taken our kids, Robert and her little boy, to pick out some new school clothes, and they just wanted to go everywhere. They were wearing us out, you know kids. So we told them to run around shopping while we stopped in for a rest at the Sweetwater Saloon. You know that place?"

I was thinking that sending a seven- or eight-year-old, as Bobby must have been then, roaming unsupervised around the mall was not a good idea. Instead I said, "Is that the place that used to be on the mall?"

"I think it's still there," Sherrie said. "Anyway, I remember a 49ers game was on, and there was your dad sitting with his friend at the bar. Good friend of his, what was his name?"

"Maybe Larry Bell?" I said, throwing out the only friend of my father's whose full name I knew.

"That's it!" Sherrie looked seriously first at Bill, then at me. "And I'm not kidding you." Her voice had softened to a conspiratorial whisper. She held her arms forward as though stroking an invisible hand. "When I walked in and saw your dad at the bar, I told my friend, 'That's him. That's the man I'm going to marry.' " Bill and I looked at each other with gee-whiz eyes to provide the effect she wanted. "And your dad told me later that he turned to his friend and he said, 'That's her. That's the woman I'm going to marry.' " Sherrie paused to let the drama settle in. "No kidding," she said, her voice high enough to crack.

"So we sat there across the bar from each other for an hour or so, and I told my friend, 'Listen, I'm going to get up and go to the bathroom, and you tell me if he checks me out.' And so I got up, and sure enough his eyes were glued to me. And then when I got back, he bought me a drink and we just hit it off, watching the game together."

"That's sweet," Bill said to wrap the tale.

But Sherrie wasn't done. "So we're talking for about an hour, and the kids come back, and it's time to go home. And your dad says, 'Let me give you a ride.' Well, I didn't know this guy, taking a ride from a stranger, you know, but I could just see how sweet and honest he was. So we walked out to his car. You remember that beat-up old truck with the camper shell?"

"Of course," I said. "Baby-blue-and-white-striped, with all that janitorial equipment in the back."

Sherrie threw her head back with laughter. "Not exactly a chick magnet! But he opens up the door, and there's a fishing pole in the cab. And I said, 'Oh, graphite,' because I liked to fish, you know. And his jaw just dropped because I knew about fishing."

"He loved fishing," I said to Bill, shoring up the story's poignancy.

"He sure did," Sherrie said. "Do you remember all the fishing trips we used to go on?"

"Some of them." I had a vague recollection of one, at least.

"Your dad would have us go to the river, and to get to the best spots he'd have us load up in this canoe—a lot of fun until you had to paddle back and carry it back to the car, right? You remember fishing in that canoe?"

"I don't remember a canoe." The canoe, I figured, was true even if I didn't remember it, and asking what I remembered was a natural enough game at a reunion like ours. But I also wondered then if Sherrie was testing how much a ten-year-old could still remember, all these years later. And if she came to think I had gaping holes in my memory, all the better.

"And do you remember our dog?"

"The boxer," I said.

"That's right!" she said as though thrilled to find these common links of recollection between us. "Rocky. You remember the time we took him camping with us?" I shook my head no. "Well, we'd bought this fancy tent with all kinds of zippers, and we left him in there while we went for a walk. You don't remember?"

I had a feeling I knew where she was going with this. This was her explanation for why the dog had disappeared just before Dad died. "And we came back and he was gone. And we just couldn't figure out how he'd gotten out, you remember this now?"

"Huh. I don't. I don't remember it." And then the story took a sharp turn.

"Well, we looked and looked for hours, and finally Rocky comes running back to camp. But we never could figure out how he got out of that tent."

"No kidding," I said as though following her drift. But I was lost. What was the point of this story? Bill looked lost too. And neither of these stories was terribly revealing or damning. The first one, the story of their meeting, seemed appropriate enough if slightly overblown. Perhaps this was what she would offer us all day, sentimental remembrances and non sequiturs, but no speculations about my father's death.

"Should we go sit down?" Sherrie said. We followed her back into the living room.

I peered across the room at the photos next to the TV. "I spoke to Bobby—I mean, Robert—last night. Is that him, in that picture?"

"Here, I'll show you the whole family tree." Sherrie grabbed a pewter tree hung with oval picture frames and ran through each shot with Bill and me: her husband, her husband's kids from his previous marriage, her mother, her father, Bobby's daughter. She didn't bring up her brother, Steve. And then she came to the picture of Bobby. He was smiling, not posed but spontaneously. He was simply a bigger version of the boy I remembered, with the close-cropped hair and the untrusting glint in his eye.

"You know, Robert had a rough patch," she said to Bill. "But the way he was going with drugs, maybe prison was the best thing for him. It was looking like either prison or death, and I think prison saved his life."

Bill nodded solemnly. "I'm so glad he's doing well now," I said.

We heard a car crunching on the gravel, and then an engine shutting down. "Oh, good, that's Andy, that's my husband," Sherrie said.

A short man, maybe five foot seven, wearing dusty jeans, a thick leather belt, a white short-sleeved button-up shirt, and a trucker cap walked in. He was olive-complexioned, with a bulbous nose, wiry salt-and-pepper sideburns, and a wrangly air about him. "Andy, this is her, this is Stan's girl," Sherrie said.

"I've heard a lot about you," Andy said, shaking my hand, and Bill's. He crossed the room to stand next to Sherrie. "Seventeen years. Wow. How'd you find her?"

I had my answer well prepared and produced it without hesitation. "My uncle heard that you'd gotten married, and someone around Merced told him the last name." And then, as though freshly amazed at the simplicity of the process: "And you're in the phone book."

Andy sat down and looked at me piercingly, hands braced against knees. I got the feeling that his last question had been a test. "Did she tell you we found the guy who did it?" My heart froze. "Stupid Mexican. But he's put away now—well, Sherrie'll tell you all about it."

"You're kidding," I said. "Wow, she'll have to tell me." I was trying to project a mix of surprise, sadness, and foreboding, not to appear too giddy. So she would pony up a story after all. I'd get my accounting. I felt delirious and fearful at once.

"Didn't I tell you, Andy, I knew she would come find me, when she was grown-up, when the time was right." Sherrie hummed this wistfully, but I couldn't help thinking they could have exchanged these same words in a very different tone, outside my presence.

"Such a stupid crime," Andy said, eyes screwed up in disgust. "Got all kinds of crazies in the valley."

I hastily agreed and ran down the list of them: the Steven Stayner abductor, the Yosemite killer, the Laci Peterson case. Andy wagged his dusty head. Then he straightened up. "You give her those things?" he asked Sherrie.

"I was just about to," she said, grabbing three clear plastic zippered bags, the kind that might hold sheet sets purchased at Mervyn's. "I've always thought you should have this stuff," she said to me, and I smiled but wondered silently why she'd never sent the packages to my grandparents'.

I leaned in, like a mesmerized child about to unwrap gifts at Christmas, as Sherrie unzipped the first bag. She pulled out a big brown leather belt with STAN H. written in black marker. "His weight-lifting belt!" I said. I hadn't thought of this belt in years, but the moment I saw it I recognized it, and I felt transported back to the reality of Dad's life. The leather was sweat-stained, the block letters rendered with cartoonish, rounded corners. I flashed to the second-grade nights I'd sat reading next to the gym's entrance, waiting for Dad to finish pumping iron.

Sherrie nodded. "He was such a fitness buff." She stood up. "Maybe you don't remember this, but sometimes when he'd lift, he'd need more weight on the bar, and he'd have me hang on and he'd pump me up and down . . ." Sherrie made vigorous motions with her arms as Andy cast his face on the floor uncomfortably. I glanced at Bill, whose face had wrinkled as though watching a graphic sex scene. "Up and down, up and down," she said, laughing, and sat again to shuffle through the plastic bag. "And these were his papers."

I rifled through them. There was a stack of photos—mostly of me and the Howards, a few of Dad and Grandpa Ben assembling the old commercial waxing machine—along with his high school diploma, various school certificates of merit, and his Boy Scout badge. My immunization record. A Valentine's Day card to me signed, "Love, Mom and Dad"—"Mom," of course, being Sherrie. And a Bible with Dad's name in gold letters.

Sherrie unzipped another bag. "And this is what he was carrying, the day he died." She handed me a blue-gray leather wallet. Inside it held a gas station credit card, a phone card, a fishing license, and a packet of photos. The first picture was of Sherrie sitting on their bed, looking up sexily from beneath those skinny eyebrows, lids coated with blue eye shadow. The next photo was of me, my second-grade portrait, and the third was of Bobby.

"Remember this?" she said, handing me a musty blue polo shirt.

"Look, Bill!" I said, and held it up. The patch on the front said HJS, and the red printing on the back said HOWARD'S JANITORIAL SERVICE.

"And this was his too." Sherrie handed me a big black leather-bound book. Gold letters read BEATLES COMPLETE. I flipped through—it was a songbook. "I guess he liked the Beatles," she said. I received the book as though picking up a baby, but I felt a wave of disappointment. I had never remembered Dad as a big Beatles fan. There was just one singer I remembered Dad being crazy about.

Then Sherrie straightened with a fresh bolt of energy. "Maybe you don't remember," she said, pointing, letting her words hang. "But your dad was the *biggest* Rod Stewart fan."

"Of course!" I said.

"No, I mean he was just *crazy* about Rod Stewart. Fanatical." She rolled her eyes. "I mean, every album Rod Stewart ever put out, that man had it."

"I know!" I said, bursting with genuine excitement. "We listened to him all the time! See, Bill, I told you!"

"Your dad had just one fantasy," Sherrie said. "His *big* fantasy was to be the drummer in Rod Stewart's band."

I grinned ear to ear. This was my dad, the man who loved Rod Stewart. Even as I sat on alert for lies, I was thrilled to hear this indisputable truth of his existence.

Maybe Sherrie sensed the wave of sincerity in me. Because we paused, basking in the memory of Dad's love for the scratchy-voiced, swaggering singer, his hero.

"I better be getting back to the fields," Andy finally said. "Why don't you guys go out for lunch?"

We decided that we'd head into town to eat at a nearby truck stop. I took a photo of Andy and Sherrie together on their front porch before he headed out for work, and then Bill and I climbed into Sherrie's truck, a white, mud-splattered, extended-cab Chevy, and Sherrie drove us down the long driveway and past miles of unending brown fields, toward the freeway.

At the truck stop restaurant, intermittently poking at my rubbery chicken teriyaki, I was anxious to cut straight to Sherrie's explanation of the murder. Her husband had given me the door I needed to ask for her accounting without bordering on interrogation. And during the ride over she'd shown signs of working up to the subject. She'd taken the drive as occasion to ask after everyone in my family, expressing goodwill toward all but Uncle Brad ("There was always something off about him," she said) and Grandma Mae and Grandpa Ben.

"I had to get out of your grandparents' house fast, even though I had nowhere to go," she said as we approached a collection of truck stops and, in the center, the restaurant's parking lot. "That man. Your grandfather acted so weird!" Her voice climbed toward pitches of hysteria. "He wouldn't lock the sliding-glass door! I mean, I was so scared, and I begged him. 'Please, are you crazy, please lock that door.' And I just couldn't stay there."

I'd loosened up while she'd given me Dad's things and even started to enjoy myself at the start of the drive, but this story jarred me back into vigilance. Grandma Mae had been terrified after the murder too, and she'd never have stood for keeping the back door open. It struck me as an incredible bluff, this explanation for why she'd moved out so soon after the murder, but I rode along with it, feigning sympathy.

"I know the fear you're talking about," I said inside the restaurant, after our food had arrived. "It took me months to sleep with the lights out. And even today I have to have a piece of blanket covering my neck, because it feels like protection."

"Me too!" Sherrie said. "Exactly. And I can't sleep next to the door."

I hoped this might segue us toward her theory of who had killed Dad, but she wanted to cover more nostalgic topics first.

"I'm just so sad your dad's not going to be at your wedding to walk you down the aisle," she said. The tears started flowing, running straight over the edges of her eyes like an overflowing bathtub, without any of the grotesque grimaces people make when they're fighting against crying. She dabbed with a Kleenex as I furrowed my brows in unfelt sympathy. Bill looked strangely unmoved as well, barely pausing from hunting chunks of blue cheese in his Cobb salad.

"If your dad were alive today, we'd still be married," she said. "I know it. Because that man—that man taught me how to love."

I could hear the violins enter on cue as we launched into the epic love story of Sherrie and Stan. She'd had it with men when she met my dad, she said, too many bad ones out there. She put up the walls, but Dad climbed them all. He put her on a pedestal, and she started to like it. She was happy now in her marriage, but she'd never love another man the way she'd loved my dad.

"And I really believe," she said, tears still flowing freely, "that it was fate that your father was killed. Because they came in for me, not your dad. It was a rapist, you see. And your dad never would have been able to go on if he'd seen me violated like that."

This was my big chance. I could wait no longer. "So who was it?" I said. "The man you figured out did it, the guy your husband was talking about."

Sherrie didn't wait a beat to kick off her explanation. The first part was winding, tough to follow. She'd gone to a psychic right after the murder, who'd confirmed Sherrie's hunch that the perpetrator had come to the house for her. And then, around the time my dad was killed, there'd been a serial rapist on the loose. "Same pattern, entering the house, taking a weapon from the kitchen—just to the letter."

She said he'd killed two or three girls—I lost count as Sherrie digressed into each of their cases. One of them had run out of her house during the rape and he'd stabbed her more than a dozen times, in the street, she said. She'd survived, but lost consciousness. This seemed convenient to me, and I felt Bill perk up with the same thought. But Sherrie turned down another road. They'd arrested him and tried him, in a nearby valley city. And Sherrie just had a feeling, reading about this guy, that it was him—the man who had killed my dad.

Then the story took another turn. "There was this button. You know, a shirt button?" Sherrie said. "After the murder, that we found in the house. And nobody knew who that button had belonged to." Bill looked at me. We were mentally recording every word.

"That was the one piece of evidence," Sherrie said. "But no one collected it, and then the carpet cleaners came, to get the bloodstains out, and it disappeared."

"Wait a minute," Bill said, as I shot him a wary look. "So you're saying there was this button, this piece of evidence, and then—what? The carpet cleaners took it?"

Shut up, I wanted to tell him, just let her keep going. "See, I don't know," Sherrie said, a little flustered. "There was just this button, and then the cleaners came, and it was gone."

"No kidding," I said with full gravity. I nudged Bill under the table. He kept his mouth shut.

"And see, I hadn't been able to see the face, when your dad was killed, it was so dark," Sherrie continued. "But I saw this big figure, kind of short and stocky, and he was wearing a plaid shirt." I nodded.

"So I decided to go to the guy's hearing. I just had to know if it was him. I had to look him in the face and see if he recognized me. And the day of the hearing I sat in the front, but he had his back to me, facing the judge, you see. And finally he turned around and I could see it in his eyes, he remembered me. And he was wearing a plaid shirt, missing a button." Sherrie let the full import of her story sink in. It took every last reserve of insincerity in me not to burst out laughing or roll my eyes, and I could feel that Bill was teetering too. But we hung on, and Sherrie continued.

"Because, you know, your dad's truck wasn't parked out in front of the house that night."

"Right." I regretted it the moment I said it. It revealed that I'd done some research into the circumstances of the crime, that I might know more than I was letting on. But maybe Sherrie had let her guard down.

"And the only thing I can't figure out," she said, "is how this rapist guy knew me. I told Robert about it and we went over it all together, trying to figure it out. And the only thing Robert could figure was that I'd do a lot of work outside the house, in the front yard, see?"

"That's right, we were always painting or planting or something out there," I said.

"And Robert remembered that he'd seen this truck drive by while I was out there and slow down like he was getting a good look. A couple different times. You know, we were out there in the country, it was strange to have a truck slow down like that, and Robert noticed it."

"I see," I said, drawing it out as though all the pieces in the puzzle were fitting together in my mind.

"They'll never convict him in your dad's case, because the Sheriff's Department, they just botched it," Sherrie said. "But at least he got a life sentence. At least we know he's shut away for good."

There was a tense pause. I wasn't sure how to fill it. Clearly Sherrie wanted me to jump on her theory. But Bill and I couldn't swallow it, surely she realized that—although I wasn't certain, at that moment, that she did. I decided to project intrigue, to sit contemplatively as though processing it all. And of course I was doing just that, but not in the way Sherrie probably hoped.

Her eyes snapped into focus, as though remembering a crucial line she'd missed. "It was so strange the way that dog disappeared a few weeks before your dad died." This too involved a long explanation. She'd work with Dad some nights two a.m. to seven a.m., and so she bought the dog, Rocky, to stay with Bobby. "The dog was his babysitter, you see." Every night she'd shut the dog in Bobby's bedroom to watch over him. And then she came home one day and opened Bobby's door to let the dog out, and the dog just wasn't there.

All I could do was feign wonder on cue. "How strange," I said as Bill stared in ostensibly rapt agreement.

She seemed to remember another element she'd missed and shifted topics abruptly. "We only fought once, you know, me and your dad— you remember?"

"I think so. You mean the time Bobby and I had to call the police?"

Sherrie hung her head. "He'd been drinking, you see. I always knew when he'd been drinking, because he'd turn yellow. Because he had hepatitis."

"No kidding. I never knew." It could well have been true, though I'd never heard it. I nodded my head as though it were gospel.

"He got it way before I met him, when he was doing heroin. God, I'm so glad I missed his wild days!" I laughed as though to say, "Oh, that Dad of mine, he did the darndest things!" But the idea of him shooting heroin jarred me. I wasn't sure I believed it.

"And so that day, the day of the fight," Sherrie continued, "he came home with you and he was bright yellow, I mean he was sloppy drunk. And he was so angry!"

I waited for her to answer the obvious question: Why would he have been angry? But that wasn't part of her script, evidently.

"And he was just screaming! That was the one and only time I was ever scared of him. That was the only time we ever fought, that day."

The hitting, the police arriving, any explanation as to why Dad had been angry—all that was left out. But now it was time for more nostalgia. "I'm just so sorry he won't be there for your wedding." The tears flowed again, as though she'd simply reached inside and turned the faucet.

I'd lost the energy to respond to her crying. I was exhausted, after hours of remaining on alert, reading Sherrie's expectations, trying to look like I felt the things I thought she wanted me to feel. I couldn't keep it up much longer. The check had been sitting on the edge of our table for at least twenty minutes. I reached for it.

"Oh, no no, no," Sherrie said. "Let me get this." I insisted. She insisted more forcefully. She picked up the check and put it on the seat next to her, not reaching into her purse for her credit card. She was not done reminiscing. She went on again about how much she missed my father. I excused myself to the bathroom, hoping the bill would be paid upon my return. Instead Sherrie was telling a wan-faced Bill how happy she was to see me healthy and grown, getting married.

Finally I had to cut her off. "Unfortunately Bill has to get back to work. We need to hit the freeway before traffic." Luckily for my line, it was closing in on three o'clock. But we weren't in the clear yet. Sherrie had to get some cigarettes before heading home. Bill and I waited in the truck. The first gas station didn't have her brand, Capris. We waited at the second station. Each wait felt like we were under surveillance, like the truck was wiretapped. Alone in the cab, Bill and I talked about the weather. I was loving the sunshine. Bill thought the valley light too harsh, blinding you with its pollution. When Sherrie opened the car door, we stopped talking midsentence, like schoolkids swapping secrets.

Back at Sherrie's house, the ordeal wasn't over. Sherrie's husband had come back in from the fields. They took pictures of me. I took pictures of them. Sherrie kept introducing new topics of conversation, asking about my wedding dress, where Bill and I would honeymoon, trying to keep us talking. I gave sweet but short answers. We hugged good-bye. "You come back and visit us," Sherrie said as we embraced. "Call me anytime: 555-DO ME. Isn't that funny? Bobby figured that out, with his dirty mind." And then, as I stepped away: "But I know you won't. You won't be back."

I tried to look back at her in a way that said "Sure I will." But I feared she knew too well that I wouldn't, that my nostalgia for our days together was a sham.

Bill and I waited until we had reached the interstate to let it all out. "My God!" I said. I still didn't know what to think. Sherrie's murder explanation had sounded fishy to me, but I needed Bill to confirm my impressions.

"That was some elaborate theory," he said. We ran through all the details, laughing incredulously at the mysteriously missing button. "Wouldn't you like to be a fly on the wall of their conversation?" he said.

"I bet they'd like to be a fly on the wall of ours."

We ran down the list of Sherrie's statements that we didn't buy. Most conspicuous of all: She'd said nothing about her brother, Steve.

I told Bill my suspicions that Sherrie's husband had been onto me when he'd asked how I'd found her. Bill said he wasn't sure. We couldn't get a read on what they'd thought of our visit. And I couldn't possibly assess how much of what Sherrie had said to me she actually believed. In sharp contrast with my family and Nanette, she'd had every last detail ready to provide, as though she'd been honing her narrative for years. But then it seemed reasonable that she would practice her story, waiting for me to call for it, whether or not she or anyone in her family had had anything to do with Dad's murder. It seemed reasonable that she'd assembled a whitewashed and sanitized version of events, as a way to deal with her guilt.

And she didn't have to be in on Dad's murder to feel guilty. She could simply feel guilty about the money she'd talked Dad into spending, the harsh way she'd spoken to me as a girl, who knows what else. She was leading a clean life now, that I didn't doubt. But was she honest?

I knew it would take weeks or months or possibly years for me to satisfactorily decide which of Sherrie's statements had been lies and which facts, that I might never be able to decide. But about the insincerity of her feelings, I had no doubt. In fact I felt a tinge of guilt at writing off her showmanship so quickly. As someone who had come to know grief early in life, if someone was sad or in pain, my natural urge was to offer comfort. And yet I'd had no stirrings of compassion while Sherrie's tears had rolled. Bill said he'd experienced the same eerie disconnection. He'd never sat with someone crying like that without feeling the slightest bit of caring. We hadn't cared, we decided, because Sherrie's tears hadn't been genuine.

A little while after we reached this conclusion, a hearse passed us on the freeway, followed by a limousine. I looked inside the limo's window. A middle-aged man sat with his arm wrapped around a woman's shoulder, and both stared at the road with one of the most disconsolate expressions I'd ever seen. They looked like they didn't know how to go on living. The pain in their eyes was so without self-consciousness, so raw, that I sank in sadness with them. "I've never seen someone so sad," I said to Bill.

That was grief. What Sherrie had felt during our visit, I couldn't tell.

THEORIES

TWO WEEKS AFTER VISITING SHERRIE I drove an hour to the nearest Parents of Murdered Children meeting. The chapter met on the first Monday of each month, and since December I'd made every meeting but one, paying to rent a car and fighting commuter traffic on the Bay Bridge to get there by seven p.m. I knew from the *Atlantic Monthly* article that the organization was not just for parents: Anyone who had lost a friend or relative to violence was welcomed and treated with respect. I liked the longtime members' bluster and bravery. One man, a sweet retiree with Mr. Magoo eyes, had a bumper sticker on his car that read MY CHILD WAS MURDERED in red block letters. That kind of survivor's pride was common and strangely endearing among the veteran members, some of whom had attended for more than fifteen years.

The new faces, though, were timid, shuddering with relief at the opportunity to talk openly about what they'd been through. The stories of their murdered loved ones were often gruesome, and badly in need of telling. One woman's sister had forbade her to cry at her nephew's funeral, not wanting to give the killers the satisfaction of seeing the pain they'd wrought. But at POMC we passed the box of Kleenex and let the tears roll.

Parents of Murdered Children helped me find my own point of normality. I'd come to the organization with a thick residue of shame over Dad's murder. The members had pushed me past that forever, encouraging me to talk to my grandparents. The POMC regulars were full of procedural advice as well, since most had watched their own victim's case drag on through the criminal justice system. One woman informed me that I was entitled to a copy of Dad's coroner's report, and because of her I'd seen more of the paperwork on Dad's case than I'd ever hoped to. Now I wanted the group's expertise once again. I wanted to see their reactions to Sherrie's theory.

We gathered in the seniors' center cafeteria and went around the circle stating our victim's name, date of death, and whether the case was open or solved, then sharing whatever was on our mind. Most of the nine members present were old-timers, familiar with my dad's story, so I jumped right in. I told them I'd met with Sherrie, and that she'd run her mouth mightily. I told them about the rapist theory, the plaid shirt, and finally, the missing button. I knew the button would probably be the clincher, but I tried to deliver the story dispassionately. Several people groaned, the guy across from me rolled his eyes, and the woman next to me waved her hand as if to say "Get out." "Puh-leeze," one man said.

"You really think so?" I said. Heads nodded.

The lead accuser ran over the established facts. "She was sleeping next to him and wasn't hurt? The back door was open? She got the insurance money?" The group obviously felt they were looking at a shut case. "Reminds me of that woman who used to come to meetings, what, ten years ago?" The guy looked at the chapter leader for confirmation before telling the story. The woman's children had been murdered and she'd come to meetings for months, he said, crying a river each time before being arrested and convicted for the deaths. I was fascinated by the story and energized by the members' certainty, but I still wasn't convinced of Sherrie's guilt. I had too many family members stacked against her, making me overwhelmingly biased in the way I laid out the case, and no evidence. I drove home in darkness, through the Caldecott Tunnel, over the Oakland hills, searching my gut for conclusions as the Bay Bridge twinkled ahead and the city lights glowed comfortingly across the water.

"I don't think she did it," I said to Bill that night as he climbed into bed. I replaced my toothbrush on the sink and stood in the bedroom doorway.

"Really," he said. "Go on."

"Maybe her brother did it, but I don't think she told him to. Maybe she knew right afterward that her brother did it, maybe she covered up for him. But I don't think she wanted my dad killed."

I slipped into bed next to Bill, who set down his magazine. It was nearly midnight, and Bill was due into the office at eight a.m., but he urged me to continue. "Interesting," he said.

"You don't think so? You think she set it up?"

"Well, let's go over what we know." His eyes had turned bright, like a child eager to stay up past bedtime for the chance to play amateur detective. We ran through all the basics again. Detectives Marshall and Parsley had told me they believed Steve had done it. But they were mum on the possibility of Sherrie's involvement. They felt the killer had known the layout of our house. And other detectives had told me that stabbing was a personal, heated crime, usually committed in anger. The back door had been left unlocked. Sherrie's explanation, as recorded in the newspaper, was that Dad had stepped outside just before bed to water some plants.

Bill wasn't sure he swallowed that one. He asked if I had seen or heard Dad go out back after we had gotten home; I said I couldn't remember. He asked if Dad was a night-watering kind of guy, perhaps trying to conserve, what with the ongoing California drought and all; I said I had no idea. Bill charged forward with his questioning, quizzing me on irrelevant details such as what kind of toppings we had eaten on our pizza the night Dad was killed, whether we'd had just Canadian bacon or pineapple too. His inquiries were absurd but his demeanor was serious. I half-expected him to push his finger into my chest and bark that I was hiding something.

The pizza-topping line of interrogation was too much for me. "All right, Matlock," I said. "This is ridiculous." I rolled over and pulled the covers around me in a huff.

"Wait a second. I'm just trying to get you to remember as much as possible." I highly doubted that there was any method in his approach, but I let him carry on. We reconstructed the night before Dad had died: Bobby and I being left at the stock car races while Dad and Sherrie saw a movie, eating pizza and dancing to the jukebox way past

Bobby's and my bedtime. Then a jolt of recognition ran through me, as though everything I'd always known had just rearranged itself around an overlooked piece of information.

"I forgot," I said. "He was dead tired. That's why he didn't hear the killer coming into the bedroom. My uncle Brad told me. Dad had worked the night before, and then gone straight to Brad's to help him with a garage sale. And then he hadn't taken a nap all day and we stayed out late that night, past midnight."

"Isn't it strange then that Sherrie would have him stay out late?" Bill said. "Dancing and everything when he was exhausted?"

I was already thinking the same thing, and the thought was turning my stomach. Bill shifted back into Matlock mode again, prodding me to remember whether Sherrie had instigated the dancing, whether she'd rallied for us to stay out later, even whether she could have turned on a porch light as an "all-clear" signal to the killer. The level of detail Bill was pushing for made me roll my eyes, and the "all-clear" signal, especially, struck me as an absurd flight of fancy. But the idea that Sherrie had tired Dad out to make him sleep soundly did not appear to me, now, far-fetched. And so my annoyance at Bill's persistent poking was drowned by a queasy feeling—realization. Maybe she had done it. The setup seemed so perfect. Her stories struck me as too elaborate.

It was one a.m. when Bill switched off the light. He fell to snoring within minutes, as I realized with dread that I needed to use the bathroom and skittered across the apartment, my back against the wall.

The next day the packet of stories I had requested from one of the valley newspapers arrived in my mailbox. I took them to the gym and read them on the StairMaster, careful not to drip sweat on the pages. There were fourteen articles on Sherrie's rapist/murderer, from his first arrest for rape, barely out of high school, to his sentencing to life in prison not many years later.

Everything was roughly as Sherrie had described. The guy had been caught on one particularly gruesome rape and attempted murder, then linked to two other rapes and one other killing. He used knives or knife-like objects to threaten his victims. And he received life in prison without parole.

The newspaper articles corroborated Sherrie's account but they didn't tie up her theory. For one thing, all the crimes had taken place an hour or more away from Merced. For another, it seemed highly unlikely that the rapist would have worn a plaid shirt—forget about the missing button—to a court hearing.

I called Sergeant Marshall to see whether he could tell me if Sherrie had indeed attended the convict's hearing, and if he could have been wearing a plaid shirt. "Real nice guy, eh?" he said when I mentioned the convict in question. When I told Marshall I'd gone to meet with Sherrie, he sounded unimpressed, but offered to grab Dad's case file and check out the convict's hearing immediately. "Yep, she went to that hearing," Marshall said. "Says right here." Sherrie had indeed driven an hour from Merced to look the guy over; a detective had accompanied her to check out the potential suspect. I told Marshall about Sherrie's tale of the plaid shirt and the missing button. He offered no commentary but made one thing clear: "A guy in jail like that would not have been wearing civilian clothes to his hearing. He would have been wearing a jail-issue jumpsuit." My heart sank. Did this mean I needed to call Sherrie and ask why she'd said otherwise?

"I just don't know what to think," I said. "Why would she say all of that, about the button?"

But Marshall wasn't biting. Apparently this was all about as intriguing to him as the nutritional facts on a bag of Doritos. "All I can tell you is she did go to that hearing," he said, as though impatient to get off the phone. I caved in. I said thanks, and good-bye.

But five minutes later I called Marshall back. I'd gotten intimidated again and let him off too easily. "I forgot something," I said. I asked if he still thought he'd be able to contact Hector Garibay, the original detective on the case, and see if he'd be willing to talk with me. He'd promised to get hold of Hector for me at our last meeting, more than a month ago, but I hadn't heard of any follow-up.

"I told you I would," Marshall said, then softened as though hearing the defensiveness in his own voice. "He's a hard one to get hold of, Hector, always off touring the world, enjoying the good life with his cushy retirement. I'll try him again."

"I can't tell you how much I appreciate it," I said as we hung up. But

I doubted I'd ever hear from Hector if I left the search to Marshall. Instead of counting on him to come through, I was already scheming to have my private-detective friend find Garibay for me. I'd talk to the original detective on Dad's case one way or another.

But the next morning the phone rang, and a voice remarkably similar to Marshall's, only grandfatherly, asked to speak with Rachel Howard. It was Hector Garibay. He was willing to talk.

I fumbled for an opening question. Fortunately Garibay just began talking, the creaky wheels of memory turning in the hesitation between sentences. He started in with Steve, the person I had long been led to believe had done the stabbing.

"We looked into her brother," he said. "The wife had indicated it might be him."

This was a significant revision of everything I'd heard. "Wait a minute," I said. "So Sherrie told you she thought it might have been her brother?"

"Yes, yes, she did," Garibay said. "She said the man she'd seen had the same shape and build as her brother. But we cleared him. And there was no one else to focus on. We couldn't find any reason why something like that would happen, and we checked into your dad's background and Sherrie's background."

"But the brother had an alibi?" I asked what the alibi was and Garibay said he couldn't recall. "But you felt certain it wasn't him?"

"Yes, we were confident. We gave him a polygraph and he passed it."

"And you felt the wife, Sherrie, was cooperative?"

"Yes, completely cooperative," Garibay said. "She was definitely shaken up that night and continued being shook up for a few days. I mean, she was kind of screwed up there for a while, calling us with different information and theories. She was scared."

"I met with her a few weeks ago," I said. "And she gave me one theory in particular. She says she knows who did it."

I told him about the convict, the plaid shirt, and the button. I asked him to confirm that Sherrie had attended the hearing. "Yes, I accompanied her," he said. "But she said it wasn't him. Otherwise we would have followed up on that. She gave us a negative ID." My stomach dropped.

I asked about the plaid shirt. "Huh. That's what she'd told us her brother was wearing—a plaid shirt," he said. "And, no, if you're at a hearing, you're not going to be wearing civilian clothes, you're going to be wearing a jumpsuit. But I do recall going to review the guy, and it was definitely a negative."

I was speechless. There was nothing to do at that moment but accept the information. Sherrie had gone to see the rapist's hearing. And she had told Garibay that the rapist wasn't the guy. So why had she used this theory with me? Had she thrown the detectives onto the rapist to cover her brother's tracks? Had she then given him a negative ID because she knew she couldn't sustain her accusation against him? But then why had she implicated her brother in the first place? Or was Hector Garibay wrong, his memory flawed—and how, without the case file, would I ever know for certain?

Instead of pushing Garibay I let him meander through what he could remember of investigating the case: the tracks from the dew on the lawn that proved someone had entered our house, the days he and his partner had spent canvassing the neighborhood. I asked how long it took for the case to go cold. Garibay told me the first twenty-four hours were always crucial—and they'd had only the weakest of leads in that time. Within a month the file was dead. I asked how many cases he'd had go that way. "A lot of times you find a dead body in a field someplace, and those are tough," he said. "But here you had three witnesses—you, your brother, and Sherrie. I'll tell you, in my thirty-year career I've only had three cases where we had no known suspect. And in one of those cases I know who did it but the DA won't file."

Garibay seemed to realize the grimness of what he was saying and feel a need to retract it. "But this is an open case—people do look at it from time to time," he said. "And sometimes when people get older, their conscience gets to them. A homicide is never closed. It's not forgotten."

I appreciated the sentiment but doubted much truth lay behind it.

SECOND THOUGHTS

IT TOOK TWO MONTHS for the guilt to hit me full force.

During the weeks after I visited Sherrie, I theorized endlessly, with anyone who would listen—my mother, my friends, Bill, even Bill's dad. These conversations were like the Choose Your Own Adventure novels I used to read in grade school. If you started with one premise, say that my father actually had stepped into the backyard to water plants before bed, you went down one path. If you started with a different premise, you went down another, but at every step of the theory you had to choose what was true, and the paths were endless. The theories people offered when I laid out the facts of the case grew so far-fetched that I had to catch myself from glaring in response. Maybe, some well-intentioned listener would say, someone had been in the house when you guys arrived home and had hidden until you'd fallen asleep? But then why would they bother to walk into the back bedroom, take nothing, and kill my father? I'd be tempted to shout. One night when the case came up during dinner on the town, an acquaintance said, "Wow, so were you a suspect in the case, since you were there at the house?" I was *ten years old*, I almost screamed in reply. Still I had to admit none of these theories stretched the imagination as far as one that I held silently: Maybe Sherrie had set the whole thing up after all—but had put another person, not Steve, up to the killing—and maybe she'd implicated Steve to throw the detectives off the real trail?

And here was another theory at the back of my mind, one that I could not ignore: What if Sherrie had absolutely nothing to do with it?

Because if that was the case—and it certainly was an enormous possibility—I had done a terrible thing. Whether or not I had become a writer, I probably would have wanted to face Sherrie one day. The visit had not just been about hearing her theory; in the months since I'd gotten engaged and begun feeling secure enough to think about the murder, I'd been overcome by a compulsion to make Sherrie real to me. But when I had gone to see Sherrie, I had known that I was working on a book. I had known that the book would probably one day be published. And I had not told her this, in part because I was afraid of how she would react, and in part because I had wanted her to talk freely, without the inhibition of knowing that what she said might eventually see print. I had presented myself as simply thinking about her after all those years. I had lied.

I felt tinges of regret over this immediately afterward, but the need to settle on next steps conveniently distracted me. Somehow over the last six months, I, who had never entertained fantasies of delayed justice, had been possessed by the idea that I had to decide who had killed Dad. I had to check out her rapist-convict theory. I had to talk with the original detective on the case. And then what? I had no answers. I thought I should be crusading, "investigating." I'd read books by James Ellroy and Mark Arax, gripping books in which they pursued every last lead on their parents' murders. I knew I was not a criminal investigator by nature, and I doubted that choosing a murderer to seek vengeance against would make my life complete. Yet I'd begun to feel I would be inadequate as a daughter if I didn't keep pressing.

Flailing for an obvious action to take, I called the private detective who had helped me find Sherrie and asked him to track Sherrie's brother for me. He could do it, he said, but first he wanted to know—what good would it do me? I had to admit he had a point. If I found Sherrie's sibling, if I looked over his criminal record and saw him with my own eyes, what would that tell me? How would that edge me closer to knowing who had killed my dad?

What you need, this private detective told me, is the case file. It was like I was trying to read a book, he said, when I only had half the pages. But I'd been trying to get the case file, or at least more of it, for more than a year, sweet-talking the Sheriff's Department, with nothing to show for it.

I wasn't afraid to look at even the most explicit documentation of my dad's case anymore, but I couldn't get a clear answer on whether I had a chance of getting my hands on it. I called around to every investigative reporter and private detective I knew of. Some said I might want to try filing a request under the Freedom of Information Act, but they didn't sound optimistic about it. Others offered to try to get the case file for me themselves—no promises—for a cool fee of $3,000. Finally a friend of a friend put me in touch with a veteran author of true-crime books, someone who'd been in the business for two decades. He didn't hedge with his answer or give me any wishy-washy line about trying a FOIA. "Listen," he said. "That case is still open. Unless you've got an inside track with someone at the Sheriff's Department or know a crime reporter with a tight connection, you're never going to see that file."

I was surprised to find that my immediate reaction was relief. I was off the hook; there was nothing to be done. But before I could let this release sink in, I was taken with anxiety. How could I want to let go so badly? Shouldn't I say that I would keep on fighting, that I would never rest as long as the killer was unidentified? How could I be such a wimp? Didn't I owe it to my father's memory to never give up?

Over the next week I waited for these feelings, this vigilante mindset, to seize me. But it didn't, and finally I had to admit to myself that I would never be a criminal-hunting crusader. I was trying to live my life according to some made-for-TV script wherein the heroine, haunted by her father's past, devotes her life to bringing his killer to justice. But that heroine wasn't me. I'd never had that burning desire for vigilante justice. Beginning as a teenager, I'd been staunchly anti-death-penalty, and I'd always felt that if my father's killer were convicted, I would want him to live. I'd never set out to "solve" my father's murder. But then what had I set out to do? And how would I know when I had done it?

I had set out to make sense of things, to move on. And I had, to a degree. I had come to understand my dad better and had rendered what I knew of his story as faithfully as possible. I had faced the reality of his gruesome death. Most unexpectedly and most importantly, I had reconnected with my dad's family, most of whom, to my astonishment, were now planning to travel two hundred miles to attend my wedding.

And then, biggest of all: I had faced Sherrie. She was no longer a shadowy phantom to haunt my dreams. As fear-inducing as my encounter with her had been, it had made her a real person, a farmer's wife, smaller and less threatening than what my imagination could conjure. But the more I thought about it, the more I realized I did not feel good about this supposed triumph.

It wasn't until my conversation with the no-bull crime reporter, the one who told me I would probably never see Dad's case file, that it sank in fully. I hung up the phone with him and sat on the couch, staring across the room, absorbing the reality. I would probably never know who killed Dad.

How do you move on from a tragedy like murder when you have no answers? You blame someone. You have to. Why did this terrible thing happen? No one can tell you. You create an explanation in your mind. My explanation was simple: Sherrie. Maybe, I'd told myself, she was involved in Dad's death. Maybe she'd just been a nasty person. It didn't matter. She was the mysterious evil force that, by calculation or even just by mere presence in his life, had brought him to his end.

But now that I had met with her and deceived her, I was sick with guilt. She hadn't treated me well as a child; I knew that and trusted my memories. She'd been manipulative and quick-tempered and cold. But even knowing that she had been all of those things, did that make her a murderer? If she had had nothing to do with Dad's death, how deeply had I wronged her all these years? How could I live with myself if I kept blaming her, when I had no proof?

About two months after we met with Sherrie, Bill and I drove down to Santa Barbara to stay at his parents' house while they were out of town. Our first night there I was nearly asleep when I saw the hallway light flicker on. I woke Bill, who got up to investigate and found that several other lights he knew he had turned off were back on now too. Someone, it seemed, must be in the house. It was two a.m. But I didn't stand on guard. I rolled over and pulled the covers up over my neck to fall asleep as Bill searched the house.

The next morning he asked how it was that I could just roll over and go to sleep like that, when it seemed certain someone had broken in. I simply wasn't that afraid, I told him. Whatever happened to me could not be worse that what had already happened in my nightmares for more than half my life. It wasn't a defeatist attitude: If someone did come after me, I would fight, just as I had in all those terrible dreams. But something had clicked in me since I'd met with Sherrie. I could not live my life in perpetual fear. Between paranoia and naïveté, I would err on the side of naïveté.

The next night as we were eating dinner, we saw several of the house's lights flick on of their own volition. Bill's parents, we learned, had set them on timers to ward against burglars while they were on vacation.

The whole episode shored up my conviction that I now had nothing to fear. The moment Bill and I got home, I wrote an e-mail to Sherrie, asking to see her again.

THAT NIGHT

I HADN'T HAD A BREATHING ATTACK in nearly five years, but standing in front of the truck stop restaurant, waiting for Sherrie, my inhales grew short and sharp until I thought I might hyperventilate. My body was rebelling against me. It didn't matter how brave my mind wanted to be. My swallows were lumpy, my stomach was leaden, and my right leg shook. But then I saw Sherrie cruise in aboard her white truck, the cab gliding a full foot above the parking lot's pickups and SUVs, and the adrenaline gushed, and my lungs opened for a full inhale. My body would come through for me after all.

I hugged Sherrie and tried to make asinine small talk about how her farm's crops were handling the hundred-degree weather. We took a booth in a dank corner of the main dining room. "Bill's at the bar around the corner," I said. "I was hoping we could talk alone." I watched carefully for suspiciousness or caution to flash across her face, but Sherrie just shrugged. "Kind of early in the day to start drinking," she said, and winked. At our table, I ordered a side of fruit salad, knowing that my nervous nausea would not allow me to eat it, and Sherrie ordered onion rings.

"It was really great to meet with you a few months ago," I said. "I've been trying to work through everything that happened, and talking to you really helped."

"It was good to see you too," she said. "Like I said, I always knew you'd come looking for me." When I glanced into her eyes, her gaze seemed to be searching mine. Her eyes looked puffier to me than when

I'd seen her two months ago. I told myself to just keep talking—too much hesitation would make what I was about to say sound more negative than it needed to.

"There's something I didn't tell you when I saw you last," I said. "I just hadn't seen you in so long, and I wasn't sure how you'd take it."

"Okay," she said with a casual cheerfulness.

"I'm writing a memoir, about my childhood, and about life after the murder." This was the moment when Sherrie was supposed to go on alarm, slam the table, explode with anger and betrayal. Instead she dipped her onion ring into the ranch dressing.

"That's great," she said. "Everyone has to work through these things in their own way. I always knew you'd be a writer, reading all those books."

Surely, I thought, she must guess that she would not come off as a patron saint in this book. To assuage my own conscience, I had better be clearer with her. "I just thought you should know, because you're in the book. And you know, after the murder there was a lot of . . . well, *weirdness*, between my family and you. And I thought you should know, I have a publisher." I wasn't quite saying it. I wasn't saying that I had always disliked her as a child, that I had spent half my life suspecting her. I couldn't get myself to do it. I told myself that it was in between the lines. She was smart enough to read the subtext. And if she wasn't going to seize this chance to throw up red flags, I had still given her an opportunity. Or tried.

But not a hint of concern flickered across her blue eyes. "Great," she said again.

"So you're fine with that? That I'm going to write about you, and about what we've said?"

"Sure."

"I was thinking about using this picture in the book. I was wondering if you'd be okay with it." I rifled through my purse for the photo of me, Dad, Sherrie, and Bobby.

"Oh, don't tell me," she said, excited. "Is it the one with the four of us at Christmas, at the apartment?"

"Well, actually, I'm not sure where it was taken." I laid it on the table.

"That's it! I have a copy of it at home. I've been looking for my old photo album, with other pictures of us, but I don't know if Robert took it . . ."

"This is the only picture I have of the four of us together," I said. And come to think of it, Sherrie had probably been the person who'd given it to the detectives in the first place. But she didn't ask where I had gotten it.

"*I* don't care if you use it," she said. "But I've got some better ones, if I could just find them." She picked up the photo. "Look at him, so handsome. Do you know what he said to me, about the wind?"

"Wait, I think I remember this. On the steps outside the Sheriff's Department, the little tornado?"

"And do you remember what I said?" She cocked her head wistfully. " 'That's your daddy, giving us a kiss.' Because right after we got married, we were talking about death. And he said to me, 'When I die, I'm going to be the wind, and every time you feel a little breeze, you'll know it's me kissing you."

"I remember." I remembered it very differently, of course—I remembered it as a lie. And here I had met with her again to come clean with her, and I was not telling her that I had always thought what she was saying was phony. But how far did I have to go? Did I have to say, I always thought that line of yours was bullshit? And what if, which now that I thought about it was highly likely, Dad really had said the cheesy spiel about the wind to her on another occasion and had said the thing about returning as an eagle later? What if I had misremembered the incident entirely? What if what I had counted as a lie had always been true?

"That night," she said. She was going to recount it for me again, unprompted, unprovoked. "It was so dark. But I just felt this—this *presence*—and I looked up and I saw this figure. And then your dad threw his arms up like this"—she crossed her arms over her chest, then circled them above her head. "And then he sprang up from bed.

"Your dad ran out of the room. And I sat up and I knocked over the lamp, trying to get to the phone, trying to call 911. And then your dad came back in, and it was so awful, he was holding his arms out like this"—she reached out her arms, palms forward, like Jesus on the cross, as I shook my head, pained by the idea. "He was begging me for help. But I couldn't do anything to help him. And then he collapsed, at the foot of the bed. I was on the phone to 911, and I couldn't see him. I was just trying to hear if he was breathing. And I told the operator, 'I don't think he's breathing.' And then I heard this big gasp"—she pushed all the air from her lungs, reenacting it—"and I just knew he had died."

She was crying again but this time I felt for her. I found myself on the edge of watering too. I hadn't been in that room, but the scene was too real in my mind.

Finally, she continued, she heard the knocking at the front door and came running. "It was Dave, an old friend of mine," she said. The sheriff's deputy who'd reported to the scene had been an acquaintance of hers. "He just goes, 'Oh, no, Sherrie, not you,' " she said. "And I couldn't think straight, I was a mess, but I go, 'Stan's in the bedroom.' "

She paused, cast her face down, picked up a cold onion ring. "At the hospital they asked me if I wanted to see the body. But I just couldn't, I didn't want to see him like that. And then the detectives took me into a room. They pulled out this plastic bag with a knife handle in it, and they say, 'Does this look familiar to you?' I recognized it. It was from our kitchen."

She paused again and poked her onion ring morosely in the ranch dressing. She took a bite and perked up. "I can't wait to see him again, when I die. Because I know I will. I believe in fate, I believe everything happens to us because we were meant to learn from it. And I know that when I die, he'll be there. It won't be like we're married again. It will just be love."

"I don't know," I said. "I have a hard time believing that anything happens to us after we die. I mean, I go to church every week, but I still feel that what's in front of us is what we've got, and maybe that's okay."

She seemed disappointed for me. She told me how her spiritual beliefs had gotten her through all her traumas and made her whole. Then she looked at the photo again. "So cute," she said, putting her finger on Dad. "And so horny!"

She proceeded to tell me all about my dad's sex life, that he had wanted to screw every night, that if she ever came to bed with her panties on, he would tell her to take them right off, and that because of his rule there had been a big embarrassing pile of panties on the floor when the deputies had come into the room. One time, she said, she jokingly asked him to dance. "And *your* dad came into the living room wearing nothing but a pair of Speedos. I swear! And he started doing this ridiculous striptease"—she lowered her lids seductively and rolled her shoulders to demonstrate—"to Rod Stewart, of course!"

I snorted—the image fit so well with the picture of Dad I'd pieced together over the last year. This was the kind of sexual detail that Sherrie had shared with me as a child, that had turned me against her. Had she just been clueless as to how uncomfortable it would make me back then? She certainly appeared to have no notion of how uncomfortable it was making me now.

"I forgot!" she said. "His weight-lifting gloves. I found them after you left last time. I meant to bring them."

"I'd love to have those." I finished off my fruit salad—I could eat now that my nausea had evaporated. I paid the check and we collected Bill from the bar. Bill and I followed Sherrie back to her house, where we said hello to Andy and checked out the new equipment shed. Sherrie showed us the tiny stitches on the corner of her eyes from recent plastic surgery—the reason her eyes were puffier, the reason she had searched my gaze, to see if I had noticed, as we sat at the restaurant. She handed me Dad's old gloves in a felt pouch. I took them out and pulled the Velcro open and closed, just as I had the night he had died. The gloves were stiff with sweat and white as I remembered, but so grimy they were really the color of concrete.

"Call me anytime," Sherrie said as we climbed back into the car. I wondered if she'd be saying that if she ever read the book I was writing about Dad's murder. But I had come back out here, I had told her about it, I had given her a chance to sniff it out. I hadn't been entirely forthright. But I had tried. Perhaps if she really had nothing to do with Dad's death, she would read the book one day and understand—the oddity of the crime, the truth of how we had gotten along when I was younger, the need I had had for so long to blame someone. And if she had had something to do with the murder—I didn't want to think about that anymore.

*   *   *

I called Bobby from Merced that afternoon. Sherrie had given me his cell phone number; he had moved out of the apartment his ex-girlfriend and daughter shared and was now crashing at friends' places, so that his cell phone was the only way to get in touch with him. But he answered on the first ring. "Sure, I got time to meet," he said. He was hanging out at a "woman friend's" house, waiting for her to finish her hair so they could head to Modesto for a night out. He'd meet me at the Starbucks—the one downtown, there were *two* of them in Merced now—while she primped.

If I hadn't been on the lookout, I would never have recognized him. He wore an electric blue sports jersey, baggy shorts, a visor, and pristine white Nikes. He was just a few inches taller than I, but he was big now, broad-shouldered. "Got a lot of free time to pump iron in prison," he said. But the greatest surprise about him was his eyes—rich amber with lush, dark lashes, almond-shaped lids. They were snakelike, and gorgeous. I'd forgotten all about his beautiful eyes.

I hugged him as I would my own brother, surprised at my tenderness. "Would you like something to drink?" I asked, strangely solicitous, and he sat down and said he'd like a blended iced mocha, without offering to pay or accompanying me to the counter.

He was slumping beneath his visor when I returned with his drink, making small talk with Bill. The visor was obviously not just slick street fashion, but a prop to hide behind. He recoiled beneath it, like an easily spooked animal looking out from a protective cave. He spoke in a whisper, so that the café's big-band jazz tunes drowned out his words. I had to lean in inches from his mouth to hear him.

"So how've you been?" I started. It turned out to be a loaded question. He had just quit his job driving a milk delivery truck, scoffing at the long hours and $60-a-day pay, and he was feeling nostalgic for the good old days of pulling down $300,000 a year—illegally, but he wouldn't tell me exactly how. He described one scheme, the one that had landed him in prison. Home Depot had a policy of refunding merchandise without a receipt, as long as you showed a California ID; Robert had taken to collecting scrap from construction sites and using his friend's driver's license to get the cash. One day he took in $400 worth of scrap and the store told him that for any return over $300, they'd have to send a check to the address on the ID. He waited weeks for his friend to give him the $400 check but kept hearing it hadn't arrived yet. So finally he broke into his friend's apartment, searched through his girlfriend's purse, and found the $400 check. He left the check but took her credit card and charged $400 on it. The friend turned him in.

"Thing is"—he shook his head—"that's one strike against me, state law."

"Well, you're not planning to get strikes two and three, are you?" I sounded like a mother. I couldn't help it. He wagged his head, but as if to lament his bad luck, not as if to answer no. He was headed straight for strikes two and three, and he was perfectly resigned to it.

Bill, sitting right across from us, continued flipping through the newspaper. He couldn't hear a word Robert was whispering.

"So I was out at your mom's place today," I said, trying to spark a brighter conversation.

"Yeah, I don't really see her no more," Robert said. "After she married Andy, she just changed."

Robert said he'd run away at fifteen and ended up at a youth home in New Mexico, where he'd finished high school. Then he'd come back to Merced, tried to get work, fathered a child, and gotten into trouble. He showed me a photo of his six-year-old girl, and a "naughty" shot of the mother, wearing a black lace bra. He didn't talk to his own mom much now, he said. And although his biological father lived in Merced, he had no contact with him or that side of the family. As for close friends, his best pal had been murdered a few years back.

The conversation was growing too grim, and as many times as I tried to say "Well, I'm glad to see you're doing all right now," it just sounded more and more false. "Listen, I better let you pick up your friend for your night out," I said, and we headed for the door.

But back outside in the nintey-five-degree afternoon, I had another thought. "I hear you still go by *Howard*," I said brightly. Robert pulled out his wallet and flashed his driver's license: Robert Howard Chavez.

"I really loved him," he said even more quietly, head bowed. "I started telling someone about the murder the other day and I started tearing up—and I *never* cry."

"Can I just ask you something? That night, at the house. Do you remember sitting on the sofa together, and then you picked up one of his weight-lifting gloves and said maybe we should keep it?"

"I don't remember that. I remember everything else, though."

It was true. He remembered it all as one continuous scene: waking up when he heard his mother scream, seeing my dad run past his door. Not a moment had been blanked out in his mind.

"I ran to your room, and I was going, 'My mom's hurt! My mom's hurt!'—you remember?"

"It's weird," I said. "I always remembered you as saying something about Dad cutting himself shaving. I must have thought you were saying, 'Dad's cut! Dad's cut!' or something."

"Nah, I was saying, 'My mom's hurt.' And then, remember, my mom going, 'Stay in your rooms, kids! Stay in your rooms!'"

"Yeah, I do now. But before I just remembered me and you, sitting on that couch, looking at the glove."

"Nah, first there was the knock at the door—you remember? And you and me, we were standing right next to the front door, but we were too afraid to open it. And then my mom comes running through and lets the cops in."

"That must have been when you and I were looking at the glove—after the sheriff's deputies showed up," I said.

"Yeah, and then my mom came running up to us when they were taking him out."

"I'll tell you what I remember. I remember your mom covering our eyes and telling us not to look. But I did. I just saw his feet as the paramedics were carrying him down the hall."

"I looked too. I saw a lot more than that. He was dead."

"What about when we got back to my grandparents' house? I tell you, I could swear—I remember it so clearly—you went straight to the chalkboard and you wrote out 'CREMATED' and the date. And I was just wondering what the hell *cremated* meant. And then the fishing show. It was the only thing on TV, so we watched it together until my mom showed up."

"Nah. I don't remember any of that." But he didn't deny that it was true. And I knew absolutely that what I remembered was true, and that what he had remembered was true too, and that between us we finally had the truth of that night, if nothing else.

"I've driven by the house a couple of times," I said. "It creeps me out."

"I've been by too."

"You ever go back inside?"

"Nah, I don't want to bother no one."

"Me either."

There was a pause, a quiet reluctant feeling that it was time to go. And just as I was about to say good-bye, Bobby had something more to say.

"You remember that night, before we went to bed, that meeting in the hallway?"

"What?"

"Yeah, my mom called us into the hallway, and she goes, 'All right, kids, close your doors.' "

I was completely thrown. I'd often thought about Sherrie's insistence that we close our doors, but I'd never recalled for certain whether she'd stressed it again that night. What was I supposed to think of this specific memory of Bobby's? What could he possibly mean by it, bringing it up at the end of our meeting, except to cast his mother into suspicion? And yet he'd said nothing else to implicate her. If he intended to make me suspicious of her, he was being supremely sly about it. I decided he had no intention, that he'd always remembered the hallway meeting clearly, that it had stuck in his mind as strange and noteworthy, that perhaps he had never thought about it long enough to figure out why. And so, instead of asking why he'd brought Sherrie's directive up, I let it go.

"I better let you take off to meet your lady friend," I said, but Bobby just stood for a moment, staring intently at the sidewalk.

"It was so bizarre," he said. "I would really like to know who did it."

"Me too," I said, and we hugged good-bye.

EPILOGUE

FOR WEEKS I ANGUISHED over whether to call Sherrie again. I still hadn't been forthright with her. Every night, trying to fall asleep, I played out hypothetical conversations in my mind. I would call her up, be utterly honest and sympathetic, give her the benefit of the doubt. I'd tell her I'd spoken with the sheriffs, and that they'd sworn she'd cleared the rapist convict. And then what? And then what did she have to say to that?

Even delivered in my sweetest voice, the call would come off as an interrogation. I couldn't know whether she deserved one, and I was beginning to feel I didn't deserve to deliver one either. Because when I tried to imagine a desirable outcome from this hypothetical call, my mind went blank. She would be livid at my implied accusation and scream at me and threaten my life. Or, if she truly had something to hide, she would offer flimsy lies in fawning tones. But what if she had the magic answer, an explanation that absolved her forever? What if she decided to pour forth about why she had implicated her brother as a suspect, if in fact she had? About why she'd given the rapist convict a negative ID, if that was true too? What if she was right about who had killed Dad, and with a few simple revelations was able to end the mystery of the murder?

All of that was possible, but I could not conceive of it. I could not believe in the rapist convict as the true murderer. And I could not believe another conversation with Sherrie would be of any use. I didn't yet realize that the resolution I was seeking could not be forced by identifying a killer, and that I'd already found it—in my father's memory, in his family, in a story that, even with all its uncertainties, felt true.

My wedding day was rapidly approaching. Happy thoughts of the celebration I'd planned in Santa Barbara had begun to vie for attention with unease about the murder, and the happy thoughts were winning. A year and a half earlier, when I'd gotten engaged, I'd decided to invite everyone on Dad's side of the family, but more out of obligation than affection. I hadn't gone to the detectives yet, I hadn't talked with Mae and Ben and Brad and Ric about Dad, and I'd felt certain that few of them would want to attend. Now RSVPs were flooding my mailbox, and all of Dad's siblings, even Aunt Dana from Oregon, were coming. And now, after finally opening up with Mae and Ben about the murder, after talking with my uncles and sharing in their grief, it felt momentous to me that they all be there, far more important than any crusading I could do on Dad's case.

Still, I decided to call Sergeant Marshall before calling Sherrie, in case he might be able to clear up some of the contradictions himself. "You know Hector's an old man now, and his memory isn't what it used to be," he said when I told him about Sherrie swearing the rapist had done it, and Hector claiming she'd cleared him.

"Believe me, I do know," I said. "Because I've been writing this book for a year and learning the hard way just how delicate memory is, especially mine. I don't know whose account to believe. And that's why I called you. I thought you might be able to help me clear this up."

"I'll call Hector," Marshall said, "and see what I can figure out. I'll call you back next week."

But Marshall never called me back, and I never called Marshall back either. And I never called Sherrie to see if she could refute Hector Garibay's account, too excited over the wedding to let worries about the murder enter my mind.

Three days before the wedding Mom confessed to me how nervous she was to see all the Howards again. I found it surprisingly easy to tell her to calm down. I myself was no longer anxious about the Howards' presence, no longer fearful of old hurts or taboos, no longer certain those old hurts and taboos existed. And then the night before the wedding, at the rehearsal dinner, there Mom was, rising from the table where my uncles Brad and Ric and Dennis and my aunt Dana had been sitting, ushering me giddily into a hallway. "I've been talking with your dad's family for almost an *hour*," she gushed. "And we've been catching up, and—I mean, I haven't really talked with them in *years*."

I smiled at her knowingly. "See?"

The next afternoon, at the reception, I hugged my aunt and my uncles so eagerly I nearly ripped my dress. The ceremony had gone off without a hitch. I'd had Grandpa Ben deliver the final reading, from the New Testament, charging me and Bill, in his deliberate cadence, to "cloak yourselves in love." "Did you hear your grandpa pause for a sec in the middle of the reading?" Uncle Brad's wife, Lisa, asked me as trays of hors d'oeuvres circulated around us at the cocktail hour. I hadn't, too focused on Bill and carried away by adrenaline over the vows to come. "He was tearing up. I thought he was going to lose it for a minute there, but he made it through. He told me afterward he was thinking of your dad."

I was far too exhilarated to let any tears fall that day. My love for Bill was thrill enough, but the wedding felt as if it was about so much more than just us. Bill's college friends were there. My color-guard buddies from high school, Cori, Kristal, and Britten, had even come. Nanette had driven down, with her little girl, Marina, and her mother, Rose. Grandma Mae was in high spirits, gabbing on bravely, despite a sore throat, about her bladder to Bill's grandma Betty, who enthusiastically replied in kind with revelations about her colon.

During dinner, as Bill and I made our rounds visiting tables, I headed straight for Uncle Ric. He rolled up his sleeve to flash the rose tattoo. "Did you hear, we talked your wimpy uncle Dennis into getting one!" he said. "When are you getting yours?" We considered putting the tattoo on my ankle or my derriere. "Thing is, you've gotta put it somewhere you'll see when you get out of the shower, you know? So you see it every day and remember him."

Over at the other table of Howards, Aunt Dana leaned in close to my ear. She was a robust, hearty woman, and I'd seen her maybe five times since my father died. My grandparents had told me that she'd taken many years to come to terms with the murder, that it didn't feel real to her until half a decade later, when she visited his grave and broke down sobbing. "I'm so glad I'm here," she said, gripping my shoulders. "We've got to see you more."

"Yes," I said, "especially now that my mom has a house in Merced, I'm sure we'll see each other more and—"

"No. We should have seen you more, talked to you more, before. But things are different now." She winked.

The tinkling of silverware against champagne flutes filled the room, announcing the time for toasts. Bill's best friend spoke, and his brother spoke, and my bridesmaid spoke, and finally Bill spoke. At last I took the mike to let Bill know how much I loved him. I told of our bumpy road to the altar, and how I'd known so quickly after we'd met that I wanted to marry him, and how grateful I was that he had always believed in me as I believed in him. But in the rush to declare my love I forgot to acknowledge Dad's family, an omission that made my heart sink as I sat back down and Aunt Lisa scurried over. "We have to pack up and get back, it's getting late for the kids," she said. My face washed pale with regret. I'd wanted so badly to tell Dad's family how important it was to have them present, how it had made the day—and, I was beginning to think, my life—complete. And now I'd never have the chance again, except . . . I grabbed the microphone.

"Many of you here tonight know that my father passed away when I was ten," I said as, from across the room, Grandpa Ben's eyes locked on mine. "Well, all of his siblings, his brothers and his sister, and of course his parents, my grandparents, are here tonight. And I want to tell them all how much it means to me to have them here on this day we all wish he could have seen."

For the first time that evening, my eyes threatened tears. But the musicians began to play and the party carried on, and I set the microphone down feeling that I had done something life changing, that I had entered a new era.

I walked back to the table where Aunt Lisa and Uncle Brad and my cousins were gathering their things to leave. Earlier, I'd told Grandpa Ben that I wanted someone to take my wedding bouquet back to Merced and place it on my father's grave. Now Lisa reached for the bouquet in my hands. "Ben told us about taking this to the grave," she said. "And Brad really wants to do it, he's really excited about it."

I smiled at shy Uncle Brad and handed the flowers to his wife. And I thought about those roses and hydrangeas and their pretty pink ribbon sitting on that little plaque in the Merced cemetery, and about how pleased my father would be to know they were there, and not about the words engraved on his headstone, which didn't matter anymore. And I felt an enormous love for my father, my husband, and my family. I felt whole.

AFTERWORD

At the end of my search for the truth of my father's murder, I did not uncover convincing evidence of the identity of his murderer. I cannot assert, nor is it my intention to assert, that either my father's third wife, Sherrie, or her brother, Steve Serrano, was involved in my father's murder or made any attempt to cover it up.